I Only Dress
the Wounds:

Notes of a Country Doctor

I Only Dress the Wounds: Notes of a Country Doctor

By Ted Merrill

ISBN 0-9773348-0-5

Published by Homeostasis Press, 315 SW Brent Drive, John Day, OR 97845.

For Janis,
who has put up
with a lot.

Acknowledgments

My first thanks go to my parents, who brought me into the world and who, along with their extended families, did their best to point the way. I am grateful to all the teachers, formal and informal, who throughout my life have helped me assemble a vision of how the world works. And I thank the many people who have graciously permitted their names to be used in the book.

Robin Dutcher provided valuable editorial insight and gentle guidance and advice. The cover design is by Gerry Patenaude, with photographs by Acynthia Sanford. My sons David and Richard have led me through the maze of the computer world.

The following chapters have been previously published in magazines: Chapter 30, "Hearts and Minds," in *Vietnam*; Chapter 35, "Rights and Choices," in *Medical Economics*; and Chapter 50, "Somewhat Informed Consent," in *Humanist in Canada*.

Apology and Disclaimer

The English language is the best I can do, but it has a serious problem: its pronouns of gender.

I have decided to follow, in this book, what in the past was accepted tradition, using the word "man" to mean "humankind" and "he" to mean a person of either gender unless the context indicates otherwise. To fill the book with "she/he" and "his or hers" or alternating "her" and "him" would put more sand in the verbal gears than it's worth. I humbly beg the politically correct reader's forbearance.

Contents

Introduction

Who can say where it begins, and how shall we mark the finish? Time has no edges, and every story floats in a sea of other stories not told. Here are glimpses of eight decades of living and a half-century of medicine in a rapidly changing world. The stories are true and the names are real. The era is past, but the earth still swoops in its orbit and always a new story is about to happen.

Amphibia

"Nanan, may I have an apple?"

It was in the year before my fifth birthday.

"Yes, Teddy, you may go and get an apple."

My grandmother's kitchen was small, warm, and fragrant of cinnamon and soup. Just by the kerosene cookstove was the yellow door. I stepped down onto steep unpainted steps, down into murky shadows, dank earthen walls and floor, air moist and heavy with cellar scents of soil, roots, organic things. From a small naked bulb dangling at the far end of the room, strands of yellow draped thinly over obscure surfaces. Jars of jams, jellies, pickles, fruit filled a tier of shelves. At another wall, below the light, a gunnysack of potatoes stood beside large baskets of apples of different kinds. I remember best the winesaps.

Gripping the wooden hand rail, breath clutched high in my chest, I paused on each step, listened to the silence and peered into the gloom below. As my full weight shifted off the last step into the rectangle of blackness, my sandal sole encountered something soft, pliant, unfamiliar, and I heard a faint squishing sound.

I scrambled back up the steps and cried out in panic, "Nanan, there's something . . . ." She came with a flashlight and I followed her, cringing on the stair.

"It's all right," she said.

Moments later she turned and showed me, lying on her dustpan, the crushed and barely recognizable remains of a small toad.

I knew toads, had seen them hiding in cool parts of the yard and under flowers by the big willow tree. I had in fact held one, carefully, in gentle defiance of warnings that their touch might cause warts. I respected toads. Added now to the fear of a few moments before was a deep and burning remorse: the first time I had killed any living creature bigger than a spider.

2

A faint moist spot on the bottom of my shoe grossly understated the hideous and total destruction I had wrought. That it was unintentional gave little consolation. To this day I can feel that moment of contact, the yielding and sideways slip of my foot, and the suffocating blanket of guilt, a sense of having committed a grievous crime.

On a golden morning at the crisp dry end of summer I stood idly on the sidewalk in front of our house, feeling out the day. The sweet cool gave way slowly as the sun climbed into a cloudless sky, and the scent of wheat harvest hung soft in the air. My friend from the last house on our block, at the end of the street, by the slough that some called a creek, had just pedaled by but was out of range before I got to the door. I loitered by the gate. When I kicked at the tall weeds, big orange-winged grasshoppers flew up with a clickety-ratchety sound.

Then I spied something on the cement a few yards away - a frog, as long as my finger. His eyes seemed bright enough and all of his legs appeared intact, but down his right side was a long tear from which mysterious and slippery inner parts protruded. The bicycle tire must have delivered just a glancing blow. He waddled a few steps, made a half-hearted jump but didn't move as I approached. When I picked him up he struggled vigorously, then lay still.

I could easily see that salve and adhesive tape would not do for this job; the wound needed to be sewn up. I cupped the frog between my hands, brought him into the kitchen and laid him gently on a wet cloth in the bottom of a saucepan.

At thirteen I was modestly experienced at sewing. When I had explained my intent, my mother let me pluck one of her long, jet-black hairs and lent me her finest embroidery needle.

Restraining the patient gingerly with one hand, and by careful tucking and stitching, tucking and stitching, I closed the wound. The final tie in the hair was a bit tricky, but Mom consented to hold the frog's legs while I finished the knot. At last, in a jar with some water and a flat rock to climb up on, the creature seemed alert and showed a remarkable semblance of normal frogliness.

A week later the frog was lively and had eaten several insects. The wound was barely visible.

Mom looked at him closely. "Maybe you'll be a doctor!" she said.

As I headed out the door to release the frog in the slough she turned back toward the kitchen. I thought I heard her mutter, "Maybe a brain surgeon!"

The question sometimes nibbles at the edges of my self-esteem: Was it my mother or was it I who decided I would be a doctor? Not that it matters; it's all I ever wanted to do. But to be safe, I'll just give the credit to the toad and the frog.

Opening Door

"I once treated a woman with diabetes," he says, as we meet in Lamson's grocery by the flour and salt. "It causes acid in the blood, and she was in a bad way. I boiled a solution of baking soda and shot it into her vein and she got better."

I know nothing of diabetes, nor of acid in the blood, but I know from his telling that it was out of the ordinary, maybe even heroic.

In all those years I never knew his given name. Even the archives of the Idaho State Board of Medicine have him simply as "W. B. Parkinson, MD, Medical University of Illinois. Internship Cook County Hospital. License issued April 7, 1931."

He was well into middle age, short and serious, with dark brownish gray hair and a toothbrush moustache. He must have smiled sometimes but I can't remember seeing it.

This was a town of only 400, and the nearest other doctor was forty graveled and tortuous miles away. He was starved for someone to talk to about medicine. Then he found that I would listen.

"Is the boy home?" he casually asks my mother on the street. "Have him come over after school today." He shows me some books, maybe lends me one to take home. He asks me to read his medical journals to him because "my eyes are getting weak," and then explains to me what the articles are about.

His family lived in the back of the big house and upstairs over the office. His wife helped with the phone and the bookkeeping. Margaret Geisler, legal aide and Justice of the Peace, was also a nurse and could be called over from the Court House for special occasions. Otherwise he worked alone.

The Hippocratic oath speaks of teaching, as well as of healing and of moral rectitude. Dr. Parkinson delighted in teaching, and by the time I was in eighth grade I hovered around him whenever I could find an excuse.

I knew nothing of his background except that the skeleton standing in the corner of his office, a stabbing victim, died in the emergency room at Cook County Hospital while Dr. Parkinson was an intern there.

"You know," he said one day, crossing Main Street as I came out of the drug store, "one of the most exacting kinds of operation is an anastomosis - sewing cut ends of intestine together. You have to place the stitches so that the edges turn in all the way around, otherwise it won't heal."

A few weeks later he came to our house to check my younger brother's fever. "Esther," he said to my mother, "I'd like you to stitch me up a gut - a piece of cloth into a tube about the size of a broom handle. I want to show the boy how to sew two ends of intestine together."

I ran with the grey flannel "gut" to his office the next day. He produced a short curved needle, threaded it, and grasped it with a plier-like needle holder.

"The stitch goes in, and out," he said, taking a bite of cloth with the needle near the edge of the tube, "then over to the other piece" - he brought the other end of the tube around - "and in, out, and over; in, out, and over." Sure enough, in a few moments the two ends of the "gut" were joined, a flannel doughnut with the raw edges turned in and out of sight.

Days and months glided by. I met Dr. Parkinson on the street.

"Would you like to see a tonsillectomy - some tonsils taken out?" he asked.

"I sure would," I said, trying to control my eagerness.

On the appointed day the patient arrived just after I did. He was a gruff, burly wheat rancher from south of town; we'll say his name was Roy. He removed his shirt and complained about the silliness of the skimpy white thing he was asked to put on. No, he hadn't had any breakfast yet. Hell, no, he wasn't nervous about all this. Reluctantly he lay down on the narrow, thinly padded table.

Margaret Geisler sat at the head of the table and made soothing comments. The doctor buckled a heavy leather strap across Roy's hips, and a shackle about each ankle and each wrist. Roy raised his head and shoulders and surveyed this arrangement with an apprehensive scowl, then lay back down under the comforting hand of Mrs. Geisler. A small can stood close by; she pushed a large safety pin through its soft metal dome. She covered Roy's eyes with a strip of vaseline gauze, instructed him to "just take normal breaths," and placed over his face a wire-screen mask covered with cotton gauze.

So far, so good. Roy was tense, but determinedly cooperative. Mrs. Geisler picked up the can and tilted it so that drops of ether fell onto the gauze mask, while she continued crooning her advice to "just breathe easy."

The drops fell slowly, one by one. Roy, his voice muffled by the gauze, said, "Jesus, that stinks!"

"Yes," said Mrs. Geisler. "At first it does. Just take slow, deep breaths." The drops came faster. Roy coughed, and the fragrance of ether drifted over to my corner of the room.

I had given up my tonsils a few years before and remembered well that acrid smell of ether, and the sensation and sound of riding a spinning, whining wheel into darkness toward a small receding point of light. Beyond this I knew nothing about anesthesia.

"Wait a minute!" cried Roy's gauzy voice. His head thrashed from side to side while his assailant tried to keep the mask in place and the drops fell briskly.

"Keep it out of his eyes!" said Dr. Parkinson. Roy's eyes, freed now from the vaseline strip and wide open, swung to and fro like search lights, confused and frantic.

"Just blow it away, just blow the smell away!" shouted Mrs. Geisler, wrestling valiantly with Roy's jerking head and lurching shoulders. Dr. Parkinson laid his short, portly torso across Roy's middle. His glance at me seemed to give permission to help, and I stepped over and threw my trivial weight onto the struggling man's knees.

Mrs. Geisler, with the mask now clamped hard over the beet-red face, was pouring furiously, while Roy's struggles eased only slightly and his now unintelligible protests between coughs did not abate. While Roy's legs bounced me up and down, I noticed that the strap-encumbered hand near my face

7

had a bluish tint. Roy made loud and alarming stridorous sounds as he breathed in, and by peering over the top of Dr. Parkinson I could see that Roy's face had turned purplish blue. I was scared.

After what seemed like a very long time, "This isn't working out," said Dr. Parkinson. "You'd better stop."

"Yes," said Mrs. Geisler. She set the can down and removed the mask. Roy's struggles didn't cease at once, but the noisy breaths gradually evened out, and his color returned to a normal pink. He began looking about in wide-eyed confusion. Soon he had returned to the land of the living and breathing, and was talking again.

Within a few minutes, released from bondage, Roy sat up, a bit teetery, and asked what had happened.

"Putting children to sleep this way is easy," the doctor explained (to Roy, or to me? I wasn't sure). "But with big folks it sometimes is hard to get 'em down deep enough so they can relax and breathe right. You just weren't getting enough air, so we couldn't safely go ahead with it." He paused. "Maybe we'll try it again later."

Roy looked at his wrists where the straps had chafed them. Looked around the room. Stared at me. Wiped his hand twice over his face. Put on his shirt. Slid off the edge of the table and leaned against it for a few moments. Then without a word he strode unsteadily to the door, slammed it behind him, got into his car and sped away, tires throwing gravel as he swept out of sight.

Late one winter night I hovered with my family near a window and watched, a block away across a vacant lot, a light in the kitchen of the postmaster's house. The talk was that Claude's boy, out of school with pneumonia, had pus collecting beside his lung, and that Doc was over there tonight to cut into his chest and drain it out. My thoughts were a writhing tangle: fear at the very idea of cutting into a chest; wishing I could be there to watch; wishing the doctor a successful outcome - and, of course, sympathy and anxiety for my school acquaintance.

8

The light was on until 3 am. The operation was accomplished, the crisis passed, the fever broke, and the boy was back in school in the spring.

I would be graduating from high school in a couple of months and summer was drawing near when Dr. Parkinson sent for me.

"You know Alf Baldwin is the dog catcher," he said. "If I spoke to him, he'd probably let us have a dog that he was going to do away with, and I could show you some surgery, some operations. If you'd want to."

If I'd want to! "Oh, I would! When do you think he'll have a dog?"

"I'll let you know."

Weeks went by. Had he forgotten? I was afraid to ask; I had carefully let him set the tone and tempo of our relationship. I went to his place only when invited; but I tried to find ways of accidentally crossing his path, finding him on the street, even passing his house though it was on the farthest edge of town from ours.

One day after school Dad (who was principal of the high school) told me that Doc had called and wanted me to come and see him. I ran across to his office, walking the last half-block so I wouldn't appear breathless.

"He has the dog. It's a stray that has to be shot. If we're to use it I have to pick it up tomorrow night and we'll have to do it the next day. I can't keep a dog around here."

Perfect! That would be Saturday, meaning there would be no school.

He seemed a little uneasy. "We need to keep this private. Your father said we could use the upstairs of the high school; nobody should bother us there, and I don't want anybody to know about this. People might talk."

I hadn't conceived this as something to be covert about; such an educational and scientific venture should be cause for celebration. My mother explained to me later that some people might be offended by the idea of "cutting up a live animal." To

9

some folks it was bad enough that the dog catcher took the dogs at all.

"You get the ether," the doctor said. "You can get it from the drug store. Better get two cans. But don't tell Barkley what you want it for." I spent the rest of the evening figuring out what I could tell the druggist that would let me buy the ether without telling a lie or revealing the secret.

Dr. Parkinson had never before been in the "upstairs" of the high school. It was actually an attic, and the stairs a slightly modified ladder that swung down from the ceiling behind the stage. The place was used for storage of athletic equipment, but in a space near the trapdoor and ladder, under the gable, you could easily stand up and there was a single bare light bulb overhead. I warned him of the deficiencies of the facility, but assured him that we could fix it into a suitable operating room by adding some more lights. There was no running water but I would have water available.

On Saturday morning the doctor's car pulled up close to the back door of the school gym. I had been there for hours, fussing with the preparations. A tabletop rested on wooden crates, and there were two chairs and two extra lamps. A five-gallon can of water (warm) stood to one side; a couple of basins, waste bucket, soap and some towels - all the things Dr. Parkinson had asked for, and just as I pictured from stories I'd read.

I ran to meet the doctor and the patient as they furtively entered. The dog, led by a short length of rope, was a bit hesitant and confused but not hostile, just a miscellaneous sort of dog, and I tried to remain clinical and not get too chummy with him. I suddenly understood better why all this was being kept unpublicized.

Getting a forty-pound dog up a ladder and through a trapdoor was a new experience for all three of us. I went up first and the doctor carried the dog under one arm to where I could reach down and assist. Finally we were all on top, the dog soothed and temporarily tethered to a brace, while the doctor brought up his bag of instruments and regained his composure and dignity. He surveyed the place and agreed that it would do.

He had rigged a cone of cardboard, with the small end cut off and covered with layers of gauze. He inserted a safety pin through the soft metal top of one of the cans of ether, and showed me how to drip it onto the gauze held over the dog's face. The smell was powerful, a little intimidating but not unpleasant. I recalled the picture of Mrs. Geisler and Roy, but hastily brushed it away.

It was surprisingly easy. Soon the dog was well asleep, resting on his back on a pad of old blankets, his feet tied out to the sides to keep him steady, and his belly soaped and shaved.

Though not familiar with the ritual of the real operating room, I vaguely realized that compromises were made here. We didn't wear gowns; the patient wasn't painted with iodine; the doctor washed his hands but I did not believe that it was with the surgeon's traditional vigor and thoroughness. After all, this patient was not intended to wake up and recover. We were the surrogate executioners, which was the whole justification for our being permitted this adventure.

Once the white towels had defined the rectangle of the surgical field, the scene changed. The dog's personality dissolved under the drapes and the ether cone. The creature identity disappeared from view and all that could be seen was the part, a square window into the anonymous life of a dog.

The doctor laid out his instruments on a towel. Five years later in medical school I found that surgeons had gone entirely to disposable, snap-on, pre-sharpened scalpel blades; but Dr. Parkinson had a set of three sizes of well-used scalpels, all meticulously honed to fine edges.

As the knife bit daringly through the skin and drops of blood appeared, I marveled at the deftness and confidence with which his fingers moved, how the tools were controlled, how he placed the narrow-tipped clamps to stop the bleeding from each cut blood vessel and tied each ligature so the clamps could be removed.

He pointed out the anatomical structures to me as he worked. Finally the intestine, stomach, and liver came into view. He placed long clamps across the small intestine in two places and cut out the section between, carefully tying off the

11

blood vessels that fed the short section that he removed. Then, with needle holder in hand he sewed the ends back together: "In, out, and over. In, out, and over."

During all of this I struggled to divide my attention between what he was doing and my assignment of dripping ether. The dog's breathing became too shallow and the doctor reminded me to stop the drip for a few minutes.

By the time the intestine was repaired, quite a long time had gone by. He stitched up the abdominal incision in three separate layers.

"What operation will you do next?" I asked hopefully. But suddenly he seemed tired. It was hot - stifling, I realized - and we were sweating heavily.

"You're well into the second can of ether," he pointed out. "You need to use the rest of it to put an end to him."

Reluctantly I agreed. The drops fell faster. The breathing gradually waned, skin and tongue turned a dusky blue. Finally there was no movement of the chest and belly, though a faint thump of the canine heart could be felt under the ribs for a few moments longer.

"Should we open his chest and see - " I started to ask. But he cut me off and muttered, "I don't cut on dead flesh!" He seemed suddenly in a hurry to be finished with the whole thing. He washed the scalpels carefully and wrapped each one in a soft cloth, and threw the other instruments into his bag after a cursory rinsing. I untied the corpse and put it into a gunnysack.

Going down was easier than going up. He put his things in the car. I promised that I would bury the dog out in the country where it wouldn't be turned up by accident, for he still seemed sensitive on the matter of publicity.

After thanking him yet again I went back inside to put the attic right again and to remove all traces of our clandestine activities, except for the lingering scent of ether.

I only saw him a couple of times after that. I went off to college in the fall, and he died that winter - kidney failure, they said. He must have been sick for longer than I knew.

His wife sold what she could of his medical things, and gave the rest to me - the skeleton; a box of old instruments with obsolete design and dull and corroded finish; a few books; his old German microscope with the high-power lens cracked; and his doctor's bag with a shallow latched drawer in the bottom and a few tiny vials with labels - morphine, codeine, calomel, strychnine - and that haunting smell. The scent of the bag was the odor of iodine and much, much more: a scent of time and of quiet power, of generations - a time-honored brotherhood. To receive those things into my possession - the skeleton, the microscope, and that aromatic bag - was a rite of passage beyond measure.

Now, sixty years after I last talked to him, I have one of his hemostats in the pocket of my fishing jacket to remove deeply-swallowed hooks. The skeleton - gaunt, grinning, and sagging on his stand, his costal cartilages ratty and moth-eaten and his twice-cracked cranium lovingly wired together - comes down from his box in the attic at Hallowe'en, or to charm the pupils in a school health class.

College

The approach to the University of Idaho climbed a slope between rows of Greek-letter houses. At the crest of the hill a long sidewalk led obliquely through grass to the Administration Building. This massive brick structure with castle-like turrets, its shoulders clad in ivy, exuded a grand aura, a promise of wisdom and permanence and truth.

One balmy afternoon I swooped down that hill on my bicycle as golden leaves of autumn fluttered down. Entering the turn at the bottom I tried to wave at a young lady standing on the steps of her sorority. My lunchbox tweaked the handlebars, and a painful clattering crash erased any amorous possibilities.

Across the street from the Ad Building stood the Infirmary. Here I learned to irrigate with Argyrol the urethras of worried young men returning sheepishly to campus late on a Saturday night.

Beyond these buildings, jumbled randomly in my memory, were the Armory, where we marched around stiffly in ROTC uniform; the athletic field with its bleachers, on which a few of us ate our sack lunches; and the "I-Tank," a water storage container atop a tall skeletal metal tower, target of frequent pranks by rival students from Washington State University a few miles away.

At the epicenter of all this - educationally if not geographically - stood the Science Building, the hub of my mental exertions and preoccupations for two years.

College for me was a time fully engaged in learning, and though I've forgotten most of the specifics, much of what I now know rests on foundations laid at the University of Idaho. The purpose was sharply focused, the name of the game boldly laid out: "Bachelor of Science (Pre-Med)."

There were English Composition, Algebra, German, and Introduction to Philosophy. But the memorable courses were Zoology and Chemistry.

The wonderful complexity of critters, and my increasing personal identification with each one that I saw or dissected, went from the microscopic amoeba and rotifers through fat earthworms and on past the dogfish shark and frogs to birds and mammals, the fetal pig and the cat. Mammals are all anatomically analogous to my very self - astonishingly so, their bones and muscles and various organs named almost the same as mine, as I learned and drew in detail in Comparative Anatomy.

That was fun; but equal beauty and excitement lay in Inorganic Chemistry - its logic, the plain simplicity of principles, even the predictability of chemical reactions. Once you grasped the meanings of the Periodic Table of Elements, it all made sense: the Cosmic Erector Set.

Dr. Cady stands behind the lectern, by a table laden with chemistry apparatus, with a modestly genteel air. You know at a glance that he is in his element. Tall, slender, impeccably dressed with silver hair neatly trimmed, he gets your attention merely by standing there. His voice is clear and decisive, but so harmonious that even the subjects of his lectures - elements, molecules, compounds - seem to carry a soft, warm patina.

He announces today's topic: sequential, delayed reactions. On the table stand two beakers, each containing what appears to be clear water. Halfway into the lecture he briskly pours the contents of one beaker into the other, which is now full of the colorless fluid. He turns to the blackboard, starts writing chemical formulas and equations.

"The rate of reaction," he says over his shoulder, "depends on concentration and on temperature. When the first slow reaction is complete, the second reaction takes place quickly and the solution turns blue." We all gasp. He still stands with his back to the table, writing, but in the very instant that he utters the word "blue," as if with a flick of a switch the solution in the beaker is a brilliant, dense indigo color!

Dr. Cady is not only a teacher but a consummate showman who loves his work.

In the second year we carried the principles of chemistry into exciting and precise action in Quantitative Analysis.

At the Dutch-door window of the Chemistry Storeroom a short jovial man issues a small envelope containing an "unknown" white powder - a silver salt, we are told. The assignment: determine the exact percentage of silver in the powder, accurate to three decimal places.

We wait in line for the electric furnace; heat a fragile porcelain crucible smaller than a shot glass to a glowing red to remove the weight of absorbed moisture and fingerprints; let it cool. Wait in line for the chemical balance, and weigh the crucible to the nearest milligram. Repeat as needed, until the weight is constant.

Put about a quarter of a teaspoonful of the mystery powder into the crucible. Repeat the heating, cooling and weighing. Dissolve and wash the powder from the crucible into a beaker of water without losing the tiniest speck. Add sodium chloride solution drop by drop to the beaker to form white flecks and clumps of insoluble silver chloride.

Strain the white clumpy stuff from the beaker through a funnel lined with filter paper.

Cram the filter paper with its delicate load into the crucible and fire the whole thing again until the cellulose filter paper has burned away, leaving pure silver chloride. After the cooling, one final trip to the scale, a breath-holding adjustment of the foil rider on the calibrated beam to balance the two sides perfectly.

Knowing the atomic weights for silver and for chlorine, and with the exceedingly accurate weights which I have determined, I can now calculate what percent of the sample is silver.

At last I take my lab notebook, showing all the scale readings and equations and calculations, to Dr. Cone over in the corner.

Dr. Cone is a study in black and white. A gruff but kindly gentleman of Russian origin with a barely noticeable accent, small but well proportioned, he always wears a shiny black suit and bow tie over a tastefully rumpled white shirt. He carefully inspects my notebook. Then he runs his hand over his short, crew-cut white hair, and from the inside breast pocket of his coat withdraws a small black leather-bound book. He checks again my sample's code number. He peers into his little book, hiding its contents like a high-stakes poker hand. He slips the book back into his pocket and in my notebook next to the silver percentage he writes with a red pen the grade - 93.

I shall never know the exact silver content of that powder, nor how many different powders are dispensed by the storeroom man, nor how Dr. Cone figures the grade. But I trust Dr. Cone, and his small wry smile shows that he wishes me well.

I stress the term Inorganic Chemistry, the one that I found so beautifully logical. Later, when we shifted to Organic Chemistry - those compounds prominent in the living organism - the beauty faded, the logic blurred, the whole scene was disappointingly obscure. The valences, the electron transfers, and the sheer size and complexity of the molecules did not seem to enjoy the straight-forward kinds of relationships to which I had become addicted. The molecule of silver chloride which I pursued in Quantitative Analysis had only two atoms, one of silver and one of chlorine, and they followed honest, clear-cut, electron-governed rules. But now carbon, hydrogen, and oxygen clustered together endlessly and the electrons seemed to make their own whimsical rules as they went along. We memorized the characteristics of a host of carbon-based substances because it was not obvious, from their formulas, how they would behave.

Perhaps this explains why I have always felt more confident in surgery, based on anatomy, than in pharmacology, derived from biochemistry.

The experience of quantitative chemical analysis moved me toward a realization that has amazed and comforted me for most of my life: the quantitative fidelity of the world. By this I mean that throughout the universe, any amount or package of matter or of energy that can be measured will always remain constant under even the most diverse conditions. If you can find it and measure it again, it will be the same amount as before. It may change drastically in form or in location, but it won't cheat you. When it appears that you have been cheated - say, in Michaelson and Morely's experiment to measure the speed of light - you may be forced to change the rules, the concepts, as Albert Einstein did by squeezing time and bending space to produce his Special Theory of Relativity, and that sets everything right again.

The U.S. Navy

The questions rattled in my head as I left Dr. Wiens and his German class and headed down the hall: *Mit oder ohne?* (With or without?) *Mit oder ohne was?*

Near the bottom of the stairs in the Ad Building was a bulletin board, and I gave it my usual casual glance in passing. This time something caught my eye - a bulletin from the U.S. Navy.

It was the spring of 1942, a few months after Japanese planes bombed the U.S. Navy at Pearl Harbor. The war effort was building up steam, and here a bulletin from the Navy announced a program for filling anticipated needs for doctors, dentists, engineers, and pilots: the V-12 Program of the Naval Reserve. As the notice urged, I went to the Administration Office for further information.

The promise was that we would stay in school in the pre-med program; that in several months or a year we would be ordered to "active duty" in the Navy but continue in school at the Navy's expense, even through medical school. In return we would remain in the Navy as doctors for some unspecified period.

"If you keep your grades up and keep your noses clean, you stay in school," they told us. "Foul up, and you go to boot camp and out to sea." It sounded like a pretty fair deal - and a grand solution to my precarious financial state. I signed up.

A physical exam was required, to prove we were actually capable of defending our country.

"I'm sorry," said the naval corpsman, "you have to weigh 132 pounds or more. You're only 130."

"You mean for 2 pounds I'm out of the reserves?"

"No, we can take you in a special category, but not on the regular status."

"What does that mean?"

"I'm not sure. They might assign you to a different kind of duty."

"I don't like the sound of 'special category.' Isn't there some way around this?"

"Well," he said, "I can only write down what the scales say. But I will tell you this: a pint of water weighs a pound, and if you want to come back in half an hour, I'll weigh you again."

And so, having been weighed 30 minutes later into Regular Category at 133 pounds, I spent the rest of the afternoon at the urinal making amends to my kidneys.

The second year began. We took Medical College Aptitude Tests, and plodded on with classes.

The United States Navy is an old, honorable, and efficient organization. It has clear, detailed plans and protocols for every contingency, for every situation however large or small. Except one: This new V-12 Program kept the Navy baffled for a while.

The Ad Building bulletin board carried current information and directives from the Naval Bureau of Personnel. For months the notices didn't require any action. Then one day: "All V-12 (Pre-Med) personnel will apply for admission to medical schools in the customary manner."

Dr. Stough, the zoology instructor, was also the premedical advisor.

"How do I do this?" I asked. "What are some good schools? I don't know anything about medical schools."

"Most people," he said, "apply to at least three schools. Northwestern University has a good medical school. So does the University of Chicago. Columbia University is good, and they usually reserve one spot in the class for somebody from the Northwest."

He helped me find the addresses. I wrote for application forms, filled out questionnaires, requested transcripts and MCAT scores to be sent, and scraped up money for application fees.

This done, we all went on about our business of studying and "keeping our noses clean."

Several weeks went by. Another bulletin appeared:

"All V-12 (Pre-Med) personnel will be assigned by the Navy to medical schools when the time comes. Do not apply for admission to medical schools. If you have already done so, withdraw your applications."

A few days later, as I still pondered this order, a telegram arrived:

From Office of the Dean, Northwestern University Medical School:
We are pleased to inform you that you have been approved for admission to the first year class, beginning in September 1944. Please notify us by return wire whether you intend to accept this position. You will receive further information by mail within 3 weeks.

I sent a telegram of explanation and regrets.

A week later I had the same exchange with the University of Chicago.

It took almost a month to receive a telegram from Columbia. Again I sent my regrets.

The following day another wire:

From the Office of Dr. Willard Rappleye, Dean, College of Physicians and Surgeons:
You have been misinformed. Our Dean is on the committee in Washington which has been developing the V-12 Program. You may come to College of P & S if you wish. Please give us your decision immediately.

I ran all the way to the telegraph office to say "Yes!"

Near the end of the school year the hall bulletin board spoke again: V-12 personnel would go on "active duty" as apprentice seaman - meaning put on a uniform, live with others wearing uniforms, get $50 a month and board and room, and continue in school. Individual orders would follow.

On July 1, 1943, I reported to my new Naval duty station - the U.S.S Gravely, which floated bravely in the hot semi-desert of southern Idaho.

The Navy had taken over the University of Idaho, Southern Branch, in Pocatello, and had nauticalized it as thoroughly as possible. Graveley Hall had been rechristened as a ship. Its hallways were changed by proclamation into gangways, the latrines were now heads, the doors (the few that hadn't been removed entirely) were hatches, and the windows were portholes.

I arrived by bus, clad in the double-breasted wool suit in which I had graduated from high school. By 9 am the sun glared onto the already hot field of sand and brown grass where we were rounded up, lined up, and jerked to attention. For a half hour, as we stood in ranks, a Navy person oriented, instructed, advised, and warned.

Our first order of business would be "strength tests," the results of which, it was vaguely hinted, could in some way affect our futures. We spaced ourselves out more widely on the bristly field. To a shouted cadence we did pushups and sit-ups and squat-thrusts and jumping-jacks. Scores were ostensibly being kept, though I could not identify a scorekeeper. Suspecting that some unspecified future advantage might be at stake, I tried to continue each exercise until most of the other victims had come to a gasping halt.

We again lined up at attention. My muscles trembled from the efforts. Perspiration had seeped outward to the wool suit and beyond. I stood, rigid and motionless, and tried to concentrate on what the instructor was saying.

I awoke and found myself lying on the harsh ground in a four-foot patch of shade cast by a stingy sapling, with a few people hovering over me and the instructor saying, "Get back in line there! He's just passed out for a minute. He'll be all right."

It was the only time in my life that I ever fainted. Someone suggested that I remove my wool coat before we went inside the gym for the pull-up testing.

It turned out as they had promised: the main action on this ship was study. We lined up and marched to mess. We had room inspections and P.E. classes and the cross-country 3-mile run and the obstacle course, and a class on Naval Organization. Otherwise it was just college continued.

The physics classes reminded me of dear Dr. Cady. No, not because the teacher (call him Dr. Blank) resembled Dr. Cady, but rather because of the comical contrast.

Dr. Blank gave us a physics lecture, and a demonstration of some sort, every week. We could hardly wait for the demonstrations, because invariably they went wrong. The lab assistant failed to provide a needed item; Dr. Blank dropped and broke a vital instrument at a crucial moment; a pulley fell off the clamp as the weight was applied; a light bulb burned out so the function of lenses happened only in our imaginations.

The school year ended in the middle of February; my class at Columbia wouldn't begin until September. This interval had been left by the Navy as a black hole in their planning. But they got it figured out and sent me with four others in my group to Sun Valley, Idaho, which the Navy in the meantime (we were now into the third year of the war) had taken over as a Naval Convalescent Hospital.

At Sun Valley we were still aberrations, some sort of freaks, mysteriously different from the other swabbies. They saw us as vaguely medical, and assigned us to the best jobs in the place - Lab, X-ray, Ear-Nose-Throat Clinic, Surgery, or Central Supply. No KP, no brig watch, no policing the grounds or swabbing decks. On my second day there we soaked in the heated outdoor pool in a snowstorm. Later in the spring, after the snow, we had use of the ice skating rink.

The patients here were sailors or marines from the Pacific Theater who had been wounded, sick with exotic diseases such as malaria or filariasis, or disabled by "battle fatigue" (in the previous war called "shell shock," and in a subsequent war "post-traumatic stress disorder").

They also had their share of sexually transmitted diseases. Gonorrhea was routinely treated with sulfadiazine, but a few cases persisted despite treatment. It was rumored that a new substance, extracted from a fungus called *Penicillium notatum* and now available experimentally as a medicine, might cure gonorrhea. A recent newspaper story had reported that some penicillin had been flown from the east coast to Salt Lake City for a small girl desperately ill with pneumonia, and she survived.

I worried about using such a precious resource on sulfa-resistant clap, but the decision was not mine and I was glad to help with the trial. First we would confirm the diagnosis by microscope, and then, every four hours night and day, inject 10,000 units of penicillin into the backsides of three cringing but hopeful victims. Even in such minuscule doses it did work very promptly.

After three months, nine more V-12 characters arrived. By then the commanding officer had figured out that we were not really a special category of sailors, and began assigning us to less glamorous jobs.

A few times I drew brig watch. This was interesting and challenging. For four hours in the night, supplied with a night stick, a master key to the four cells in the dungeon under the hospital, and no clue as to what to do, I walked slowly and continuously the length of the musty and dimly lit hall and back, peering into each cell to ensure that all was well (usually there were from one to three prisoners) and tapping big cockroaches on the cold concrete wall with my stick to help keep me awake.

One night a new client in the last cell, no doubt aided by intoxicating chemicals, suddenly went berserk. Rattling the bars, he shouted and berated and challenged me in colorful phrases. He threw his mattress aside and, picking up his bed frame, pounded the bars and walls with it; then he leaned it against the wall like a ladder in order to reach the small transom-style window. To his surprise - and mine - he found the window unlocked, and prepared to clamber out.

I tried to visualize a heroic scene: I rush into the cell, wrestle him back down and subdue him. Considering his drunken rage, bulging muscles, and 70-pound weight advantage, I couldn't get the scene to come into focus. Instead I abandoned my post and ran upstairs to the desk of the Officer on Duty. He and a colleague hurried outside, intercepted the fugitive as he was nearly out through the window, smote him to unconsciousness, dragged him back to his cell, and locked the window from the outside.

My embarrassment at my cowardly retreat cast a harsh new light on the term "apprentice seaman."

While I was away in college my parents had separated, my brother had graduated from high school, and Dad had quit teaching but now had a little photo studio in the village of Ketchum, two miles from Sun Valley. Sometimes after the day's work I would climb out the back window of the living quarters with my fly rod and fish down Trail Creek to Ketchum, have dinner with Dad, and hike back up the road in the dark to bed.

All in all, this was a rugged duty station!

It is most of 3,000 miles from Fairfield, Idaho, to New York City. On a remote branch of the Union Pacific Railroad, a wide-eyed country boy boarded an ancient car with a large pot-bellied stove in the middle. After two changes of trains and three days and nights of rumbling along clickety-clack tracks trailing a plume of black smoke, and an hour creeping and clanking past the sooty back yards and gloomy fringe of a strange new world, I got off at Grand Central Station.

The largest city I had ever seen was Boise, population 35,000. New York, I can tell you, was not like Boise.

I quickly learned the first rule of travel in a strange place: ask directions from at least three people. If two of them give you the same answer, it's likely to be right.

Carrying all of my luggage (a large suitcase and a heavy duffel bag), I found my way onto the subway and headed uptown for Columbia University. At 116th Street, emerging like a prairie dog from its burrow, I saw a lot of buildings, but none clearly declared its identity. The first three people whom I stopped all pointed vaguely in the same direction. I finally found a promising entrance, and someone in an office who appeared official.

"I'm looking for the Columbia University medical school," I said.

"Physicians and Surgeons? That's up at 168th Street."

"Oh. I was told that Columbia was at 116th Street."

"That's right. This is Columbia's main campus. Physicians and Surgeons is at 168th Street."

"Thank you," I said. "Will the same subway take me there?"

"Yes, it will," said the man, his clipped voice softening a bit.

I picked up my bags and reentered the burrow. At least by now I knew to put the nickel in the slot before trying to go through the turnstile.

I fished out a paper and rechecked the address. It was true; my correspondence with the medical school had said 168th Street; but the three-person-query result had seemed so conclusive! I got off this time with renewed confidence, meanwhile inhaling deep draughts of the distinctive city air amid the constantly changing yet somehow congruent environment.

It was not hard this time to locate the building. Inscribed over the entrance, in letters that I fancied were carved by a reverent old stonecutter, were the words: "College of Physicians and Surgeons, School of Medicine, Columbia University."

I pushed through the doors, gratefully dropped my increasingly heavy bags to the floor, and explained my mission to the woman behind the counter.

Yes, she had me on her list of students, and her checkmark after my name lifted a weight of apprehensive uncertainty from my already strained psyche.

"And where will you be living?" she asked.

"I was about to ask you that. I assume the Navy has the information."

"Have you made the arrangements through the Navy?"

My relief of a moment before evaporated. "No, not yet. I thought they would automatically take care of that. My orders just said report to Columbia University." I looked around hopefully. "Where do the other students stay?"

"A lot of them have already arranged to stay in Bard Hall, just around the corner from here."

"Is that a possibility for me?"

She gave a shake of her head. It may have signaled exasperation, or maybe sympathy. "I'll see whether there's a room available," she said, and went to the phone.

"You're lucky," she reported, and at last she smiled. "They have a vacant room, and you can move in tomorrow."

"That's a great relief," I said. "And where could I stay tonight?"

"I guess you'd have to work that out with the Navy."

"Where would I find them?"

"Their center is down at 116th Street, the University campus."

"Could I call them from here?"

"All right. I'll see if I can get them on the phone."

As I got off the subway once more my bags weighed at least twice as much as they had at the beginning of the day. I dumped them on one of six empty beds in the Navy quarters, and wearily went off to find something to eat.

Thereafter, my entire dealings with the Navy consisted of a monthly pay check and a token monthly muster with 20 minutes of close-order drill at the Armory a couple of blocks up from Bard Hall. Then apparently someone decided that even that wasn't useful any more, and our awareness of the Navy faded away, leaving only the study of medicine to concern us.

By 1946 the war had been won without us, and V-12 personnel were notified of our options: either join the active Naval Reserve, or receive a complete discharge from the Navy.

With my medical life ahead of me, my country's military future appearing peaceful but its possible implications for me entirely unpredictable, and my heart set on small-town general practice, I opted out.

The First Days

The first day of medical school! That venerable building on 168th Street had been my destination for a lot of years, a lot of courses, a lot of wonder and fantasy and midnight studying and testing and poring over applications - and a lot of life options and possibilities passed by, temptations foregone.

I don't remember just what we did that morning. Book things, paper things, listening to instructions and finding our way.

But in the afternoon we took the elevator to the Anatomy Lab and entered a whole new universe and a new phase of life.

Thirty tables stand in rows. On each table lies a long rounded object covered by a brown sheet of canvas. An unfamiliar odor meets us at the door, a potent portentous mixture of carbolic acid and something else. There are 118 of us.

"Pick a place," says Dr. Truax. "Four to a table. You won't need your dissecting kits today. Just get acquainted with your cadaver. Locate all the surface landmarks, on the cadaver and on yourselves."

Someone hesitantly pulls back the drape. We place it, folded, on a shelf under the foot of the table.

There she lies, our companion for the next few months, the second dead person I've ever seen. (My Sunday school teacher had been resting in a coffin.) Does the word "gaunt" apply here? Or "shriveled?" I uneasily concede "anonymous," though it seems somehow disrespectful; she must have had a name. Somewhere, hidden under the skin or hovering in the air, there has to be a history. Did she look like this when she was walking on the street? What did she die from? Will we be able to tell? Where did she live? Does she have family around here? Was she a secretary, factory worker, teacher, housewife? Indigent or not? And how closely and in what ways does she resemble us living ones? How much can she teach us? Or rather, how much can I learn from her?

Conversation in the room is hushed, punctuated now and then by nervous laughter. Someone lays his *Gray's Anatomy*, a thick, heavy book, on the edge of the table. This has a steadying effect on our feelings and our talk, a centering, like dropping an anchor. We begin touching, feeling, comparing, looking in the book and back at the body, feeling points and hollows and bulges on ourselves. Occasionally someone asks Dr. Truax a question.

I am surprised suddenly to realize that nearly four hours have passed. We replace the smelly canvas.

The second day. We locate our places, two on each side of the cadaver, and settle expectantly into our chairs, books in laps or on the floor.

"Start at the acromion," Dr. Truax says, "and remove the skin from the arm down just past the elbow. Work carefully so you don't damage the underlying structures. You'll want to do most of it by blunt dissection. Identify what you can as you go."

I had dissected earthworms, fish, frogs, a fetal pig, and a cat. I had killed and dressed salmon, chickens, pheasants, rabbits.

But picking up the knife here was different. When you enter a human body, even a dead one, you cross a threshold. You enter a world, a psychological space, from which there is no exit.

On the fourth day we numbered only 116. Two of the women (a few of us had already predicted it) did not appear. Aloof, with a defensively superior air - from the upper social strata of Connecticut, it was said - they clearly had better ways to spend their lives than to lean over a stinking dead body for a year. It gave some of us an uplifting sense of solidarity: we were still here, and ready for whatever might come.

Every afternoon for nine months we were in the lab. The first cadaver took three and a half months, and I thought I knew it well. Then we started another one, spent twice as long on it, going into much finer detail: identify the nerve and blood vessels supplying each muscle; dissect the head, the circulation to the brain; the puzzle of the sinuses; the six muscles that move either eye; the structures of the inner ear laboriously chiseled out of the temporal bone.

My dissecting partner was Ralph Colp, the only child of a prominent New York surgeon who had high hopes - firm expectations and intentions, in fact - that his son would follow in his footsteps. Ralph was tall, lean, with straight stringy almost-black hair and a broad friendly smile. He was one of the smartest people I've known, and well read: he could converse with authority on any subject from classical music to coral reefs to Egyptian archaeology to Greek philosophy - and yes, even anatomy. But he hated dissection, that greasy stickiness, the smell on your hands and under the nails, and even on your face after you wipe hair back from your eyes. The meticulous care in separating fragile tissue planes without destroying the things you wanted to reveal intimidated him.

"It's your turn today, Ralph," I would say, sliding my chair back from the partly dissected leg and picking up *Gray's Anatomy*.

"I know it," he says, "I know I've got to do this." He scoots into position, adjusts the light, and seizes the dissecting probe. For five minutes, clumsily but doggedly, he tears at the layer of fat and connective tissue along the sartorius muscle, determined to find its insertion on the tibia. Here the structures are tough; some force is required, with an occasional switch to the knife.

Suddenly Ralph drops the tools and pushes back from the table. "I don't know this area well enough," he mutters. "I need to read the book for a while."

Trying to conceal my delight, I say, "Are you sure?"

"Yeah." With apparent guilt and frustration, "You go ahead."

I give a sympathetic shake of my head and eagerly take his place, for I know this is where you learn, where you find the effigy of yourself, the endless revelations, and I love every minute of it.

In the mornings we lean over microscopes and study stained sections of tissues, the high-resolution views of the structures we have seen in the cadaver, moving the mental images from the gross to the microscopic and back again. We learn to recognize the cells, to distinguish salivary gland from prostate, breast from pancreas, stomach from colon, upper part of the small intestine from parts farther downstream. Looking at the confusing jumble of cells in bone marrow, I call the instructor over: "Is that cell - the one the pointer is on - is that a mast cell?" Dr. Smith, tall with thinning gray hair and large feet, has a gentle *gravitas* about him, a softly paternal manner. His voice is strangely liquid, almost a lisp.

"No," he says slowly, "that's an erythroblast." He points to the open histology book. "You can see the differences right there on that page."

One afternoon Dr. Truax summoned us into a classroom across the hall. Dr. Detweiler, Professor of Anatomy and Head of the Department, gave us a slide show of his research project on the brain. He had removed or transplanted from one tadpole to another the forebrain, midbrain, or hindbrain in various combinations. He then put the tadpoles in a racetrack improvised in a petri dish, and with a human hair in one hand and a stopwatch in the other he goosed them and timed them, goosed them and timed them as they swam around the track, to determine which part or parts of the brain worked better for locomotion.

It was here that I learned a common feature of academic hierarchy: Professor Detweiler, whom we seldom saw in the lab, had the prerogative of consigning the students to Assistant Professor Truax and keeping the tadpoles and stopwatch for himself.

For the whole first year we studied dead things: the structure, the forms from which function flows. In the second half of the year we used the mornings for Biochemistry and Physiology - the functioning of the structures - sometimes with the use of live things. We measured ourselves and each other, our breathing and heart rate and oxygen consumption. We used a jerry-rigged device - a clock-driven rotating drum covered with smoked paper on which a wire stylus scribed a trail - to graph the contraction of the gastrocnemius muscle of a cerebrally-disabled frog when we gave its sciatic nerve an electrical tweak; or the spontaneous beat of a strip of turtle's heart muscle stretched in a dish of fluid, and how the beat was affected by adding digitalis or potassium. These tactile and visual experiences were building blocks for a constantly growing edifice of understanding how a human animal lives.

A thing that struck me forcibly early on was how much we were expected to learn in a limited time. But then I realized that I could indeed learn that much, that fast, given undivided attention and focused effort, freed from distractions, the mind driven like a spike into the solid mass of material.

Freshman students at P & S now hold annually a ceremony to honor the people who gave their bodies - those rigid, scented folk who lay on the tables, quiet and uncomplaining under our knives.

I wish our class had thought of doing that.

Neuroanatomy

The sun of late summer burns down onto 168th Street, reflects upward from the sidewalk and redoubles the input of heat to the masonry. On the other side of that wall, row upon row of bodies slump in the seats, their digestive systems sullenly grinding a hastily ingested lunch. The dense, hot, heavy air lies like a shroud in the darkened auditorium, more like a tropical rain forest than a classroom. A hundred and ten pairs of lungs trade their stale exhalations back and forth, and we squirm or thrust ourselves back in the chairs to help concentrate, or just to stay awake.

The projected image on the screen is a cross-section of the spinal cord, stained with a silver compound which brings out in elegant black-and-white detail the bundles of neuron fibers (axons and dendrites) that carry electrochemical messages between the brain and the rest of the body. Dr. Elwyn, at least, is enthusiastic, his voice melodious and compelling, his long white coat demanding our attention in the darkened cavern. His pointer dances over the picture as he speaks.

"As we discussed yesterday," he says, "the dorsal columns carry afferent signals from the muscles to the brain; the pyramidal tracts carry efferent signals from the brain to the muscles. Some of their subdivisions can be seen on this slide." He pauses, peers into the semidarkness.

"Grumbach, tell us the name of this structure." His pointer abruptly comes to rest on one of the lighter patches on the screen.

From the shadows a voice promptly responds, "The lateral spinothalamic tract."

"Come down here, Grumbach." Amid shuffling sounds and stifled tittering a silhouette moves across the screen, and our compatriot moves down the aisle to the front. Dr Elwyn hands him a lollipop the size of a saucer. "You are correct," he says.

The lecture resumes. A few minutes later the pointer stops, imperatively. "Aitelli, what is this."

A pause; a faltering reply: "The pyramidal tract?"

"Aitelli, come here."

The lollipop this time is the size of a grape. "That is the ventral horn, Aitelli. A little more acquaintance with the book would be useful."

And so we struggle with the heat and darkness, with the intricately beautiful patterns of structure and function that determine our movements, and, through the summer's remaining torpor, with the process of installing all of that information within our own packages of cerebral neurons for future use.

Year Two

The second year brought a whole new horizon. Having knowledge of the normal human organism firmly laid, we now moved to the abnormal, to pathology, and to seeing some live people - sick people mostly, some fatally ill and dying. Again there was the endless poring over stained slides under the microscope, but now these tissue samples came from victims of some kind of misfortune - infections, cancers of many kinds, autoimmune diseases, degenerative diseases, diseases of unknown causes. We studied surgical and autopsy specimens, fresh or pickled in jars.

I had seen only rare bits of surgery, enough to note the style, the attitudes of the surgeons toward their material, their meticulous handling and utmost care with and respect for living tissues.

Then we saw our first autopsy. That the pathologist wielding the scalpel was a woman perhaps enhanced the effect.

She stands behind the cart in the front of the room. As she gives a brief history of the patient's final illness she lifts away the white sheet to reveal a pale form, a man clearly different from our friends the lab cadavers. Just by looking one knows that he is cold.

She picks up the knife and with a single breathtaking sweep makes a looping cut, from the front of the left shoulder arcing downward to the tip of the breastbone and up to the right shoulder. Unlike our careful dissections in the anatomy lab, this first cut is not merely skin deep; the knife has splayed open the pectoral muscles, some ribs are exposed, and the lady seems entirely oblivious of the ghastly wound she has inflicted. In moments the rest of the Y-shaped incision has reached the pubis, the rib cartilages are severed, and the front of the rib cage is swung open like the hood of an automobile.

Over the years I have done quite a few autopsies, and I can verify the truism that a pathologist does an autopsy much faster than a surgeon. Try as I may, I have never been able to relinquish my profound respect for the tissues I was cutting, structures on which I would spend uncounted hours of anxious care in the operating room. To cut casually through blood vessels, nerves, and vital organs never felt right, even in the morgue.

Second year medical students are a sorry lot, because they're so frequently ill. Take lymphoma, for instance. I looked at enough stained slides of lymph nodes and spleen and other parts so that I could pretty well recognize a lymphatic tumor; and then I read in *Boyd's Textbook of Pathology* about the palpable enlargement of lymph nodes in the neck and the groins and under the arms, slowly enlarging as the lymphoma progresses. That night I furtively felt under my arms - and found a couple of lymph nodes! In truth I had found them back when we were studying anatomy the year before, but now they carried a whole alarming new load of baggage.

Similarly with cirrhosis of the liver. Many of us, taking a deep breath to pull the diaphragm down, could easily feel our liver's edge just below the right rib margin. How does a "normal" liver feel? Or with hepatitis: is my urine really supposed to be that yellow? This went on through the litany of human ailments. Luckily we all recovered intact from the pathology book. All, that is, except Dottie, one of our classmates who actually developed tuberculosis, and died the year that the rest of us graduated.

During this year we also met bacteria. We learned how to grow them on cultures, and how to identify them by their microscopic appearances and by their habits of growth on culture media. At last I realized how totally the world is populated by bacteria - in the soil, on my skin, on doorknobs and spoons and coins, and floating in the water that I drink and the air I breathe, and within those parts of my body with direct access to the outside. Leave a Petrie dish open on the table for an hour, then cover it and place it in the incubator; the next day you can count the colonies representing the many drifters which had covertly settled in from the air.

By now P & S and Bard Hall and Morningside Heights felt like home. It was a benign and friendly environment, the neighborhood, the subways, the city, the river, and the cliffs - the Palisades, over on the New Jersey side where I went on a picnic with Ruth Alice Davis and on the way back surprised both of us on the middle of the George Washington Bridge by kissing her while the Hudson River wind blew up my sleeve and sang in the bridge cables and ruffled Ruth Alice's hair.

There was a little delicatessen across Broadway at 168th Street where a cooked turkey neck cost 15 cents, a big kosher dill pickle from the glass tub in the window was 5 cents, and a quart of milk was 10 cents. I would carry these, and maybe a piece of bread, over to Amsterdam Avenue and eat lunch in the park. Another block north was a bakery where lunch could be a big bowl of split pea soup and a roll. For an actual restaurant meal of spaghetti and meat balls, when we could afford it, there was the Tropical Gardens with a neon palm tree just across Broadway.

The first two years I lived in a single room on Bard Hall's 3rd floor. The noise and social restlessness and hallway traffic were often an impediment to studying, and sometimes, to escape the socializing, I went to bed at 8 pm with my alarm set for 3 am for a few hours of uninterrupted study before breakfast.

By now we had all become well enough acquainted so that five of us selected each other and the suite on the top floor. It worked out well, and Holmes, Bruce, Art, Horky and I lived there for two years, respecting each other's time and space, with a grand panoramic view of the river and down toward lower Manhattan where the Riverside Church spire punctuated the near skyline.

This was the year that my Navy income stopped and I got a job assisting in the autopsy room in exchange for meal tickets. I learned to peel a scalp all the way forward with cosmetic care and remove the top of the skull - with a hand saw, not today's handy electric ones - without damaging the brain; and to sew up in a hastily non-surgical manner the almost three feet of torso incision left by the pathologist.

The autopsy suite displayed a distinctive aspect of life, different indeed from the wards of living patients, but different too from the anatomy lab's cadavers. The autopsy clients were still in transition, still unsolved problems in the minds of their failed rescuers; they had not quite reached the bottom line. This fact lent a flavor of importance and urgency to the work, a counterbalance to the cold smell of blood and death and the liver balanced on the butcher's scale suspended over the emptied client on the bloody white enameled slab with rubber hose and gurgling drain.

I also worked nights in the blood bank, crossmatching units of blood for next morning's surgery and sleeping there to issue blood when needed for emergencies. This brought urgency and anxiety back into the world of the eagerly living, the would-be rescuers still looking forward instead of backward. These two jobs rounded out richly for me a broader view of life's trajectory. The connection and continuity between the living and the dead became especially vivid one sorry night when the OB resident came running in repeatedly for more blood as fast as I could crossmatch it and the woman bled to death anyway from a tear in the cervix despite all their efforts.

Diamond in the Soup

> "Big fleas have little
> fleas upon their backs to bite
> 'em. Little fleas have lesser
> fleas, and so ad infinitum."
> *Jonathan Swift*

We had just finished a several-week course on parasites, taught in part by Dr. Harold Brown. Dr. Brown had spent many years in the tropics doing research, and had written our parasitology textbook. Parasites - small animals living on or in larger animals - exist throughout the animal world. In humans these range from one-celled creatures like malaria in the blood, trichomonas in the vagina, and giardia in the intestine, to tiny worms in the flesh and worms half a foot long in the intestine.

The kinds of worms that live in the digestive tract are usually identified by using a microscope to find their eggs in the feces. Most of these creatures inhabit the tropics, and we seldom saw an actual person who was thus infested; but we had ample preserved specimens, and became proficient at identifying eggs of pinworms, roundworms, hookworms, flukes, and others, distinguished by shape, size, and how the light was refracted by the shells of eggs no bigger than pollen grains.

Third-year students were also trusted with some of the simpler lab procedures on patients on the medical wards - drawing blood, testing urine, and examining stool samples. One ordinary morning I found waiting for me a request for a stool exam on a patient whose symptoms suggested a stomach ulcer. The sample, already obtained by the nurse, was a random gob in a paper cup sitting on the counter in the lab. The patient's name was written on the cup. Let us call him Mr. Cosmo.

The doctor had ordered a test for traces of blood and also, for no obvious reason, examination for "O & P" - ova and parasites.

Familiarity had by now squelched most of my distaste for these procedures. A wooden tongue depressor served to spread a thin smear of the brown stuff onto a piece of white filter paper. A drop of guaiac solution was added, and I waited for thirty seconds, watching for a blue stain to appear. None did, meaning there was no bleeding into the client's digestive tract.

Next, a somewhat larger dip with the stick, mixed and stirred with saline solution to disperse and thin the material out enough to view it effectively. A drop of the fecal soup was put on a glass slide, a thin glass cover slip carefully floated on the drop, and the slide placed on the stage of the microscope.

Selecting the medium-power lens, I adjusted my chair and leaned forward into the "Louis Pasteur position," ready for ten minutes or so of searching for anything unusual. Feces normally contains an infinite variety of pale brown to greenish to yellow to colorless bits, flecks, gobs, or strands of the residue of assorted foods, masses of bacteria (the body's little helpers), lots of partly digested fruit or vegetable fibers, and mostly unidentifiable particles.

As I cautiously turned the knob to lower the barrel of the scope, the yellow-brown blur came into focus. A slight turn of the fine-adjustment knob. There, almost in the center of the field, as if it had been waiting for me all this time, was a gleaming jewel, the unique and unmistakable egg of *Schistosoma mansoni,* the intestinal fluke! Its elliptical form was outlined by the brightly refractile shell, and on one side was the telltale thorn-like projection, at an angle of about sixty degrees from an imaginary tangent to the oval.

My first diagnosis of parasitic infestation in a real live patient!

I stepped into the adjacent lab where a young girl, a new technician, was working with test tubes and pipettes and bottles of chemicals. The blue flame of a Bunsen burner hissed softly nearby.

"Would you come and look at something for me?" I asked. I showed her my prize. "What would you say that is?"

She peered into the eyepiece for a few moments. "It looks like some kind of egg," she said. "But I'd have to go and look in the book to say for sure."

Not the self-assured confirmation I'd been hoping for. I thanked her, resumed my position of surveillance, and moved the slide about in order to admire more schistosome eggs. They did not appear. I kept moving, but still no eggs. Finally I began a systematic search: start at a corner of the cover slip, follow along the edge to the next corner, move down the diameter of one field of view, and reverse direction, continuing so that every bit of the entire slide was scrutinized. I came across that one egg again; that was all.

Frustration rising, I prepared another slide, and another. For two hours I sat there, until forced to leave for a class, without finding another ovum.

I wrote up the slip: "Guaiac test neg. One ovum found, Schistosoma mansoni," dropped the slip into the in-basket, and scurried away.

That afternoon I caught up with the intern covering the ward, and explained the problem. For some reason he seemed skeptical - too skeptical for my liking - but said he would order another stool exam for the next day, to be done in the regular lab.

I hurried in the following day to find the report. It was, of course, negative.

I went on the ward to visit Mr. Cosmo. He lived just outside of the city, owned a real estate business, and no, he had never been in the tropics, though he had been on one brief trip to England and Scotland a few years ago. Specifically, never to "Africa, South America, some Caribbean islands, or the Middle East" where the books say *Schistosoma mansoni* is endemic.

Now I need to be perfectly clear here. Suppose you enter your kitchen and see there in the middle of a bare table, at close range and in broad daylight, a handgun, say, or a human skull, or an apple - an object that is absolutely recognizable and permits no other interpretation.

What I'm saying is, that <u>was</u> a *Schistosoma mansoni* egg.

My mind, in its spare moments, was painfully preoccupied. I went over and over the questions: Was it there? Did that specimen actually come from Mr. Cosmo? How many schistosome eggs could be present in two tablespoons of shit and still elude detection? Was Mr. Cosmo concealing something about his life and travels? Were schistosome species really as specific to certain parts of the world as penguins, pandas, or kangaroos, as I had been led to believe?

For days my concepts of reality, of seeing and knowing, of my political status in the hierarchy of students, interns, residents, and attending physicians, my very sense of self and justice and honor, all dangled from that one gleaming image.

Despite my earnest entreaties, my most ardent (though appropriately restrained) persuasions, the diagnosis of "schistosomiasis, sub-clinical" never appeared on Mr. Cosmo's chart. My attentions and concerns were urgently swept on to other matters, and I eventually quit worrying about it. But a half-century later that picture in my mind, that sparkling gem in the fecal broth, still shines undimmed.

Ivory Towers

Outside of my first eight childhood years, if there was one segment of my life that was pivotal, that was most significant in the formation of self and most formative of my style of being and believing, it probably was my years at Columbia-Presbyterian Medical Center, the shining beacon on the hill.

The Center consisted of Columbia University College of Physicians and Surgeons, more manageably called P & S; Columbia University School of Nursing; Presbyterian Hospital; New York Psychiatric Institute; the Neurologic Institute; Bard Hall, dormitory for the medical students; Maxwell Hall, residence for the nursing students; and other lesser affiliates and associations and medical, social, educational and economic tentacles that stretched out through the neighborhood, the city, and beyond. This was considered by trustees, alumni, faculty, students, and many outsiders to be the true Ivory Towers of medicine - one of the best. To the eyes of a naive country lad, only fragments of this great organism were visible, and even after four years I understood far less of the structure and inner workings of the Medical Center than of the human body.

I experienced it variously as King Arthur's Court; a vast three-dimensional maze; a feeding trough for those of us hungry for knowledge; a sort of dingy underground nest for our colony of timid, scurrying novices; and a clanking cookie-cutter hammering out an endless stream of identical medical-doctor units.

There was far more knowledge available at P & S than any one individual could ever absorb. Yet human frailties and physical misfortunes are so richly diverse that even in a place like Columbia-Presbyterian there were things a student might never have a chance to see, and we had a tightly scheduled time in which to see them. To cover these gaps, we were sometimes sent down from the Ivory Towers to other hospitals in the city for special learning experiences. Sharp mental images from four of them remain with me.

I. MONTEFIORE

Montefiore Hospital, in the Bronx, was dedicated to the care and warehousing of people with chronic, generally incurable illnesses. As part of the neurology course in our third year, we went down to Montefiore where we watched patients parade around and across the stage. We were asked to diagnose their neurologic problems just by watching them walk.

At this stage in our development we had learned mainly from models: the cadavers, the textbooks, the microscope images, the slides projected on the screen, the test tubes in the laboratories. We had not seriously interacted with any humans except our teachers. Here it was no different; we did not communicate with these people, but merely watched them as they were directed, or in a few cases led, around the stage by a nameless attendant. We had not yet learned to think of them as patients, or as actual people with richly complex lives of their own; they were presented as mere teaching models, moving images as in a motion picture, and I felt only a vague uneasiness at seeing them there, living persons making spectacles of themselves for my benefit and receiving nothing in exchange.

A tall, slender, slightly stooped man with thick mouse-colored hair laid his cane aside and moved hesitantly, cautiously, feet spread rather widely. He lifted his foot high with each step, and as each heel touched the floor the front part of the foot came down with a slapping sound. He held his arms out a bit to the side as if reaching for something to secure his balance. This one, I suddenly realized, was easy; this fit perfectly the textbook description of "the wide-based, slapping gait" of tabes dorsalis - damage, by late-stage syphilis, to the long nerve tracts in the spinal cord that normally provide automatic reflex control of feet and legs.

The next man, appearing similar in age but heavier, shuffled across the stage in short, stiff steps, arms held rigidly at his sides, face expressionless, head bobbing in a fine trembling motion: quite clearly, Parkinson's disease due to degeneration of nerve cells in the basal ganglia of the brain.

The procession continued, a dozen or so different disorders - Charcot knee (syphilis again); foot drop from an injury;

cerebral palsy; two who had had strokes; and more - some quite easy, others that none of us could identify.

Now, a half century later, walking downtown to the Bird House Cafe in the mornings for coffee with other geezers, I go through the same drill, recognizing acquaintances by the ways they walk: Bert Miller, with his Parkinsonian shuffle and body rigidity as we greet each other on the street; Bill Hudson, whose wide-base step and reaching to touch a wall for equilibrium is still being investigated by neurologists, CT scanners, and MRIs; Rex Redden, professional tree climber and lumberjack showman, who strides along as if he were leaning into a headwind; Murl Anderson, retired school administrator, whose white tennis shoes move in a quick twinkling rhythm distinctive even from blocks away; and my own arthritic, rather tense and self-protective walk with traces of bobble, stagger, and limp.

Not only in Montefiore Hospital are the ravages of time and entropy exposed and open to the eye of a discerning beholder.

II. WILLARD PARKER

Willard Parker Hospital had long been used for the isolation and the treatment (such as it was) of infectious diseases, and according to legend had been commonly referred to as "the Pest House." Immigrants unloaded on Ellis Island for processing, if found to have contagious illness - smallpox, cholera, typhoid fever, tuberculosis - were often sent to Willard Parker to recover or to die.

In 1947 it was still open, and still reserved for contagious diseases; but public health measures, both in New York City and abroad, had greatly reduced the numbers of potential clients.

We were assigned, in groups of ten, to study contagious illnesses. Traveling by subway or car, we converged at the entrance of the ancient brick structure at 16th Street and Lexington Avenue and straggled with some uncertainty into the apparently abandoned building.

A small man appeared silently from a doorway. He wore a black suit, shiny at shoulder and elbow. A dark grey tie constricted the frayed collar of a white shirt. His pink, round, almost expressionless face was surmounted by a fringe of short white hair that stood up like dry grass in a vacant lot. He asked who we were, seemed satisfied, and introduced himself as "the doctor in charge."

He led us into a room with a table, a small blackboard, and eight well-worn wooden chairs. After some uneasy shuffling about, all but two of us were seated, and the Gnome presented a lifeless lecture on the statistics of scarlet fever, typhoid fever, and other residual plagues in the city - now a pitiful remnant of the good old days when the hospital was literally full to overflowing.

We then set out on a tour of the floors to see some actual patients. Our footsteps and hushed voices echoed down dark and empty corridors. We passed room after room containing empty beds, mostly without bedding, just thin mattresses and uncased pillows; climbed some stairs; and traversed another hallway like the first, the bare boards squeaking and resounding under our feet. At last we paused at a doorway.

"Stay here in the hall," said our leader. A slender young woman was propped up in one of the four beds.

"This is scarlet fever. She's just about recovered - had a red rash for eight days, and will be out of isolation in another week."

(The person named Scarlet Fever watched us, motionless and silent, from afar. I doubt she was aware of the irony, as I learned much later, of this, my only visit here. In the 1890s a doctor at Mount Sinai Hospital felt sorry for a little girl who was quarantined with scarlet fever in a New York hotel room, and he smuggled her out to an isolation room at his hospital. Her grateful and wealthy mother put up the money to build this new hospital for infectious diseases in 1896.)

More dismal corridors, down a flight of stairs, and on through the shadowy labyrinth scented vaguely by time and antiseptics. Again an abrupt stop before a narrow doorway. Our guide made a brief gesture and we clustered just inside the room.

Against the farther wall, under the narrow window, a small boy sat up in bed as we entered, then leaned back against the single pillow. In this cavern with its high ceiling and three empty beds, he appeared tiny, vulnerable, alone. He watched us with a quiet alertness, like a little caged animal.

"This patient came in two and a half weeks ago with a severe cough. Now he only coughs a few times a day."

The Gnome drew a bottle from his coat pocket, removed the glass stopper, and applied a wad of cotton to the mouth of the bottle. As the sharp smell of ammonia reached us, he stepped across the room and thrust the cotton under the child's nose.

The boy coughed once, took in a deep breath, then coughed again, this time in a continuous and accelerating series of coughs, shorter and shorter, smaller and smaller, on and on, faster and fainter, face turning red and then almost purple, until it seemed that the last tiny wisp of breath had been expelled from his lungs and that something would burst. Just as I wondered whether he would be able to pull himself out of this, he drew in a long, raspy, high-pitched gasp of a breath - the famous "whoop" for which the illness is aptly named. This frightening series of "locomotive coughs" was repeated once; then he relaxed, cleared his throat carefully, wiped tears from his eyes with the heel of his hand, and settled back against the pillow, obviously exhausted.

Our guide indicated that we were through here, and the group filed out. I hung behind, sorry for the boy, outraged at the cruel old curmudgeon, and guilty at being part of the occasion for this heartless abuse. As I glanced back I saw the boy suddenly sit up in bed in pleased anticipation as the Gnome slid by the bed and with a furtive backhand move slipped a coin into the little outstretched palm. The boy slid down under the sheet, a definitely non-abused grin spreading across his face.

The conspiracy was clear. As I caught up with the others I looked at the funny little doctor in a different light. Suddenly everything was all right again.

Now, whenever I give an exuberant demonstration, a vivid reenactment of that cough to young nurses or doctors who have

47

never seen a case of whooping cough, they shake me and clap me on the back in alarm, fearing that I may be gasping my last.

III. BELLEVUE

In the third year we were learning physical diagnosis, and a few of us were dispatched to Bellevue Hospital to test our skills. Picking up a slip at the front desk of P & S designating a ward and a patient number, I set off by subway.

Bellevue Hospital was - and, 50 years later, I presume still is - a vast medical kaleidoscope. As a student I had only a few brief and limited contacts there; legend, newspaper articles, and personal conversations fleshed out the picture. I briefly glimpsed the emergency department, a crowded and seemingly chaotic space with orderlies rushing past each other pushing wheeled stretchers empty or loaded, sometimes bearing a long object completely covered with a sheet; interns calling for x-rays and hastily scribbling orders; blood, vomit, soapy water; IV bottles hanging; policemen questioning a patient and perhaps handcuffing him to the stretcher; a gooseneck lamp illuminating the sterile field where a doctor stitched up a lacerated scalp; moaning, a baby's cries, an urgent current of voices. I passed through the "drunk tank," and through the detox ward where despair was the predominant flavor in the air. White-jacketed staff struggled to put protective restraints on victims of delirium tremens, gaunt derelicts cried out in terror at the creatures and visions which they alone could see, and the odors of urine and exhaled intoxicants seeped out into the hallways. Upstairs or around the corners were wards for psychiatric, pediatric, obstetric, orthopedic, and postoperative patients. Most of the customers, I deduced, were indigent or nearly so.

My patient was in the second of about twenty beds that lined the walls of a long, narrow ward. The assignment was to ask no questions about the patient's history or his diagnosis, but simply, without any other clues, to examine carefully his chest and abdomen and to report my findings to our mentor.

I introduced myself. The man graciously nodded and said "Yup!"

48

Feeling awkward, uneasy, I asked, "You know why I'm here?" He nodded.

"Learning to be a doctor," I added for good measure. "Will you please take off your shirt? I'd like to examine your chest." He did so.

He was tall even sitting in bed, well developed, muscular, no doubt a strong man used to heavy work. His skin was dark brown, dry, and laced with tiny creases or grooves that gave it the character of fine soft leather. His tightly kinky hair was grey at the edges and framed a long, narrow face.

I asked him to lean forward, and began the examination of his back - first inspection of form, symmetry, movement; then palpation, feeling for irregularities, vibrations, pulsations; then percussion, tapping with the finger tip and listening for variations in resonance; and finally auscultation, listening with the stethoscope. ("Always be systematic," I could hear Dr. Dana Atchley say. "Stay with that sequence so you don't miss anything through carelessness.")

I was approaching him with the stethoscope when the man said, "Listen to the aortic valve."

What little I heard of his voice was gentle and melodious with a very slight drawl, a bit like a black man I had once met from British Guyana.

"Thank you," I said. "I'll get to that in a minute." There seemed to be a few faint crackles at the bottoms of both lungs, but I wasn't sure whether this was abnormal or not.

The pulse in his neck was readily visible. His heart beat was strong and regular, but the sounds from the aortic valve were indeed abnormal: a proper "thud" as the ventricle contracted and its load of blood forced the mitral valve closed, but then a high-pitched "swish" audible below the right second rib as the ventricle relaxed. This meant that the aortic valve was not closing completely and with each beat some of the blood that had been pumped forward squirted back through the defective valve into the ventricle again.

"Diastolic murmur," prompted the man.

"Thank you. I agree," I said with a conspiratorial smile. I checked his abdomen for enlargement of liver or spleen, and his

49

legs for accumulation of fluid under the skin. No, there didn't seem to be any sign yet of definite weakening of his heart function.

My assessment finished, I now felt it would be fair to ask him a couple of questions.

"Have you ever had rheumatic fever?" I asked.

"Nope."

"How about syphilis?"

He smiled, and nodded.

"Thank you again," I said. "That's all I need to do."

"You're welcome," he replied. "I hope you do good."

"Thank you." I pretended to belong, strove for some semblance of dignity as I made my way down the halls and to the conference room for "debriefing" and then out into the fresh, sooty, exhaust-laden air of lower Manhattan.

Thinking back, I realized that on that day our roles were oddly inverted. That black gentleman with the failing valve was the one with the "bedside manner," the one offering comfort and reassurance. I have wished that years or months later, when his heart muscle finally tired of having to do so much of its work in vain, like Sisyphus endlessly pushing the stone uphill - that in that time when his heart was at last ready to give up, I could be there to hold his hand and say, "Wherever you're going, I hope you do good."

IV. ST. LUKE'S

I think his name was Ephraim Schorr. That's the way I remember it. The doubt is disconcerting because the rest remains so clear.

Four of us were sent to St. Luke's to watch an inguinal hernia repair. I took the subway sixty blocks down and walked across to Amsterdam Avenue on one of those light spring mornings when a breeze comes in from the Hudson and sweeps the exhaust and city fumes away beyond the East River, mixing a hint of salt marsh with the perfume of a bakery on 110th Street. The world felt rock-solid underfoot.

St. Luke's presented a modest but uncompromising face of stone and concrete. Two of my classmates were already waiting

50

in the hospital lobby, and another arrived a couple of minutes later. There was probably a statue there of St. Luke, physician and historian of Biblical lore. I recall that a worried woman in a long blue dress comforted a feeble man in a wheel chair, and a young woman seated on a bench comforted the child in her arms. But my attention was drawn mostly to the subtle fragrance of hospital, and to a kind of steadiness and tranquility around me despite the earnest busyness of the people behind the desk and moving in the corridors.

"Down to the end of the hall and take the elevator to the third floor," the receptionist tells us.

Like a litter of kittens with eyes barely open we hesitantly creep through a swinging door sternly marked OPERATING ROOMS. NO ADMITTANCE. A nurse wearing a hair-enveloping cap and a nose-and-mouth-covering cloth mask scurries briskly past us through another door; she reappears after a few seconds and pulls down her mask to direct us to the doctor's dressing room. Her voice is not loud but is crisp, strong, and compelling - a drill sergeant in sheep's clothing. As instructed, we exchange our street clothes for baggy, faded-green surgical scrub suits and don caps and masks, tying the strings clumsily by feel, trying to figure out where the ears go. We move across the hall and through another pair of swinging doors, strangers to the *terra incognita* of the actual place, and are swallowed into the somber rectitude of the sacrificial chamber.

The walls, ceiling, and floor are all varying shades of white. In the center of the room stands a heavy-looking table with a thin pad on top and assorted steel rods and levers and cranks underneath and along the sides. Directly over the table, suspended by an elbow-shaped steel arm, is a shiny hemisphere the size of a bushel basket, its glass face gazing down like a huge unseeing eye. A patient - an anonymous form covered feet to nipples with a sheet, the lower part of his face visible below a rubber mask - is just being put to sleep.

Here, I realize, is where it all comes together. Here the medical theories, knowledge, and craft converge, the practitioner cuts to the heart of his understanding and tests its truths against the beat of life itself.

"Now take a deep breath," says the anesthetist, busily checking gauges and adjusting dials. A black rubber bag rhythmically fills and empties with the patient's breathing.

The drill sergeant shows us where to stand, near the wall. "I'm the circulating nurse," she says. "That's the scrub nurse," pointing to another woman wearing cap and mask but also a full-length white gown and rubber gloves, counting and arranging instruments and gauze sponges on a tray. "Stay here until the sterile drapes have been placed on the table, and then I'll show you where to stand so you can see the incision." She heads out on another errand; at the door she turns back toward us. "Dr. Schorr doesn't want any talking in the O.R. unless he speaks to you first."

The anesthetist no longer instructs the patient; the cadence of the rubber bag is smooth and unafraid. The sheet is whisked from the anonymous and now fully naked torso and the drill sergeant returns with a bowl of fluid. With dripping gauze sponges held in a clamp she scrubs a large area of the exposed skin, all of which has been previously shaved. After the tincture of green soap comes a liberal painting with gaudy, fluorescent-red tincture of merthiolate.

Something within me is disoriented by the sight, by the ritual at once irreverent but rigorously dedicated, by the part-of-a-body suspended between living and cadaverhood, the subtle movements of breathing perceptible yet so utterly defenseless, each participant's every move completely delivered over to the event. The genitals so trivial and ignored.

With immaculate choreography now enters Dr. Schorr, clad in pale green pajamas like ours, his dark brows and brown gimlet eyes showing between cap and mask. He nods silently in our direction, then steps over to the scrub nurse, who unfolds and holds out a sterile gown. As he pushes his arms into the sleeves the drill sergeant steps behind him, pulling the back of his gown smooth and tying the strings. The scrub nurse sprinkles a small packet of powder over the surgeon's extended hands, then stretches each of the sterile gloves open in turn as as he thrusts his hands sharply forward. The gloves snap into place and firmly overlap the cuffs of the gown.

52

Just behind Dr. Schorr, also in silence, comes his assistant, whom the nurses likewise gown and glove. By his deferential and faintly hesitant manner I take him to be an intern.

Now sterile towels are laid to leave an exposed trapezoid of skin over the gaily painted right groin; I cringe to see the towels secured to the skin by clips that dig their points a quarter inch into the now unresponding victim. Next the protagonists unfold a large sheet with a hole in the middle and center it carefully over the target area, overlapping the towels.

The drill sergeant flips a switch on the wall and adjusts that imperious beacon above the table so that the world contracts and only three pairs of eyes, three pairs of hands, and a small polygon of red in a field of white are brilliantly displayed. She silently escorts us to precise locations on the floor from which we can peer over the shoulder of the surgeon or of the assistant and see most of what their hands are doing, our non-sterile hands held carefully behind us to avoid touching anything. The surgeon holds out his right hand, the scrub nurse slaps a scalpel onto his palm, and the action begins.

Not a word has been spoken in the room since the anesthetist's last instruction to the patient.

The surgeon's left hand feels briefly through the drapes for the bony landmarks: the pubic tubercle and the anterior superior spine of the ilium. One swift, clean motion of the blade lays open a four-inch-long gap in the skin, an inch above and parallel with the crease of the groin, just down to but not touching the white, glistening fascia.

As the skin and underlying tissues separate under the knife, the assistant sponges away the red with one hand and with the other he clamps with precision each small bleeding vessel, flipping the fine-pointed hemostat back so its handle lies away from the incision. Then he holds up each clamp in turn and releases it after the surgeon has tied the knot with a piece of suture handed to him by the nurse.

I recognize each layer as the operation proceeds - the skin; Camper's fascia; the aponeurosis of the external oblique and rectus abdominis muscles fused together and forming the

53

external inguinal ring; and beneath this the internal oblique muscle.

But how different from the cadaver! I never cease to marvel at the nature of living flesh: its elasticity, its fragility blended with toughness, so that some parts can be easily plucked out with tweezers while other parts can be sewn almost like canvas; the constant flow of blood, through vessels from large to microscopic, on which hangs precariously the entire fate of the organism.

"What is this structure?" asks Dr. Schorr, as he points with a hemostat and turns toward one in our group.

Brief hesitation. "Poupart's ligament." Dr. Schorr nods, and glances around the group of us.

"Have you seen this kind of operation before?"

We jointly murmur, "No sir."

He returns silently to his work.

The hands and body language of the three - surgeon, assistant, and nurse - flow like the movement of a fine Swiss watch: cut, sponge, clamp, pass the suture, tie, pass the suture, tie, pass the scissors, snip, nurse unobtrusively retrieving each instrument as it is laid down. Never a wasted move. Never a sound but the clicking of the hemostats being released, and the faint hiss of gases in the anesthesia machine.

The spermatic cord, complete with nerve and blood vessels, is gently lifted, and the hernial sac (I have never seen this before except in books) is identified and teased free from the cord with a gauze sponge. Forceps pick it up, scissors open it, a finger explores inside it. It is then carefully transfixed with a threaded needle and tied tightly at its base; slender scissors trim away the excess of the thin, translucent membrane, and the ligated neck of the sac retracts and disappears under the internal oblique muscle.

Now for the actual repair. The nurse is threading needles clamped in needle drivers, and laying them out in a row.

Dr. Schorr speaks for the first time to his assistant. "Placing this first stitch to get a firm bite of Cooper's ligament is important to keep the hernia from recurring."

"Yes, sir."

Stitching in silence, six hands synchronized like violinists in a symphony.

"Reconstitute the external ring so it just admits one finger snugly." The assistant nods, and dutifully tests the space with his finger.

The layer-by-layer closure continues. The skin finally conceals all the rest of the morning's work. The scrub nurse announces that the sponge and needle counts are correct.

"That last tie was almost too tight. It's the blood flowing in the capillaries, not the forcing of edges together, that lets the wound heal." Dr Schorr's final comment to his assistant hovers over the tableau as he strips off his gloves and lowers his mask. I glimpse his face for the first time as he exits. A long oval, chin slightly squared. Faintly swarthy. "Patrician" is a word that comes to mind.

We watch as the drapes are removed, a dressing is applied, and the patient begins to stir slightly and gives a cough. The cool tightness in the atmosphere has eased, and low-key conversation resumes. We exit on cue, change to our street clothes, and re-enter the world.

As I passed through the lobby, Dr. Schorr had finished talking to the receptionist and we reached the door together.

"Are you going back up to the school?" he asked.

"Yes."

"And the others?"

"They have a car, and some other errands. I came down on the subway."

"Would you like a ride? I'm going up that way."

"Well, yes, thank you, that would be fine," I stammered.

We walked out to the parking lot in formation as if he had said "heel," and got into a silvery-grey 1941 Oldsmobile - clean, immaculate to match Dr. Schorr's person and dress. The car glided out westward onto the street, then turned north on Broadway.

I furtively watched Dr. Schorr. His movements were as smooth, sure, effortless with the steering wheel as with the scalpel and needle driver. I looked at his hands - perfectly manicured, fingers long and slender. His fingers wrapped around the steering wheel seemed as firmly in command as they had at the operating table. My romantic vision saw him alert but relaxed, energized but at peace.

He asked me a few superficial questions - where I was from, what classes I was in at the moment, how I was getting on in New York.

"Have you seen much surgery?" he asked.

"Not much. I saw an appendectomy from the gallery at Presbyterian. But I couldn't see much of the details - not like we could today."

"We haven't been doing appendectomies very long," he said, "only about sixty years. Sir Reginald Fitz, from London, was teaching at Harvard and was among the first to do the operation. He wrote the first definitive paper on acute appendicitis. Before then surgeons called it 'typhlitis' because they thought the inflammation started in the cecum where the appendix is attached."

I had never heard the word "typhlitis"; he pronounced it "tif-leet-is", as an Englishman might.

We both fell silent, but my thoughts were churning. As a surgeon, as a teacher, as a person, here was someone to emulate, a model to aspire to.

Traffic moved smoothly, and suddenly we were turning onto 168th street and pulling up to the curb by P & S, on the Babies' Hospital side. I thanked Dr. Schorr for the ride, and for the surgical demonstration.

"You're quite welcome," he said, and drove away. I never saw him again.

Mycosis Fungoides

The Grand Professor of Dermatology - tall, solemn, with closely trimmed dark hair and long white coat - strode purposefully out of the elevator and down the hall, the hierarchy dutifully in train behind him: first a Dermatology Resident, serious and close behind his superior's left elbow; then two Interns, like colts just in from the range and freshly broken, clad in hospital scrub suits and short white jackets; and last, the nervous ragtag cluster of eight or ten third-year students in short white jackets over street clothes, uncomfortable in our uncertain identity. We jockeyed for just the right place in the parade.

The ward had six beds along either side, separated by curtains and well lit by rows of windows out of reach above the beds. The Professor checked the chart in his hand and the number on the pillar by the bed, then pulled back the curtain.

"Good morning," he said crisply, as if his concerns were elsewhere. "How are you feeling this morning?" The question sounded like a routine opening gambit, like dialing the combination to a locker, rather than an actual query. I felt strangely uneasy.

The patient lying in the bed mumbled something that I could not hear from there in the back row. She appeared to be in her thirties, with light brown hair to her shoulders, and brown eyes which darted questioningly over the shuffling assortment of strangers.

"Take off your blouse, please." Our leader waited for the group to settle and for the woman to sit up and untie the strings at the back of her hospital gown and slip it down from her shoulders. She drew up the sheet to cover her as she tossed the gown aside onto the bedside table and lay back on the pillow.

"This is mycosis fungoides," said the Professor. (Strange name, I thought sarcastically, for a young woman.) "This case is not far advanced." He seized the corner of the sheet and whipped it down to the foot of the bed so that the cringing victim was totally exposed, stark naked all the way including her toes. "The skin lesions are not prominent, but you just can see these on the right side of the chest." From where I stood I couldn't see any lesions, only a wantonly violated victim.

"This tumor is already in some of her lymph glands, and will gradually invade her spleen, liver, lungs, and other internal organs. It progresses slowly; she will probably have five to seven more years."

He talked on about the microscopic characteristics of mycosis fungoides, and compared it with the appearance and behavior of other lymphomas. I heard little of what he said. Increasingly angry at his callous disregard for the patient's feelings, I waited for him to pull the sheet back up over the young woman's body. He did not. After a few minutes, without a word to the woman, the Professor turned and walked away, his entourage following like a school of fish. As I glanced back at her she reached down and grabbed the corner of the sheet and pulled it up close under her chin.

I still count it one of the failures of my life that I didn't push through the crowd, step forward and pull up that sheet.

Pop Malmberg and
the Spry Sign

The third year was the clinical year and I had just been assigned four patients on the Orthopedic Ward. One night, after studying a few hours and wanting some movement and air, I took a brief walk east past Amsterdam Avenue, around the little park by the Harlem River, then back to the Medical Center. I needed to finish some notes on my patients' charts - a new and nerve-tingling privilege and responsibility, almost like being an actual doctor. I went through the main entrance, took the elevator to the third floor, and walked down the corridor and around a couple of turns to where P & S adjoined Presbyterian Hospital.

There was not a moat and drawbridge separating these two worlds, but the change as you passed through the opaque swinging doors was palpable. On the near side of the door were the scents of labs and classrooms, and in the now empty halls the silence was simply absence of sound. On the hospital side the air was that of live people and body functions and medicines; the quiet here had substance, the faint rustle of moving feet and the textured but softly formless tones of young women, like a flock of murmuring birds settling into trees at dusk.

I arrived just at the change of shift and had to wait for my charts because the nurses were "giving report," hastily writing last-minute comments, describing in hushed voices how the woman in Bed 5 was in a lot of pain and an old man on the other side had an open wound with an unpleasant odor, or trading complaints about a doctor's poor handwriting.

Several of the flitting white uniforms were those of upper level nursing students, or "probies." They, like myself, were having their first exposure to the trenches, the proving grounds of real blood and guts and broken bones and sickness and pain. I hovered in the shadows until the tired ones had drifted away via whispering doors and softly humming elevators, and the four fresh troops dispersed to their places.

As I finally approached the chart cart, one young lady remained in the nurses' cubicle fussing with some papers. We introduced ourselves (though we each wore a name tag) and I explained my mission. Miss Elizabeth Good pointed out that she too was still a student, having been on this ward now for a month.

"And I already know you a little bit," she said, pointing to a bulletin board near the door. There, to my surprise, were photographs of me and three of my classmates who also were assigned to the Bone Yard. She turned away and did not meet my eyes as she said, "Some of the nurses think your picture is the cutest one."

Just then a husky, guttural voice came from the deep shadows in a six-bed ward across the hall.

"Nurse! Nu-u-u-rse!"

Miss Good picked up a flashlight from a shelf and hurried in to the patient's side. "What do you need, Pop?" I heard her ask in a half-whisper.

"I don't like this!" the voice drawled loudly.

I could hear Miss Good moving things around and giving gentle reassurances. In a few minutes she came out, grinning.

"That's Pop Malmberg. He's in here with a broken hip. He's pretty deaf, and he gets confused at night."

"What didn't he like?" I asked.

She chuckled. "He'd used his water pitcher instead of the urinal, and then he took a drink."

Miss Good had to get on with her work. I did my charting on the patients I had seen earlier in the day, and headed back for my quarters.

The kaleidoscope of student life kept turning. I went every morning to the Orthopedic Ward to check on the progress of my patients, learned where to find their x-rays, and bravely wrote a brief note in the chart.

It was perhaps a week before I had occasion to return to the ward at night. I waited until a little after 11 pm. Sure enough,

Miss Elizabeth Good was on duty. I fumbled with a chart or two.

"I hear Pop Malmberg is doing pretty well," I said. "Has he given you any more exciting nights?"

"No," she said, "I just make sure his urinal is easier to reach than his water pitcher."

I noticed a subtle change in the rhythm of my days. More and more errands drew me to the Orthopedic Ward after 11 pm. It was of course helpful, in tracking a patient's progress, to have regular briefings from a nurse. I also learned such useful data as the location of the combined linen closet and medicine room (where Miss Good had to fill syringes with penicillin) as well as the timing of the Night Supervisor of Nurses (who made rounds of the wards to insure that nurses did not loiter in linen closets with medical students). I learned that Miss Good had grown up in Cameroon, West Africa, where her parents were Presbyterian missionaries. And I learned that she had a stray lock of hair which fluttered down over her left eye, and which she could deftly restore to its proper place by blowing a quick puff of air upward while her busy hands never broke stride. I learned that her name was Betsy.

One morning, before ward rounds with the attending physician and residents and interns, I noticed an envelope with my name on it tacked to the bulletin board. Inside was a note:

> Since today is Saturday and a beautiful day, maybe you would like to go for a walk around 3 pm. I'll be hanging around the lobby at Maxwell Hall. If not, it's OK and you could leave a message at the switchboard.

It was, indeed, a lovely October day. Fall can come with a sweet and gentle touch even in New York City, the air tart and clean off the Hudson, sun leaning to the south and painting leaves gold and orange along Riverside Drive, and some sort of pulsation deep in the breast of the earth beyond the range of any stethoscope.

I remained diligent, in ensuing months, at my central task of becoming a proper doctor. Whether a slight decline in my

61

grades was caused by the widening scope of human frailties and hazards to which I was being exposed, or by the diversion of some of my allotted hours to Betsy's company, no historian will ever discover. A typical evening might find us in the Maxwell Hall lounge, which was usually deserted and dimly lit after 9 pm. Or we might settle - even under a frosty wind - on one of the pedestrian benches along Riverside Drive with the Medical Center's rectangles of light hovering over our backs.

The bench afforded a widescreen panorama of the New Jersey Palisades. Swooping strings of lights on George Washington Bridge framed the right edge of our view, while to the left the scattered points of light hinted at anonymous actions and artifacts of the city's shoreline. The foreground was the Hudson River, wide and black and silent but on a breezy night picking up countless gleaming reflections.

The exact center of the show, across the river, obviously placed there for our exclusive enjoyment, was a rectangular sign formed of blinking red and white neon. Viewed close up it must have been huge, for even from our bench it dominated the scene though it stood atop the cliff, across the river, in the *terra incognita* of Fort Lee, New Jersey.

"Spry," the sign said, and then "Spry for Frying. Spry for Baking . . . For Frying. For Baking. (white) Spry. (red) Spry. S-P-R-Y, Spry. Spry for Frying . . . ."

Our endless enjoyment of the Spry sign was seriously augmented, through the winter, not only by exchange of reminiscences, family lore and stories of our so very different childhoods - of playing with black children under banana trees or catching trout in the streams of Idaho - but also by our own presence, by our touches and kisses and eager caresses.

We married in May. Neither of us had met the other's parents: both Idaho and West Africa were too far from New York City. But we did our best by mail to convey the appropriate assurances, promises, requests for permission, and expressions of our mutual and reciprocal love. When my father saw our wedding picture he exclaimed, "He looks just like he did the day he caught a three pound trout!"

We were wed in the afternoon on the day of my last three final exams to end the third year. We had a brief honeymoon on Duck Island, in Long Island Sound, where the vast Atlantic lapped coyly at the gently sloping sand under a warm sun, and dogwood bloomed outside our window.

Betsy had graduated, had a job at the New York Psychiatric Institute, and supported us through my last year of medical school.

"Yes," she used to say years later, "we met over Pop Malmberg's broken hip!"

Wringer Injury

The first Maytag I ever saw did not have a spin cycle. Instead, mounted above the tub of the machine on our back porch was a wringer: two hard cylinders like kitchen rolling pins, pressed tightly together by a heavy coil spring at either end of the rack. My mother inserted the wet clothes between the motor-driven rolls, which squeezed them through and dropped them into a basket while the water ran back into the tub.

Feeding clothes into a wringer could be hazardous. The rolls were not clever enough to distinguish between cloth and flesh, and if they caught your fingers along with the shirts, they just kept turning. It was nearly impossible to pull your hand out, and wringer injuries - especially in curious children - were common.

In the second month of my surgical residency I found myself in charge of the Outpatient Surgery Clinic. A thin, frail, white-haired lady walked in with her left hand wrapped in a dish towel. She was pale and trembling, and clearly in pain as she answered my questions.

When she felt her fingers start into the wringer, she said, she tried to reach across with her other hand to the release lever but couldn't make it work, so she braced against the tub, pulled as hard as she could, and pulled her hand out.

The result, revealed as I unwrapped the towel, was startling. The entire skin of her palm, from the wrist and base of the thumb, had been sheared loose by the roller and was laid back as a complete flap, still attached across the flexion crease at the bases of the fingers.

I had been taught the principles of skin grafts, had in fact done some small ones and watched larger ones - split-thickness pieces of skin taken from a thigh or abdomen with the Padgett dermatome. But here was a different problem, a situation I hadn't encountered. I called the chief surgical resident.

Bob Rife and a visiting surgeon who came with him agreed: "You'll have to cut that flap off so you can put on a split-thickness graft."

I knew, of course, that it wouldn't work just to sew the flap back in place as it was; all the fat and shreds of connective tissue attached to the under side of the skin would prevent nourishment and oxygen from seeping up from the live tissue of the hand into the epidermis, and the whole flap would die and slough off.

But, I argued, couldn't I trim off the fat and, in effect, convert the flap into a split-thickness graft? No, they said, you couldn't trim it that fine, couldn't work from the under side and get the skin consistently thin enough to work. But why couldn't I?

Finally I persuaded them: I could try trimming the flap and sewing it back in place. At best, it might save the normal skin of the palm, with less scarring and no need to take skin from some other donor site. At worst, a proper graft could be applied in a week or two, after my flap had died and turned black.

With a scalpel, bit by bit I shaved off fragments of fat and the protruding threads and scraps of collagen fibers, holding the skin taut over my fingers like a sock over a darning egg. After an hour of this, keeping the skin moist with saline-soaked gauze, I made some perforations for drainage and sewed the flap back in place. The result looked remarkably like a hand.

Six days and two dressing changes later I was delighted to see the entire palm, except two or three tiny dark areas, a lovely living pink. It had worked!

From this I learned that it is sometimes appropriate to color outside the lines, to deviate from tradition, provided that you understand and carefully observe the imperative principles of living flesh.

Diving In

When I finished my residency at the County Hospital, Betsy and I and our two babies moved 30 miles south to the little agricultural town of Gilroy, population 6,500. I met with each of the seven doctors there and convinced them that I was qualified to join the Medical Staff of Wheeler Hospital. Dr. Oscar Carlson, who had been there for some ten years or more, offered me space in his office building.

I hired a young nurse just out of school to be my receptionist, medical assistant, and secretary. Lavern and I trained each other and gave mutual moral support as best we could. Most of the patients in the waiting room were there to see Dr. Carlson, and they peered in the door with expressions of curiosity and skepticism as they passed our office on the way down the hall.

In the first couple of weeks I was glad not to have many patients. My time was heavily occupied with the mysteries and unfamiliar details of running a business: checking account (a psychological space full of hope and anxiety); payroll (the struggle between penury and fairness in negotiating Lavern's wages); tax laws and records, including workmen's compensation (a totally new concept for me); setting up patient charts and a filing system, getting prescription blanks printed; getting acquainted with the town's pharmacists; learning where and how to order medical supplies (in the smallest possible quantities); installing a telephone; and other measures to differentiate my presence and practice from what had always been known as Dr. Carlson's place - to become visible.

In those long-ago days the process of becoming visible was vastly different from today's method. It was unthinkable - not illegal, I believe, but a serious violation of ethics and professional protocol - for either doctors or lawyers to advertise as did ordinary merchants. These were dignified professions, not mere businesses; they provided a service, not a product, and therefore held themselves to a different standard. A simple announcement in the newspaper, as a news item, reported the arrival and location of a new doctor in town; the rest was by word of mouth or the telephone directory. A small and tasteful sign in the waiting room indicated which door to enter for Dr. Carlson and which for Dr. Merrill. If you didn't want to wait three days for an appointment with the door on the right, you could turn left and be seen at once.

I don't recall, from four years in medical school, any instruction whatever on the economics of medicine nor on the tactics and techniques for running a medical business, establishing fees, and collecting money. What is the value of service? What, to a sick person or a person in pain, is the value of money? To this day I am confused and troubled by the economics of medicine.

I inquired around and learned what other doctors were charging, and figured that a safe course would be to strike an average. Since fees varied little among the seven doctors in the area, "average" meant charging the same as most of the others: $3.50 for an office visit and $6.00 for a house call.

The several insurance salesmen in town knew that they could get an appointment for a life insurance examination, at the convenience of their client, more promptly with a new doctor. A doctor had to be approved by the insurance company - a *pro forma* and same-day process - and then could accept referrals from the agent.

Most insurance companies paid the doctor from $6.00 to $7.50. I had heard that New York Life paid $10.00, so was pleased to be contacted by the local New York Life agent.

"I'm just calling to welcome you to town," he said. "I know you young doctors sometimes have a struggle getting started. I sell a lot of life insurance policies. I'm a member of the Million Dollar Club, and have awards from New York Life for being the top producer in this area. I could send some business your way if you'd like to get approved as an examiner for New York Life."

"Yes, I'd be glad to do that."

"All right, I'll send you an application."

That afternoon his secretary brought me the form. I filled it out and promptly sent it back to the agent - call him George Carter.

The next day my benefactor called again. "I have a client for you. Can you do an exam Monday afternoon?" I consulted Lavern and gave him a time.

"Oh, by the way, this is a large policy, and it's important that the form be filled out just right. This man's been working on losing some weight, and he may not be quite down to what he wants to be, but his weight needs to be put down as 165 or a little less, so he doesn't have to pay an extra premium. Not over 165."

"I understand," I said, after perhaps a slight hesitation. "I'll take care of him."

I usually started the examination with measurements of height, weight, and blood pressure; but this time I left these until the last. As I asked Mr. Smith to step up onto the scale he hesitated, then said, "The agent talked to you about the weight, didn't he? It's supposed to be 165 or less."

"Yes, he did," I replied, and gestured toward the scale.

The reading was 182.

I filled in the blanks on the form while he put his clothes on.

"What are you putting down?" he asked.

I had given this matter quite a bit of thought during the three days. "I have to put down what the scale says, 182."

"But," he protested, "I thought you had this worked out with George Carter! If you put 182 they'll reject the application or I'll have to pay more."

"I realize that. But if I falsify your weight on this application, you'll always know that I can't be trusted. If you should come to me some time with a medical problem and I told you that you needed to have your gall bladder taken out, you'd know that you couldn't really believe me. If I'd lie for you now, why wouldn't I lie again next time we meet? We'll just have to play this straight and then you can talk to Mr. Carter about it."

He left unconvinced, uncomforted, and angry.

Years later Dr. Thomas Szasz, psychiatrist and noted medical philosopher, raised the pointed question: Is the physician to be an advocate for the patient, or for the state or the insurance company? He cannot be both.

On that day I had never heard of Dr. Szasz, but it seemed clear that my honor was being tested - and that New York Life was paying for my services. And if there appeared to be a conflict among my various roles, being an advocate for the truth seemed to cover all the bases.

After completing the examination form I wrote out a letter for Lavern to type, with an extra carbon copy:

> Dear Mr. Carter:
> I examined Mr. Smith today as you requested. His weight on the scale was 182. He was unhappy that I did not record it at 165 as you had requested.
> Under the circumstances, I think it best that you not refer clients to me for examination in the future.
> Yours truly,
> M. T. Merrill, M.D.
> cc: New York Life, Home Office

I have wondered: Was it right to send a copy to the company's home office?

I never heard from Mr. Carter or Mr. Smith again.

Pouring Snoozy

In medical school I had no hands-on encounters with anesthesia, but I had an inspiring and famous teacher, Dr. Virginia Apgar. She was especially interested in the breathing and circulation of babies, and devised the Apgar Score, now used widely around the world to gauge the condition of a baby in its first minute after birth. We watched, from the gallery above the operating theater, her relaxed but meticulous skill as she put a patient to sleep, inserted the endotracheal tube, and explained to us the critical features of each move.

As an intern at Santa Clara County Hospital (SCCH) I learned some anesthesia, and in the following year took a combined residency in anesthesia and surgery. Teaching was skimpy but learning was abundant. Al Ribisi and I were the first-year surgical residents, but after three months Al caught hepatitis and was laid up for six months, so I got even more experience than I had counted on.

Until about 1840, an operation such as amputation involved several strong men, ropes and heavy leather straps, a charcoal burner to heat an iron rod, great determination on the part of the surgeon, a disconcerting fatality rate, and a high premium on skill and speed with knife, saw, ligature, and cautery.

For the next hundred years the standard anesthetic substances were inhaled vapors - diethyl ether or chloroform. When I arrived on the surgical scene the anesthetic art had advanced to the point of using several neuro-poisons at the same time, each assigned a specific part in the process.

Intravenous injection of sodium pentothal put the patient asleep quickly and gently. Inhaled nitrous oxide gas blocked pain sensation, up to a point. Curare - used on South American poison arrows - relaxed (or paralyzed) muscles. Ether, with plenty of oxygen, could do all of these things.

These were the main agents available when I was learning anesthesia in 1950. For children, ether alone was the usual choice; and for adults, pentothal followed by an adjustable combination of oxygen with both nitrous oxide and ether. A hose connected a mask to a rubber bag on the anesthesia machine into which the gaseous mixture continuously flowed, and from which the patient drew each breath.

For tonsillectomies - the most common operation at that time - the protocol at SCCH was "See one, do one, teach one." After the poor little tyke had been put well asleep, an oxygen-ether mixture was blown from the machine via a nozzle into the side of his wide-open mouth. Since both the surgeon and his assistant wielding the suction tip were hovering directly over the patient, they both inhaled a good deal of ether. It is highly soluble in the body's fat stores and takes up to several hours to dissipate from the body - and from the breath. Often when I returned home in the evening Betsy would approach me for a kiss and then say "You were taking out tonsils this morning, weren't you?"

As an additional safety feature, an endotracheal tube is used to prevent muscle spasm, vomiting, or other problems from blocking the airway. The E-T tube makes a smoothly direct connection between the anesthesia machine and the patient's lungs.

The anesthetist literally holds the life of the patient in his hands, monitoring his condition breath by breath and often providing each breath by squeezing the ventilation bag, sometimes through the entire duration of the surgery.

In those days we didn't have the technology for measuring the oxygen in the blood; it had to be continuously guessed at by watching for subtle changes in skin color, lung sounds, and breathing. If the patient's lips, tongue, skin, or the blood that the surgeon was encountering at the moment turned from pink to blue, you were treading on perilous ground.

"Her blood's looking kind of dark," the surgeon would say, and the person at the head of the table would quickly check the gauges and make sure once more that the oxygen tank wasn't empty; watch the movements of the ventilation bag; squeeze the bag to increase the depth and rate of breathing; and then glance anxiously over the top of the screen to see whether the color of the blood had returned to normal.

Surgery nurse Irene, making up the schedule for the following day, would say, "Who's doing what tomorrow?"

I might reply, "Rife has the knife and I'm pouring," or on another day, "I cut and Ribisi passes gas."

The next year, when I entered private practice in Gilroy, all of the seven doctors there were GP's, and they provided the anesthesia - mostly Dr. Elmer Chesbro, who was otherwise largely retired, and soon including me.

One of the group was Dr. Hugo Schmidt, a somewhat older German fellow and a bit eccentric. He removed tonsils and adenoids in his office. Being young, poor, and eager, I accepted his invitation to give the anesthesia for him. I would arrive at the appointed time and so would the mother with anxious child in tow. Dr. Schmidt would remind the mother, while I put her little one to sleep, that if she rounded up two more tonsillectomy customers for him, hers would be only half price.

He worked quickly. We might do two or even three children in a morning before office hours. When finished he would hand me a ten-dollar bill for each one, and I'd still be only a little bit late getting to the office for my first appointment.

I was always a bit apprehensive about doing this as an office procedure. Dr. Schmidt's facilities and his apparent level of competence would not be reassuring to me in case of any complications or emergencies. After about a year - being only slightly less young, poor, and eager - I resigned as his itinerant anesthetist.

Dr. Oscar Carlson, who had let me rent part of his office building, was the busiest and, in my opinion, the best doctor in town, and was a generous mentor and advisor. He could give anesthesia well, but was so busy that he preferred to leave it for someone else.

About a year after we moved to Gilroy a man came into my office vomiting large amounts of blood. He was already weak, pale, and sweaty, in shock from blood loss, and from his medical history it seemed pretty certain that he was bleeding from an ulcer in or just below the outlet of his stomach.

After two blood transfusions he continued to vomit blood, and his condition was not improving. If the bleeding couldn't be stopped, he was going to die. I consulted Oscar; he said he didn't think the patient could survive surgery. However, I called Dr. Bill Molineaux, a surgeon in San Jose, 30 miles away, one of my former teachers at SCCH. I described the situation, and he said he would bring an anesthesiologist down and do a gastric resection. It was probably the man's only chance to survive.

When the team arrived an hour later we had two IV's running, one with blood, and two more pints of blood ready (our local blood bank was out, and more had been brought from San Jose). The man's blood pressure was low but had stabilized somewhat.

I assisted Dr. Molineaux with the surgery, and it went very well. A bleeding vessel was found in the duodenum just beyond the stomach, and as soon as the clamps were placed to stop the bleeding the man's signs of shock began to improve. Two hours later he was back in bed, and to our great relief he appeared almost certain to recover.

The next day Oscar stopped by to talk to me. He had stood by and watched through much of the procedure, and was especially impressed by seeing the state of the anesthetic art in action - cyclopropane, a relatively new gas which, along with endotracheal intubation, allowed faster induction, a lighter degree of anesthesia, a high concentration of oxygen, complete control of breathing, and a faster recovery - quite different from what was seen daily in our hospital.

Within two weeks Oscar - in his late thirties, with two children eight and ten years old - told me he was going to quit his practice and was enrolling in an anesthesia residency in Los Angeles. He had long felt frustrated at being "a Jack of all trades and master of none," and had decided to become the very best there was at doing one kind of thing. Three months later he was gone.

I saw Oscar once more, briefly, two years later. He said he had accomplished what he set out to do, and was content in his new role. "Do you miss general practice?" I asked. I thought I detected a slight ambivalence in his reply, but couldn't be sure.

Childbirth

"So, Ted, are you ready to deliver some babies?"

"Yep! You show me where they come out and I'll catch 'em!"

Thus had begun the one-month rotation in the Maternity Ward, one twelfth of my rotating internship at SCCH.

In medical school a few months earlier I had seen six births, and had a hand in three of them. Each was a totally different experience. What had I learned? How had this prepared me for actually being the doctor in the delivery room? How to understand the birth process?

Now, after more than a half century, my memories of that time are blurred. I can only say that somehow, 60 babies later, I had survived the month with no real disasters of my own making; had experienced some of the vast diversity in the ways babies make their entry into this world of air and light; and had established in my mind and hands my own personal concepts, rhythm, and style - unique, I'm sure, to every birth attendant - that bound me to the incredible process by which a person is created.

The nurse's standard ritual with each woman in labor started - even before the paper work - with a rectal examination so she could feel and report to the doctor the status of the cervix.

The uterus with its little passenger, the size of a watermelon, rests in the cradle of the pelvis. The escape hatch, the cervix, usually can be felt through the front wall of the rectum as a soft doughnut-shaped structure against the baby's head. (Since that time tradition has changed; the exam is now generally done directly through the vagina.) If the cervix is only one centimeter dilated, the lady may as well go home and wait. If 2 to 3 cm., better stay but expect a few hours to elapse before delivery time. If 6 cm., the doctor had better have his pants on and his car headed for the hospital. At 7 to 8 cm. the baby's head is all ready to slide through the cervix, and may appear at any moment - or may not.

The ritual then proceeded to shaving the mother's entire nether region. Next came an enema. Finally the patient was ready, as if for a surgical operation.

I had learned in medical school, and it was reinforced at SCCH, that the doctor's first duty is to give the woman in labor a shot of Demerol as soon as she complains of pain. I dutifully followed this rule, and felt guilty on those occasions when nature hastened and the baby arrived before anyone could reach the patient with loaded syringe in hand.

As delivery time drew near, nurses moved the patient into the delivery room and, with shared grunting and panting and gesturing, transferred the woman to the delivery table. Her feet went up in stirrups, cold steel cradles supported her thighs, and leather straps secured her legs and wrists.

It was now the doctor's turn for ritual: prepare to cut. The conventional wisdom was that every woman, at least with her first delivery, needed an episiotomy - that the tissues around the vaginal opening are unable to stretch adequately for passage of the baby's head (the largest and least flexible part of the baby) and that the tissues will probably tear unless a cut is made to enlarge the opening. Even if the surface does not tear, it was reasoned, the underlying muscle will be overstretched and damaged, leading to future complications such as impaired rectal or bladder control. Furthermore, some local anesthetic will reduce the pain of delivery as well as the pain of the cutting and the stitching. Hence the pudendal nerve block: a 4-inch needle inserted just beside the sitting bone, slid along the inner surface of the bone, the position of the needle monitored by two fingers in the vagina to feel the swelling as the lidocaine solution was being injected.

This (if properly executed) largely numbed the rearmost portion of the vaginal region, so that as the baby's head began to press on and stretch this area, a deep cut (an episiotomy) could be made with scissors. The theory held that sewing the severed muscle after completion of the delivery would result in better healing than if the muscle had been torn or overstretched.

76

Thus a second potential source of guilt for the doctor: failing to get an episiotomy done in time.

Even the patients were aware that the nurses executed their preparatory rites with almost religious determination. One Hispanic woman in her late thirties, having her fifth baby, came to the hospital in some haste. The nurse called me from the adjacent building, then ran down the hall with her soap and razor. I was a few yards behind and gaining on her. I heard the patient call out, after a prolonged grunting sound, "Jesus Christ, nurse, I hate to do this to you!" as a fine baby girl slid out onto the bed.

During my first 4 years in private practice I presided at the births of about 250 babies, and my method changed very little.

Then I came across a book by Dr. Grantley Dick Read, called *Childbirth Without Fear.* This physician, touring rural Europe, saw how differently those societies and those women think about and deal with childbirth. There it is treated as a natural process; here, more as a medical emergency. Bicycling through Italy he saw a woman in a field lay down her hoe, squat in a grassy place, produce a baby, pick it up and walk back to the house.

His central thesis was that American women have been conditioned to expect excruciating birthing pain, to be treated by narcotics and perhaps even anesthesia; and that a combination of fear and of ignorance about their bodies causes tenseness and counterproductive muscle actions that not only increase the sensations of pain but also slow down the actual process of dilating the cervix.

It seemed only fair and reasonable to test his claims. In a magazine ad for prenatal vitamins I found a very nice full-page, full-color, side view cut-away illustration of a pregnant woman, showing the uterus, cervix, fetus in its normal head-down position facing the mother's back, with placenta and umbilical cord and the bones of the pelvis through which the little voyager must navigate.

To each mother, sometime in the last month of her pregnancy, I devoted 15 to 20 minutes explaining the picture, predicting that she would be feeling rhythmic contractions of the uterine muscle, an intense sensation of pressure; and that the purpose of the contractions is to pull upward and outward on the muscle of the cervix while pressing the baby's head down against it. This gradually stretches the cervix open to accommodate the baby's head.

Thus far the process is automatic, not under voluntary control of the mother. Pushing down, squirming around or tightening other muscles of the body or face will not only cause the cervix to tighten and interfere with nature's dilating process, but will also increase the sensation of pain. I assured her that pain relief will be available as needed, but that relaxation will minimize the pain and speed the delivery.

It did not take long to see the results of this bit of extra communication. Unfortunately, not being pregnant myself, I was never able to verify personally the difference between a "labor pain" and a "uterine contraction," but the behavior of the ladies was convincing. They needed much less pain medication during labor.

As chance would have it, in one week I saw two 18-year-old women just starting in labor with first babies. Both of these girls entered the hospital at the very onset of labor, crying and writhing about. Both had only very slight dilatation of the cervix.

In each case, instead of ordering an injection for pain I sat down beside the patient's bed, gently laid a hand on her tummy, and explained to her what was happening, what the contractions were doing, and encouraged her - with frequent demonstrations - to relax her face and limbs and to breathe long, slow, loose breaths. "Now another contraction is just starting," I would say (I could feel it before she could), "so be ready to relax and breathe."

The result was amazing, even to me - better than 100 mg. of Demerol. These two young women both did eventually get some pain medication, but didn't need it until hours after admission.

A nurse at the hospital even told me that when someone in labor walked in the front door, she often could tell whether the woman was my patient by her behavior, by how tense and anxious she appeared.

I had that colored picture laminated in plastic. It served me for another 40 years and still lies among my souvenirs.

My next obstetrical revelation didn't occur for another 25 years.

The Robert Rife Effect

During the internship at SCCH, and the next year when Al Ribisi and I were first-year residents in surgery and anesthesia, Bob Rife was Chief Surgical Resident.

The term "resident" meant someone who had completed a year of internship and was taking another year, or more, of in-hospital training. Residents usually were just that - lived in the hospital most of the time, even though they might have a home and even a family somewhere nearby. They were also called "house officers," and carried the final responsibility for what happened in their departments.

I liked and respected Bob Rife from the start - a good, kind, conscientious doctor, a good teacher, a proper role model. His face, roundish but not chubby and with a receding hairline, was friendly and there was an openness about him, straight forward, saying what he thought. He smiled a lot, and meant it, even as he delivered a corrective comment.

It is my first month on surgery, 5 pm on my evening off. I have been up all the previous night with emergencies and can hardly wait to get out the door and breathe some of that autumn sunshine and the earthy scent from the field across the highway on the way out to the bus stop, and to catch twenty minutes' sleep on the way home.

Bob Rife is sitting on the couch in the locker room and watches me hang up my white jacket with name tag on the front and stethoscope hanging out of the side pocket.

"Hi, Ted. How did it go today?"

"Pretty good. I did three tonsils this morning, the way you showed me; that makes five that I've done. And the woman who came in at noon that we thought had a bowel obstruction is pain-free with normal peristalsis and no tenderness. I just now checked her."

"Good. Did you get her history and physical done and written up on the chart?"

80

My hand freezes on the jacket. "I was tied up in outpatient clinic all afternoon, until just a few minutes ago. I figured I could do it first thing in the morning."

"But Ted," he says, shifting slightly to face me straight on, "that's not how it works. Al's on duty tonight, right? Suppose something happens to her tonight and he has to deal with it. What he finds - or doesn't find - on her chart could make a big difference." His brow tightens just a bit. "You know, once you've signed up for this business, your first responsibility is to the patient, to give the patient the best you've got. And that means that you don't leave until your part's done."

Sheepishly I pick up the jacket, trying not to show my frustration, my fatigue, my struggle with priorities, my guilt and concern for my wife.

"I get the point," I say. "I'll go and do it now."

He smiles and settles back on the couch.

During the two years at SCCH under Bob Rife's tutelage, the best part was that I got to do a lot myself, far more than most interns or first-year residents in other hospitals. He had already had two years of general surgery elsewhere, and enough experience so he was generous in letting Al and me do such "lesser" operations as hernias, appendectomies, skin grafts, even a couple of thyroidectomies and gall bladders, with him assisting. It was a priceless opportunity for hands-on practice of surgical skills and judgment, enough to feel ready to begin my own practice.

During most of those two years I was off duty every other Saturday and Sunday, and from 5 pm (or whenever the work was finished) every other evening until 7 am the next day. Usually I arrived home dog-tired and often fell asleep on the couch while Betsy fixed supper. She ran the household, paid the bills, did the shopping, cooked and cleaned, and bore two children. It will be better, we assured each other, after this is finished and we're into the real life of a private practice.

And it was better, there's no doubt about that. The rhythm was different. I was my own boss. Following the example of the other doctors in Gilroy, I closed my office one day during the week, and from noon on Saturday until Monday morning.

During the closed times we puttered around the house, sometimes took a drive over the pass to Watsonville and had a picnic on the beach, or visited some friends - did something as a family. I did a little woodworking in the half-dark of the cellar.

We met a man in his seventies, widowed and living alone in a nearby town, who had worked in the Presbyterian mission in Cameroon with Betsy's father. She hadn't seen him for many years. He invited us - including, of course, our two small children - to his home for Thanksgiving dinner.

About two hours before time to go I got a call from the hospital: one of my obstetrical patients had just been admitted in labor.

I did not have a partner, nor any regular exchange of call with anyone; and the nurse of course knew that I was in town. This would not be a good day to call some other doctor and ask him to deliver a baby for me so I could go out for Thanksgiving dinner.

Adding to the dilemma, we thus far could only afford one car. Betsy could drop me at the hospital and go to the dinner by herself, but she didn't want to do that. We settled for hoping that this would be a quick delivery. With chagrin she called the host to tell him that we would probably be late.

It was not a quick delivery; at the appointed dinner hour we had just gone to the delivery room. And to my horror, just as the baby appeared a second woman arrived in labor.

I could feel the ghost of Robert Rife stalking into our midst, into the dynamic core of my family. Here were two people, total strangers to Betsy and known only slightly to me, who had pre-empted our plans, heaped unmeasured embarrassment and disappointment on Betsy, and smothered me with guilt. And I could see no way out.

"Hey, Ted," I could hear the grinning phantom say, "lighten up! This is what it's all about!"

The United States Army

There was some sort of disturbance in Korea. A year into my new medical practice, though technically a veteran, I received an imperative piece of mail offering me a choice: either volunteer as a first lieutenant in the U. S. Army Medical Corps or be drafted as a private in the Infantry.

After deep soul searching and serious discussion with my wife for long enough to drink a cup of coffee, I filled out the forms and involuntarily volunteered. My feelings ranged from despair to adventurous thrill, and I began the process of closing my practice.

My previous illustrious military service in the United States Navy - a year of college and two years of medical school at taxpayers' expense, and no ship except the Staten Island ferry - obviously prepared me well for my new venture of defending the health of those defending our nation against a threat that was never quite clear to me.

In July of 1951 I kissed Betsy and our two little sons goodbye and flew off to Fort Sam Houston, in San Antonio, to learn in six weeks how to be a proper medical warrior.

Did this mean, I wondered, learning how to hold a stethoscope while standing at attention? Or did it mean triage and amputations and life-saving surgery?

No, as it turned out, it meant lecture after lecture, on the sun-broiled bleachers of Texas, from a full-bodied, pleasant, no-nonsense gentleman whom we came to speak of affectionately as Captain Feces Smith. He taught us that we were more likely to face outbreaks of diarrhea and stomach upset than traumatic wounds among the troops. To prove to us that the chlorination tablets we carried were not what made the water in our canteens taste like chlorine, he made us dissolve six tablets, instead of one, in a canteen of distilled water before taking a drink. He was right. The chlorine taste came only if the pills were added to water with leaves or bugs or dirt - or, he said, a bit of feces. He convinced us that a platoon getting "the runs" was not caused by traces of soap left on the trays in the mess hall, but was caused invariably by eating traces of feces from food, water, hands, or dishes.

We took a bus to Camp Bliss one day and learned other military stuff: threw dummy hand grenades, which made only a small "pop" but felt sort of real; practiced an hour or so with rifles and real bullets on a firing range; and most memorable of all, crawled thirty yards on our bellies with full gear, under barbed wire, in rain and two inches of gooey black Texas mud, with live gunfire and tracers zipping four feet above us. Now, this was really getting us soldierized!

Here I witnessed a rare exercise of power politics, a clash between the unflinching omnipotence of the military and the thinly-gloved fist of the medical profession. We were scheduled to repeat the mud-crawl at night when darkness, ripped by red streaks of tracer bullets overhead, would amplify the impression of serious reality. But three of our soaked, shivering, slime-covered comrades joined forces and berated the poor sergeant in charge.

"We're all doctors and dentists, an older group than you're used to here. We're just civilians in costume, and we're not in top physical condition. We're already cold and wet, and we'd have to sit around like this for another three or four hours to wait for you to be ready. If anybody gets seriously sick, say with pneumonia, somebody's going to be very unhappy, and it'll be on your head!"

Somewhat to my disappointment (for I was only 28 and on a roll of eager bravado) the sergeant caved in and sent for the bus. I must confess that by the time we got back to barracks a hot shower and a meal felt awfully good.

When I left home, Betsy had just started knitting a pale green skirt - figured it would keep her occupied during the lonely times when the children would be sleeping. I called home every evening or two when I had free time.

One evening I told her about a talk we heard from a member of the 101st Airborne Division. He made being a paratrooper sound inviting: physically and mentally challenging, high regard and respect from others, plus a nice package of extra pay. I told Betsy I was kind of thinking about it. She didn't say much.

By the three-day deadline for signing up with the 101st I had decided that I'd probably better stay on the ground. When I called home and told Betsy that, she seemed relieved.

Later she told me that the next day she held up her piece of knitting to inspect it, and saw that on the evening of my first call the knitting had tightened up so that the skirt was about three inches narrower. Six inches farther down, after I announced my decision to give up on sky-jumping, the stitches slacked off to normal tension and the skirt widened out again. She had to unravel it all and start over.

Half way through the six weeks I was presented with a new question: "What is your preference of duty assignments?"

"What are my options?"

There were several, but the two that I remember were Korea and Germany.

I had studied German for a year and a half in college. I could not speak any Korean.

We had post-occupation troops in Germany but no hostilities, and after a few months my family could join me there. In Korea there were bullets and explosions, and of course no family allowed.

I requested Germany. To my surprise, the request was granted.

The troop ship from Hoboken, New Jersey, to Bremerhaven, in the north of Germany, carried about 1,100 men. Conforming to the military rules of hierarchy, those of us with metal bars on our shoulders - doctors, dentists, engineers - had the upper decks, while those with cloth stripes on their sleeves got the stagnant air and sultry heat down below.

Entertainment was do-it-yourself. We watched for porpoises, and read whatever we could find. Several of us played chess a lot. In eleven days of bland weather and smooth water I didn't get seasick, and was glad to sharpen my chess game noticeably.

In Bremerhaven, on the train headed south, I was assigned a compartment with a dentist whom I'd not met before. He said he was from Minnesota.

"I only know one person in Minnesota," I said. "My cousin, Rosemary Bertelson, lives in Walnut Grove."

"Well," he said, "the week before I left home I fixed Rosemary's teeth."

Going into another culture is tantalizing and fun and a bit scary, and this was my first experience in a foreign land. But at least here I would start out with a fair command of the language.

On the first morning I sauntered out of the hotel on Augsburg's Königstrasse and set forth to savor the city. After a couple of blocks I went into a small shop. A plump lady behind the counter smiled and moved in my direction.

"Guten Morgen," I said hopefully.

"Ach! Wie gute Deutch sie sprechen!" she said, and then, beaming, began a rapid-fire dissertation - a welcome, I presumed. To my dismay, I didn't understand a word she said.

Uneasily making my escape, I moved on down the street. In the window of a bakery, seated at a small table like a carefully arranged advertising display, were a matched pair of men, sturdily and squarely built, their broad bushy moustaches streaked with gray. They were hunched forward, glaring from under heavy brows at large wooden chess pieces arranged menacingly on the board between them. As I stood in breathless anticipation one of the men moved a black knight, but hesitated with his fingers still on the top of the piece. His adversary reached over and brushed away the lingering hand and quickly made his own move. They both resumed a tense and motionless stance.

Wondering whether it would be some kind of violation of protocol, I decided to step inside to watch. As a pretense of casual purpose I moved over to the counter and, in my most careful German, asked the slender fair-haired boy behind the counter (I guessed him at about 14) for a roll, the one with kase - cheese - on top.

He handed me the roll on a piece of waxed paper, and as I sorted out the needed coins he asked - in very serviceable English - "Would you like to play?"

Startled, I hastily considered. At least I could expect not to embarrass myself, so I smiled and assented. He brought a board and chess pieces from under the counter.

In the first game he beat me in three moves. The second time it took four. I shook my head, thanked him, took my roll and left without glancing at the combatants in the window.

I was assigned to the 11th Field Hospital, which did not yet exist but was about to be created in a building which some 30 years earlier had been an old folks' home, then during the war had housed German troops, and now had been abandoned for several years. It needed a lot of cleaning and organizing. In the back of a cupboard I found a stethoscope of the original kind, a revolutionary instrument invented by Rene Laennec in Paris around the time Lewis and Clark were returning from their hike. It was a wooden tube about a foot long, nicely turned on a lathe, with a saucer-like flange the diameter of a hen's egg at one end and a smaller expansion the size of a wine bottle top at the other. When Laennec was discovering useful information from the sounds inside the human body, he also discovered that not every lady of high status appreciated having a strange physician lay his ear against her bare bosom. The stethoscope placed some distance between Laennec's ear and his patient's modesty.

Because I had been a general practitioner with surgical privileges at Wheeler Hospital, I was able to persuade the Army to classify me as a surgeon. The 11th Field had an anesthetist, an internist, and an ob-gyn specialist (there were already a lot of military wives around) but no other surgeon nor an orthopedist. I soon became the designated bone-setter, and the question of whether "real" surgical problems would automatically be sent to the 93rd General Hospital in Munich was left tastefully vague.

One of our first actual patients, while we were still getting organized, was a soldier with a simple fracture of his wrist. An orthopedist's basic needs (before the era of fiberglass) included plaster of Paris in a usable bandage form, and water to wet it with. Back home I had rolls of gauze pre-impregnated with plaster; here we had only plaster of Paris powder in paper bags, and rolls of plain gauze bandage. The idea was to dredge the gauze through a pan of the powder and hope that enough would stay on the roll long enough to get it wet and draped onto the injured limb. A dour old sergeant, a thirty-year man with medical experience and some compassion carefully concealed, came by and showed me how. It worked, crudely but well enough. I laid a piece of plywood across the tub in a spare bathroom for a work space, and the patient perched on a folded shirt on the lid of the toilet seat while I plied my craft.

This first logistical and therapeutic triumph appeared to relieve the minds of those around who had more metal bars on their shoulders than my lone silver one, and before long I had half of an actual ward, with six beds and two orthopedic patients to call my own.

The military demands here were not great, and the medical business not challenging. We Americans were in transition from a status of occupation troops in a conquered Germany to that of allies against a potential common enemy, the Soviet Union. This was confusing to both the Germans and the Americans, and flashes of resentment sometimes flared on one side or the other.

In anticipation of my family's arrival I was given a third-floor apartment in a building "requisitioned" by the Army from its German owners. As I looked out from the bedroom, over the tops of houses across the street, a sign was visible.

"Wow," I thought. "Hasen Brauerei. Rabbit Brewery. Since 1853. That's old!" Then I read it again. No! It was <u>1583</u>! Now that must be awfully old, even for a German brewery. But a few blocks away there was a building where you could go down behind and see the stone foundation built by the Romans in 1030, the ends of big wooden timbers still showing and weathered so they looked like stacks of cardboard; and the upper part rebuilt twice through the centuries, once during the Turkish period which accounted for the onion-shaped dome on the tower. Antiquity took on a whole new meaning for me.

Betsy and the children arrived in early December - just in tme for the Christmas party of the Augsburg Medical Society. Betsy spoke no German, but had studied French in high school. We sat with a German doctor who said he had been a prisoner in France during the war; he spoke French, so each of the three of us was bilingual in a different combination. He and Betsy conversed in French, and she translated to me; he and I spoke in German, and I translated to Betsy; and either she or I could pass on to him roughly what we were talking about in English. It was a nice, happy and friendly party.

After nearly two years in Germany we still knew only Bavaria, and that only superficially. Betsy sang in the choir of the local Evangelische Kirke, and we became friends with the minister and his family. We sometimes drove out into the countryside - always, for some reason, to the south, deeper into Bavaria, into hillbilly country. Their dialect and woodcarvings, the red featherbeds plumped up and hanging out the windows to freshen, a cart pulled along the road by a cow and a horse harnessed side by side and led by the farmer, the "honey-wagon" collecting animal and human wastes door to door - these are things that come rushing back to mind with the word "Bavaria." I took a train from Augsburg down to Schwabmuenchen with my fly rod and lunch, walked out from the village to fish in the Wertach and a little stream that fed it, creeping on hands and knees through deep grass to lower a fly to brilliantly spotted little trout in the crystal-clear water, then hurried back smelling of fish and sweat to catch the last train home in time for supper; or drove down a different way to cast a small brass Colorado spinner into the Lech for trout or small pike; or we drove with the children down toward Kaufbeuren and found in a tiny village a "gasthaus und metzgerei" - cafe and meat market - where the beef or veal was killed, butchered, cooked and served on the premises and the "schnitzel natur" makes my mouth water even now in the remembering.

I recently found among some old papers a Christmas card that we received the year we came back from Germany. It had a photograph of a man, a former test pilot in the Luftwaffe, who at first had refused to eat with us. It said,

"Merry Christmas to the Merrills from Peter Geiger, whom you
taught to love Americans."

My neighbor Murl Anderson laughs derisively when my
military service is mentioned.

Am I guilty, then, that while my brother Bill stared into
freezing fog and dark at the helm of a destroyer off the
Aleutians, and when my closest high school friend Jim
Wokersein crashed in flames on a bombing run over Germany, I
peered into microscopes and carved cadavers in New York? Or
while Jim Thomason, the antique and junk dealer up the road,
hunkered behind a machine gun or drove an ambulance full of
body bags in the bloody hills of Korea, I sipped wine and cast a
fly and made another baby in Bavaria?

Sometimes I torment myself with it for a little while. Then
I think of old Luis Bidasolo. For years he rode the carriage with
the log back and forth past the screaming bandsaw in the little
Oregon mill town of Bates - a town that no longer exists.

When Luis was 83 he shuffled across his kitchen and sat
down at the table. After he caught his breath he said, "Yeah, I
worked at that mill over 40 years - except I was away four years
in the army." He paused.

"I don't talk much about that. I trained for a medic. And
then I stayed that whole time workin' in a stateside hospital.
Other guys I knew were goin' overseas and gettin' shot up and
killed, and there I stayed. That still bothers me."

Then he leaned across the table toward me, intense, his
breathing fast and labored, his dark brown eyes burning into
mine. "But I went where they told me to go," he said, "and I did
what they told me to do!"

I rest my case.

Compassion and Justice

I had never been in a real prison before, only a small-town county jail with clinky doors and a view of the park. But here it was just like in the movies. We passed two armed guards, massive steel doors clanged shut behind us, and our footsteps rang deep and hollow down cold, dimly lit stone corridors.

Around the second turn we halted. The guard motioned Don into a side room. I was ushered on ahead to the third heavy grating on the right. The jailer turned the key and I entered the cell. Again the clang of steel behind me, again the chill, the involuntary tightening in my bowels. This would not be a nice place to live.

Against the far wall, below a small window, a chair was wedged against the bunk, and light glaring between the bars drew a silhouette of its occupant. I couldn't make out the face. The drooping shoulders appeared to pour down into a long shadow on the floor.

Slowly, as with great effort, the man pushed himself to his feet. I could hear his breathing. As I approached he turned so I could see him clearly.

His face, beneath sparse wisps of white hair, was loosely draped over its bones. His skin was sallow, the eyes a faded blue. He seemed at once gaunt yet heavily built. An odor of urine and antiseptic suggested that the place had been hastily cleaned up.

"Herr Milch?" I asked. "Feldmarschall Milch?"

As if amused by my halting German - or because of the terms of our encounter - he drew his flaccid lips into a thin smile; I fancied that it was an eager, wistful smile. He nodded.

"Ich bin Doktor Merrill - ein Artzt." We shook hands. He sat on the bed, and his trembling gesture offered me the chair.

I asked how he felt, how long he'd been ill, the customary list of questions. For two years he'd felt shortness of breath with exertion, and had to cut out most vigorous activities. He no longer went to the shop to make wood and brass furniture and souvenirs with the other prisoners. For two months he hadn't been able to walk around the grounds during exercise period, and now it was hard to get to the eating hall. Sometimes he had to sleep in the chair because he couldn't breathe well lying down.

I asked him to take off his shirt. It was all just as I had expected. The speaking had tired him and his breath came fast and shallow. Veins stood out slightly in his neck. My stethoscope showed his heart beat rapid and irregular, his lungs two-thirds filled with wet crackles like crumpling cellophane. His liver was enlarged, his belly slightly distended with fluid. His legs up to mid-thigh were greatly swollen, skin tight and translucent, sandal straps imprinted deeply into the tops of his feet.

I reviewed what medical notes had been handed to me. There was no mention of an x-ray or electrocardiogram, nor any laboratory tests, but none were needed. The man was dying of congestive heart failure.

In the back of the chart a brief letter from Herr Milch's son requested that his father, because of failing health, be released from prison so he could spend his remaining days at home with his wife. It stated that his long-time home was only eight kilometers from the prison, and that his wife of 56 years came to visit him on every day that was permitted - once a week. She too was in her eighties, and getting feeble.

"Danke schön, Herr Milch," I said. I again took his hand, and it lingered in mine for an instant before I dropped it. I didn't know how to express my thoughts, so I said again, "Danke schön!" He didn't speak. Old men's eyes sometimes water a lot, so I wasn't quite sure what I was seeing. I turned away, gestured to the guard that I was finished, and walked down the hall without looking back.

The small windowless room where Don waited was stark and severe, nothing but a bare desk, two straight chairs, and a bench against the wall. It was just what I needed. I took Don's chair while he had his turn with the prisoner. For thirty-five minutes, under a dim light that dangled from the high ceiling, I sat in total privacy and silence, trying to settle it in my mind.

92

When Don returned we signed out in the visitors' log, followed our escort back through the dank halls to sweet clear light and air, and climbed into our jeep as if it were a lifeboat.

The Bavarian countryside was green with spring, and tightly trimmed. A woman in a field of young sugar beets led a cow pulling a wagon with a tank on top, and a man standing on the wagon flung out brown liquid fertilizer with a scoop. Small villages showed in the distance only as white church steeples reaching far above tiny rooftops - perhaps where Herr Milch's wife waited.

Don broke the silence. "I agree with them. He's got bad congestive failure, and it's getting worse by the week."

"Those medicines he's getting," I said, "are about what I'd be giving him if he were my patient." He nodded.

I pulled out the memo I had gotten that morning.

> *From: Lt. Col. Craig Cannon, Commanding,*
>   *54th Engineer Combat Battalion.*
> *To: Capt. M. T. Merrill, MC.*
>
> I have been requested to send two doctors to Landsberg to examine a prisoner and give a medical opinion and a recommendation as to whether he should be released.
>
> You and Capt. Bancroft are scheduled to be there at 1300 hours today. This letter will be your introduction.
>
> Please submit your report to me within 48 hours.

"The first part is easy," I said. "The medical part."

"I'd say he has a few weeks, possibly months," Don said, "but he could shuffle off any day."

"That front sheet in the folder said 'convicted of crimes against humanity and sentenced to imprisonment for life.' I wonder what exactly that means."

He didn't answer. His hands eased the wheel over to pass a farmer on a bicycle carrying a scythe over his shoulder. Then, "He said his wife always brings him fruit tarts when she comes."

I was annoyed. Why did he have to tell me that?

"He doesn't look much like a field marshal now," I said.

93

"He's been there six years. He must have been pretty old already during the war."

"Yeah," I said. I realized I was tense, frowning. I tried to relax. "I wonder who sentenced him," I said.

"I think it was one of those military tribunals after Nuremberg."

"No, I mean the people, what individual persons. I'd like to talk to them." He shrugged.

"We haven't heard what the crimes were. What was the testimony?" He didn't reply.

"What is life imprisonment? Does that mean stay in until you're dead, or just until you get sick?" He stared at the narrow road, and didn't answer.

I continued my questions in silence:

Who am I to second-guess the members of the court who had heard it all? I don't even know what crimes he committed, against whom, or why.

Should difficult breathing and an old woman baking tarts be reason enough to override an internationally constituted court's decision?

He certainly isn't any danger to the world now. But what does that have to do with it?

We pulled into the compound, and Don stopped the jeep in front of my apartment building. "I've got to take my wife shopping at the commissary this afternoon," he said. "I'll see you in the morning at the dispensary and we'll knock out the report for the colonel."

"Sure," I said, feeling sarcastic as I got out. "I'll do the heart failure part and you do the judge and jury part." He grinned and waved, and the car moved down the street and out of sight.

I sat down on the steps. The sun was pleasantly warm - a soothing contrast to the dungeon-like experience of two hours ago - and a light breeze had come up. I looked across the corner of the compound, beyond a patch of cabbages and a row of trees, to where the stone tower of the Evangelische Kirke, the largest building in Leipheim, still presided over the village. It was built in the year 1300, with a spiral staircase contained in

94

one wall and slot-like windows near the top for the archers. The moat around the village was mostly obliterated now, but the births and deaths and weddings were still being inscribed in the old register in the chamber under the tower. Our new son was in that book.

As I sat there a sort of peace settled on me, a comfort in reflecting that time grinds all of us to dust at last - the archers, and the people in the latest war, and Field Marshal Milch and the tart lady, and me and Don and Colonel Cannon. Maybe some day even the old stone tower.

I got up and went inside to start writing the report.

Pulmonary Embolus

Deep vein thrombosis comes creeping into your life like the padded paws of a cat the color of shadows.

Something causes the blood flow in one of the veins of the leg to slow down, to stagnate, and it begins to coagulate. At first the clotting causes little or no symptoms. The blood takes a different route; there are detours available. The clot grows slowly, hour by hour, day by day, blocking more branches until few alternative routes remain. Maybe now there will be some swelling, a little aching or cramping in the calf, a bit of tenderness - nothing to get very excited about.

By now the clot is like a fragile, slimy, dark red snake, maybe a couple of feet long, filling the largest vein in the leg and clinging loosely to its inner wall. From ankle to groin the veins, like a river, are larger and larger as more branches join. Perhaps now the upper end of the clot is a narrow strand hanging loose and waving in the stream of blood.

The clot, in place, is a thrombus. The thrombus, or any part of it, breaking loose and floating free, is called an embolus. Suddenly set adrift, the embolus floats into larger and larger veins until it reaches the largest one of all, the vena cava, which carries all of the blood from distant parts of the body back to the heart. Unimpeded, the clot floats into and through the two chambers of the right side of the heart and on into the pulmonary artery, which carries all of the blood out of the heart into the lungs.

Here the artery branches again and again, the branches now growing ever smaller until the clot cannot proceed. It jams in place, blocking the vessel and preventing any blood flow beyond that point. A part of the lung is now without blood, therefore non-functioning for oxygen exchange. The oxygen deficiency makes you breathe faster and feel short of breath; but the movement of air isn't affected by the embolus, so the lung sounds and even the x-ray picture are still normal. It takes a radioactive lung scan or an injection of dye into the pulmonary

96

artery to prove the nature of the problem - but that does nothing to correct it.

If the embolus is small it will block only one small branch and affect only a small part of one lung, and thus may cause little or no symptom. If it is very large it can completely plug the main pulmonary artery, with immediately fatal result.

There is an ignominious aspect to dying from a pulmonary embolus: it has a disconcerting tendency to happen while you are seated on the toilet. Straining to pass a stool causes increased pressure in the veins in the legs, which stretches them, dilates them, and thus may free the clot to start on its journey - a trip of but a few seconds from thigh to lung.

In Santa Clara County Hospital a robust man about 50 had an appendectomy, uncomplicated. On the third day, his first time out of bed, he walked into the toilet, sat down, and abruptly died in his wife's arms.

Tony Filpetti, age about 33, came home to Gilroy from San Jose four days after back surgery, wearing a body cast. His wife helped him into the bathroom. He suddenly became short of breath, blue and frantic. His wife made a panicked call and she and a friend brought him to the hospital. I met them there, and he was dying as they arrived.

An elderly man, 8 miles out from Gilroy, had been sick with congestive heart failure but doing pretty well. He sat on a commode by the bed, then got back in bed and got very short of breath, gasping. His wife was so distraught that she couldn't give clear directions as to how to get there. When I arrived, after some delay from taking a wrong turn on the country road, he was dead.

Franz Kranenberg, retired Prairie City postmaster and husband of Izetta, our surgical scrub nurse, had flu symptoms and stayed in bed a couple of days. A week later he had sudden shortness of breath. His lungs sounded normal and the chest x-ray was negative, but he had the typical overbreathing and slightly dusky color, and mild swelling in both legs.

We gave him heparin and coumadin, anticoagulants that theoretically should keep further clots from forming. But in a few days, after some gradual improvement, he had another similar episode. We discussed sending him to Portland for vena cava ligation, a new and still controversial procedure, but he didn't want to do it. "Let's wait and see how it goes," he insisted.

Finally, three weeks later, another one hit, worse than the others, and in the hospital he and I discussed the options as he lay there turning blue and gasping his last.

Even as I write this, 32 years later, I feel the frustration and the guilt of not being able somehow to stop the process, of letting Franz die; and I have to recall the details of the event in a form that absolves me of any negligence, any failure in handling the situation given the knowledge and resources available at the time. (See what I mean? ". . . resources available at the time.")

In 1986, walking the streets of Hong Kong, I came by chance to Kwang Wah Hospital. The receptionist found someone who could speak English, and I had a delightful tour of the hospital, including a conversation with a surgeon about our new policy of "early ambulation" after surgery - such as the cholecystectomy patient he was showing me.

"Oh, yes," he said, "we do early ambulation."

"On the same day as the operation?"

"Well, not that early. The patient would be afraid his incision would burst. Maybe the third or fourth day," he replied.

I couldn't get any good information on how many of his patients had pulmonary emboli; but in our country the aggressive policy of getting patients up and walking within hours after surgery had made a very great reduction in the frequency of this catastrophe.

Surgery isn't required to start a clot forming. Anything that slows down the return of blood from the legs to the heart will do, like lying in bed, or a long trip on a bus or airplane. It's even been called "Greyhound disease." On any long trip, be sure to get up and walk in the aisle for a few minutes every hour. I guarantee you'll appreciate the fact that you don't die abruptly three days after you get home.

May Dye

Mae Dye was in her early sixties, but one might have guessed her older. The nondescript light gray of her hair hinted that she may once have been a redhead. Her S-shaped posture, translucent skin, and bird-like frame suggested a bamboo-and-tissue kite - delicate, fragile, yet with sturdy resilience and flexibility.

I never got much of a picture of Mae's past; she seemed to keep it hidden away somewhere in a hope chest. I learned that she had a grown son who lived far away, and that she had lived alone for many years in a neatly kept little yellow house on the back fringe of town.

Mae and I first met when she came to me with abdominal pain, sharp and crampy. It had started the day before, and she had vomited several times. Her tummy was moderately distended but soft, with very little tenderness. It didn't require a stethoscope to hear the high-pitched tinkling sounds made by loops of small intestine trying to push a fluid and gas mixture past a place where it wouldn't go. In the midline below her navel was an old scar, and she confirmed that she had had a hysterectomy many years before.

When a surgeon removes a uterus he inevitably leaves behind a number of raw, irritated areas where vessels have been tied and things have been cut away. Each of these places, as it heals, may stick to nearby loops of intestine and eventually form an adhesion - a solid attachment by scar tissue. An adhesion may not cause trouble for years, maybe never; but it also may kink or even twist and obstruct the intestine at any time.

The rest of Mae's organ systems - heart, lungs, kidneys, circulation, blood count - checked out well. But after half a day in the hospital with a tube in place through her nose into her stomach to keep it empty, her abdomen had not improved, there was a little more tenderness, and the x-ray confirmed the "ladder pattern" of distended gas-filled loops, the hallmark of small bowel obstruction.

There was no sign yet of strangulation of the bowel, nor of peritonitis, but the safe period for waiting was past. It was time to cut.

She had adhesions, all right. Several loops of bowel had to be cautiously dissected free before we could get to the actual point of the trouble, where a loop had been constricted and laid back on itself like folding the finger of a glove. Once I released this kink the problem began to resolve itself before our eyes as the collapsed loops beyond the blockage started to fill again with air and fluid.

This is always a gratifying operation. The downside, however, is that every place where an adhesion is dissected free leaves two raw surfaces where new adhesions can now form, and one's anxious hope is that an even worse problem won't eventually develop.

Mae recovered from the surgery very well, was eating normally in two days and home in less than a week After the stitches were out I didn't see her again for several months.

Late one night she called me and said that she was having that pain again. She hadn't vomited yet, but felt that the situation was starting the same as before.

I went to her house. A brief examination confirmed her diagnosis: she was obstructed again, almost certainly by new adhesions. I shuddered at the thought of trying to whittle through the mass of scar tissue which I now envisioned. Mae shuddered at the thought of undergoing another trip to the operating room. Quite aside from the pain and misery, few people in those days had medical insurance, and she apparently lived on a very restricted income.

There is one procedure from nursing lore that has now, I believe, been largely abandoned, but which sometimes has served as a last resort in trying to unplug the intestine: the return-flow enema. If an ordinary enema has proven fruitless, one fills the enema can with warm water, inserts the black torpedo-shaped nozzle well up into the suffering victim, and elevates the can two or three feet above bed level. When the can

100

is nearly empty or the patient protests, the operator lowers the container, allowing the fluid to run back into the can. This is repeated slowly, over and over according to the tolerance of the two participants. If some gas bubbles appear in the can, they ignite eager hope.

This activity is generally done by women, by nurses. They're paid to do this sort of thing. But the stakes here were distressingly high, and it was my job to make her well. This had to be done right, and I had to do it. I explained my intention to Mae, and in an agitation of embarrassment and anxiety and cramping she gave her assent.

I went to the hospital and returned with the borrowed equipment. Mae lay on the bed on her left side. Joined by four feet of red rubber tubing, she and I slowly and patiently traded a quart of water back and forth for perhaps ten minutes. No gas bubbles appeared, and she continued to wince frequently from both the obstructed bowel and from my determined efforts.

I must say that, in theory, I can see no reason for a return-flow enema to succeed. There is no way the water is ever going to make its way up through all that length of limp and tortuous plumbing to the point of the obstruction; and even if it did, there's nothing solid to be washed away. Maybe it's a sort of internal massage effect, just moving intestinal loops around; or maybe it triggers some sort of muscular reflex in the bowel. But past teachings, and having previously seen apparent successes, were enough to persuade me to pursue this as the procedure of first, last, and only choice short of the knife.

I desisted for a bit to give Mae a rest, and at her suggestion even fixed myself a cup of tea. Then the hose and can and I went back to work.

After a few more passes with the gleaming bucketful of liquid desperation, suddenly the gurgling sound of bubbles could be heard issuing from the can. Another in-an-out cycle and more bubbles appeared, and the can was fuller than before, the fluid now green and turbid. At her request I removed the apparatus and she went to the bathroom, and through the closed door I could hear more signs of success. Her cramping stopped, and we exchanged tentative congratulations. I instructed her to eat no solids, and to take only a couple of ounces of liquids at a time for the next twelve hours, to make sure she didn't start vomiting. Then I went home and stumbled into bed.

Between 1954 and 1958 I saw Mae occasionally for minor things, but our relationship largely congealed around the threat of the adhesions. She had two more episodes of obstruction, and by the third trip she and I had the drill well developed: She calls and reports the symptoms; I pick up the equipment, drive to the yellow cottage, and knock on the slightly sagging screen door. Her voice, faintly audible, calls from her couch, "Come on in." My hand and stethoscope quickly confirm the situation. Mae assumes the fetal position on the neatly made bed with the hand-stitched quilt turned back, knees drawn up, her pale blue nightgown clutching what shreds of modesty and decorum are left to her. I solemnly go to work with hose and bucket.

Little conversation is needed. Her humiliation, my feeling of silliness, and our mutual dread of what failure will bring remain acknowledged but unspoken bonds between us, and we treat the process as if I were there simply to help with a clogged drain in her kitchen sink.

The sacrificial choreography and the rhythmic dance of magic water seemed always to be accepted by the deities of the bowel as sufficient, and she was spared the knife once more.

I don't know the rest of the story. One day I moved away, and never saw Mae Dye again.

Jack of All Trades

We settled into our chairs on opposite sides of his desk. Casual in dress and posture, Dr. Microbe gave me a reassuring smile.

"What topic have you chosen for your quiz?" he asked.

This was a traditional medical school dance, the second-year Oral Examination and Career Conference. I had been assigned to the Professor of Bacteriology.

"I've chosen Rocky Mountain spotted fever."

He nodded, just barely.

"My Sunday School teacher died of it when I was twelve," I added. His eyebrows rose briefly.

"Yes." He glanced at the ceiling, and back at me. "What is the causative agent?"

"*Rickettsia rickettsii*," I replied, hoping that my voice sounded italicized. "A rickettsia is a very small organism, sort of between a bacterium and a virus."

He frowned faintly. "What are the clinical features?"

"Fever, aching, malaise, and generally a rash in the first few days. It's often difficult to diagnose in the early stages. The main damage is to the small blood vessels, so the rash turns into petechiae or purpura - little hemorrhages into the skin."

"And into the internal organs, too."

"Uh, yes," I said. "Blackie looked a blotchy purple there in his coffin."

He winced. "That was most likely postmortem changes," he said with obvious distaste. "Purpura is not usually prominent."

"Oh."

Dr. Microbe shifted in his chair. "And how is the disease spread?"

"By the bite of a wood tick - *Dermacentor andersoni*. There are other ticks that can carry it in the eastern United States, but that's the only kind of tick I've ever seen. In Idaho the sheep carry them around."

"What is the treatment?"

"There's no specific treatment. Just supportive measures and nursing. Maintain hydration."

I quoted this from the book, and had never discussed it back home with Dr. Parkinson. He had been noted for his skill in treating spotted fever, and had been called to places as far away as Montana for consultation. But he still hadn't saved Blackie.

"What about prevention?"

"A vaccine has been used. They gave it to our Boy Scout troop. But I don't think it's considered now to be very effective." He nodded, and was about to speak. "The main thing," I hurried on, "is to avoid tick bites. When we were camping my brother and I used to strip down and inspect each other for ticks before we went to bed."

Dr. Microbe moved some papers on his desk two inches to the left, then settled back loosely in his chair and looked up at me again.

"And what are your plans for the future?" he asked

I too relaxed; the hard part had been surprisingly easy. "I'm going back out west and into general practice."

He leaned forward abruptly, arms resting on the desk, brow now sharply furrowed.

"Oh, no!" he said emphatically. "You don't want to do general practice! A Columbia man's too good for general practice! You should go into research, or a specialty, or maybe teaching."

I was startled. I had lived in small towns, and all the doctors I had ever known outside of medical school were general practitioners. Dr. Davis in Twin Falls, who delivered my younger brother; Dr. Cromwell in Gooding, who lanced a boil on my neck; Dr. Kerns, Dr. Parkinson's successor in Fairfield, who drove me 50 miles to Wendell the previous summer and took out my appendix - all of these had seemed to be real doctors, whole doctors. I was surprised to hear them disrespected in this way.

"Think about it," said Dr. Microbe.

"Yes," I said. "I'll think about it."

At that time there was no formal internship program in Idaho, and I chose an internship at Santa Clara County Hospital in San Jose, California. This turned out to be the perfect preparation for general practice. Despite a few gaps in the quality of available teaching, there was much more opportunity for hands-on experience than in the first years at any large teaching hospital.

In the rotating internship we spent one or two months on each service - male medicine, female medicine, surgery and anesthesia, pediatrics, obstetrics, orthopedics, tuberculosis and geriatrics, emergency room. After each move to a new department I always felt the need to go back and check on the progress of patients I'd been caring for. Each new area was challenging and exciting, but never to the exclusion of any of the others. There were always more skills and more knowledge to learn - obviously more than any one person could ever assimilate.

Clearly a good general practitioner must master the skills of surgery, at least for the commoner operations, including the kinds of surprises and complications one might encounter in even the most "routine" procedure. Thus I stayed on at SCCH a second year for a residency in surgery and anesthesia. When I set out the next year into private practice I had limitations in some areas but felt confident of my skills in others, and in my ability to know the difference and to get help when I needed it.

After hospital rounds one morning, in the parking lot I happened onto Al Cary - 20 years older than me, a fine doctor and one of my favorite colleagues at Wheeler Hospital.

"Ted," he said, "you should join the AAGP. I think you'd find it enjoyable and useful."

"What's the AAGP?"

"American Academy of General Practice. It's a new medical organization - a new kind of medical organization. I'll bring you some information about it."

Wheeler Hospital's medical staff had no specialists, only general practitioners. They decided who, on the basis of his training and experience, would be granted the privilege of admitting patients and using the hospital's facilities. But I later learned that in larger cities competition and jealously made staff membership a tightly guarded bastion dominated by specialists. GPs often were denied the use of the hospital, especially for surgery or deliveries. At about the time that I was a student being admonished by Dr. Microbe, unknown to me there was growing despair and demoralization among general practitioners throughout the country.

Many years later I read an account of the problem written by Dr. Stanley Truman of Oakland, California. He wrote that "In 1946 the general practitioner was at the bottom of the totem pole." A city's medical society president said, "Our general practitioners are twenty years behind the times." Even a doctor's wife, when asked in what field her husband practiced, said, "Oh, he's just a general practitioner."

Later that year, at the annual meeting of the American Medical Association in Chicago, the general practitioners got together and, under the leadership of Dr. Truman and several others, began the creation of the American Academy of General Practice. The year I graduated from medical school the Academy was officially established. It introduced a unique idea: to require continuing education as a condition of membership - a feature not then existing in any other medical organization. To remain a member one had to have 150 hours of postgraduate courses, lectures, or other types of study every three years, half of which had to be courses put on or specifically approved by the Academy.

I was gone from my practice in Gilroy for two years in the army, and by the time I was ready to accept Al's invitation and join the Academy he had tragically been killed in a plane crash; but through all my 45 years as a member, Al Cary was *in absentia* my sponsor and inspiration.

During the next few years the concept of mandatory continuing education was adopted by almost all other medical organizations, and spread increasingly to other professions as

106

well. Continuing Medical Education (CME) is now widely required not only for membership in organizations and on hospital staffs but also, in some states, to maintain licensure.

The next round of jousting over turf took place in the late 1960s. The morale of GPs and the respect accorded them had indeed improved, but there was still rivalry and conflict between generalists and specialists, focused especially on surgery. This was accentuated by the rapid growth of medical insurance: a surgical specialist generally was paid more than a GP for the same operation. The president of the American College of Surgeons proclaimed, "There's no such thing as minor surgery, only minor surgeons."

Some GPs tossed around the ironic idea of a "specialty" in general practice. After some years of negotiations and arguments, a compromise was reached: the emphasis on surgery in general practice would be reduced, the term "general practice" would be dropped, and a specialty in "family practice" was approved, with recertification required every 7 years. The American Academy of General Practice was renamed the American Academy of Family Physicians. And everybody settled down and went back to work.

I was certified by the American Board of Family Practice in 1971 and recertified in 1977 and 1984.

The vast increase in knowledge and technology, as well as changing politics and economics, have made general practice in the old sense a thing of the past; but if I were starting over again now, I definitely would choose the "specialty" of family practice - encompassing in breadth, if not in depth, the whole of medicine. And if I could meet Dr. Microbe now I would tell him, "Oh, no, you have it all backwards! Only a Columbia man is good enough for general practice."

Emigration Time

Gilroy was then a quiet little agricultural town near the southern end of Santa Clara Valley. To the north, stretching past the villages of San Martin and Morgan Hill and Coyote, toward San Jose, were fields of tomatoes, strawberries, and broccoli. Japanese farmers used short siphon tubes to direct water down each long furrow from a precisely tailored irrigation ditch. To the south and west were prune orchards tended by resident Portuguese, the prunes picked by migrant Hispanics. To the southeast were fields of garlic, and more garlic, and Gentry's garlic and onion packing plant. Gilroy called itself "the garlic capital of the world." Whenever I stepped out from an examining room into the hall I could tell after one breath whether there was an employee from Gentry's in the waiting room. In the east edge of town stood four tall white pipes gleaming in the sun, enveloped during tomato season by sun-brightened clouds of steam - the smoke stacks of the cannery. It was a lush, productive little piece of the world. I lived there with my family for eight years.

In the early 1950s the townfolk grew restless. "We've got to get more industry in here," they said, "bring in more people to share the tax burden." They formed committees, flogged the Chamber of Commerce, sent out scouts.

They got more industry, more people. New housing covered some of the fields. They had to build more schools, a new sewage treatment plant, more streets. The tax burden doubled.

The postmaster, nearing retirement, had built a dream home in a wooded area well out of town. Four years later, surrounded by new neighbors and a drive-in theater, he put his house up on rollers and moved it two miles farther up the road.

Meanwhile, driving every few weeks the 30 miles north to San Jose, we would usually see a new sign, a big billboard: "Castro Villa. Thirty new homes ready by September"; or

108

"Westfield Estates. Nothing Down for Veterans." The food basket was being rapidly paved over.

Farmers deepened their wells as the water table under the valley subsided, overdrawn by increased pumping from the aquifers. Nearer the coast, some wells brought up salt water sucked into the ground from San Francisco Bay. In San Jose, shifting sidewalks and cracks in the basement of the courthouse showed how the entire floor of Santa Clara Valley had sunk a few inches as the water was drawn out of the sand and gravel that supported it.

My wife and I, though we had met in New York City, were both small-town folks at heart and felt ourselves drowning in the onrushing tide of civilization. There was no sense of stability, no picture of the future that we could hang on the walls of our minds.

On a camping trip up into Oregon we liked the scenery, the atmosphere, and what we heard and read about the people and politics and attitudes. It was 1958, and it was time to go.

First I needed a license to practice medicine in Oregon, which required passing the Board of Medical Examiners test. This covered the clinical parts of medical knowledge - treating heart failure and diabetes, reading x-rays, managing fractures, recognizing complications in surgery and pregnancy, and so on. But if one had been out of medical school for ten years or longer he also had to take examinations in basic sciences: anatomy, physiology, bacteriology, biochemistry, pathology. I had graduated just ten years and four months before the next available test date, so I did some hasty reviewing.

I flew to Portland, took all the tests, and asked the members of the Board if they knew of any small towns that needed doctors. They said a fellow just finishing his residency at Physicians and Surgeons Hospital had looked at John Day, in eastern Oregon, as a possibility; maybe I should talk to him.

They gave me his name, I found him by telephone, and we made a date for lunch. By the time we finished eating, Howard Newton and I were partners, aiming for John Day. I needed only to check the town of John Day myself, and discuss it with my wife.

Settling Into the Outback

After a 7-hour ride eastward on the Trailways bus, I climbed down at sunrise into the fresh cool air and the scent of pine boards and shavings from a nearby sawmill.

First I talked to John Day's only doctors, the husband-wife team of Drs. Jerry and Martha Van der Vlugt. They had remodeled an old residence into a private hospital, and cordially invited us to work with them. This, it was clear, meant to work <u>for</u> them. I thanked them, and explained that we would look forward to working cooperatively with them as occasion called for, but had decided to practice as a separate partnership.

The Blue Mountain Hospital, owned by Grant County, was in Prairie City, 13 miles farther east. It had been closed for a year and a half because there were no doctors to use it.

Francis Cole, a local banker, gave me a ride to Prairie City to see the town and the hospital. Thirteen miles of river bottom land, hay fields just showing green, hereford cattle clustered around hay bales scattered by ranch hands earlier in the day. It was February, and calving time. Francis pointed to a calf lying on a pile of hay near its mother and said, "There's $70 lying there on the ground. If it wasn't for those, the economy here would be hurting; those calves are the ranchers' bread and butter."

He filled me in on some of the history of the area, and skirted around the edge of the politics. From him, and from other assorted stories and rumors, I gradually learned that political tension, medical and otherwise, between Prairie City and John Day was so thick you could cut it with a knife. At least six doctors had come to the county during the past decade, and somehow the Drs. Van der Vlugt had managed to drive them all away. Everyone in the whole area seemed either to adore the Van der Vlugts or to dislike them passionately; there was no middle ground. But that was only part of it.

Until 1933 Prairie City sat at the end of the Sumpter Valley Railroad that came in from the east and was the main supplier for much of the John Day valley. The town's school had burned in 1901. In 1904 they built a new school, but converted it a few years later into a hospital. Being the economic center of gravity, the town was able in 1930 to build a new hospital. This was added onto once or twice and had been used steadily, but now was languishing and vacant.

After the railroad closed down and freight arrived instead by truck, the economic action in the area began to shift to John Day because it stood at the intersection of two main highways. When I arrived in 1958 John Day had the Grant County Bank, a theater, three grocery stores, two pharmacies, three dentists, an optometrist, a jewelry store, a shoe store, a mortuary, three sawmills, and 1,625 people - twice the population of Prairie City. The Grant County Court House and county offices were located in Canyon City, whose city limit was only a few hundred yards south of John Day's.

Their hospital had been a source of pride and status for the people of Prairie City. But when the city had suffered an economic squeeze and had trouble maintaining the hospital, they deeded it to the county with the stipulation that it would always be operated as a hospital. Now, with nobody using the hospital, the city was suing to regain possession of it on grounds of breach of contract: it was not being operated as a hospital - nor as anything else.

To make matters worse, topping off the animosity of Prairie City toward John Day, the county's voters had just passed a bond issue to build a new hospital in John Day, to be completed in about two years.

Our arrangement for visiting the empty hospital involved meeting Harvey Wilhite, pharmacist and Mayor of Prairie City, who had a key to one lock; and Barbara Reynolds, clerk of the hospital's board of directors, who had a key to the other lock. They stood outside the front of the hospital glowering at each other while Francis and I made the inspection tour inside.

Betsy and I made a trip up together a few weeks later, and agreed that this was the place.

At last, I thought, I've found a place where growth will be limited by how fast the trees can grow and how fast the grass can grow, because it's strictly timber and cattle country. And it was remote, way out in the center of the state, from 70 to 150 miles over a mountain pass north, south, east, or west to the next larger town. A place for a doctor with either some self-confidence or some cold indifference!

We found a house for rent, and a building for an office. I talked with members of the hospital board, and they agreed to open the hospital and have it staffed and ready for Howard and me to use when we arrived on July 1. We decided to have our office in John Day, where the new hospital would be, and meanwhile commute to the hospital in Prairie City. (This choice ruffled some additional feathers in Prairie City.) Betsy and I returned home to Gilroy and started packing.

The day after our arrival in John Day I went excitedly to the hospital to admire the details and final tuneup of our new workshop. Alas! The hospital was neither open nor staffed.

"Well," a board member told us, "we decided we'd kinda' wait and see whether it looked like you'd be staying around here."

Staying around here? Without a hospital? What a grand prospect!

A couple of weeks later Gordon Wilson, a local attorney, and his wife held a cocktail party to welcome Drs. Merrill and Newton to town. Some twenty or thirty of the town's prominent citizens stood around chatting and gossiping in the Wilsons' back yard. Dr. Martha Van der Vlugt was busy at their hospital, but Dr. Jerry was there. He was a small man, wiry, with angular features and wispy reddish grey hair. He greeted me and Betsy amiably. We spoke of where we were living, how many children we had, where I had gone to school.

Nursing a scotch over ice, he turned so that speckles of afternoon sun shining through an elm tree flickered over his face, and it was hard to read his expression. He suddenly said, "I just don't think it would be in the best interests of the community to reopen that hospital in Prairie City, and I think I have enough clout to see that it doesn't happen."

There it was, the situation clarified, the game plan revealed. Howard and I had intended to keep our relationship with the Van der Vlugts friendly but separate, and here was even more incentive to maintain that resolve.

Sipping my gin and tonic bought me time to choose a reply.

"Then I guess we'll just have to be patient and see what happens."

The next move had to be ours. Within a week Howard and I had obtained "courtesy staff" privileges at the hospital in Burns, 70 miles to the south.

There are both ethical and practical problems in using a hospital 70 miles away over a mountain pass, especially when there is a hospital, owned by others, right here in town. Our solution, however, proved to be manageable.

When we have a patient who needs hospital care, we first ask ourselves, "Is this patient safely transportable to Burns?"

If "No," then we have to tell the patient, "You need to be in the hospital. Sorry, but we don't have a hospital available, so you'll have to go over and see Dr. Martha or Dr. Jerry."

If "Yes," then we say to the patient, "You have a choice: either go and see Dr. Martha or Jerry, or we will take you to Burns and treat you in the hospital there."

This, of course, was long before the concept of Emergency Medical Services. Ambulance service, such as it was, was provided by the only businesses which had equipment for moving a human body: Driskill's Mortuary in John Day, and George Sanderson, undertaker in Prairie City. Thus we would either meet the patient in Burns or provide the transport ourselves. Jean Willey rode over the mountain in the front seat of my station wagon to give birth in Burns. I took out a gall bladder in Burns, and admitted a couple of other patients there, as did Howard.

After three and a half months, the Blue Mountain Hospital Board apparently began to feel a little foolish - or had decided that we were going to stay around here - or maybe Dr. Jerry's clout had worn thin. They opened and staffed the hospital in

Prairie City, and the two of us gratefully used it for two years until the new hospital was completed in John Day.

The old structure in Prairie City, after remodeling and additions, eventually became the Blue Mountain Nursing Home, which is still operating today.

Freddie Youngren

Perhaps Freddie Youngren's was a political death.

The call came in by Blue Mountain Mill's CB radio, relayed to Carl Driskill, who called me. A logging accident up on Rail Creek; a Caterpillar tractor had rolled over onto the driver and crushed his leg.

I grabbed a kit of dressings, a Thomas splint, some liter bottles of saline solution, and my black bag, and hurried down to Driskill's Mortuary. Carl had his rig ready and had good directions to the place, about 30 miles out. We found it without any trouble.

We were near the landing, at the foot of a steep hillside crisscrossed by trails cut into the hill by the blade of a D-6 cat. While we hurried over to where a man lay on a stretcher, a couple of the loggers told us the story.

It was to be the last skid of the day. The cat-skinner would drive across the bare sidehill to hook onto three logs, all chokered and ready, and bring them down.

The cat-skinner, however, didn't feel good about this part of the hill; it was too steep for safety, and he told his foreman, Freddie Youngren, that he wasn't going to drive across there. Freddie was impatient.

"Get off, then," he said. "I'll take it across."

I have to digress here for fairness, clarity, and the futile quest for accuracy. It is said that "history is what historians agree to write down." I have recorded here my memory of what I was told on approaching the scene. Forty-two years later, recalling this day, I talked with two old loggers who knew of the incident by hearsay but had not been present; both told me the story as they had heard it: The crew were eating lunch when Freddie started up the cat-skinner's D-6 and started across the hillside, but "somehow got onto some slick rock" and the cat slid and then rolled. The original cat-skinner's version has been washed away by the stream of time.

The men describing the accident had been standing on a trail about a hundred yards downhill. They heard a noise and looked up.

"This cat," said the older, bearded one, "looked like a toy. It was tumblin' ass-over-teakettle down the hill toward us, and we started to run. Then it bounced once and sailed about ten feet over our heads and rolled on down to the bottom." He pointed to a yellow and mud-colored hunk of battered metal lying beyond some trucks. "It threw Freddie off and caught him on the first roll." The men had carried the stretcher up and got him down here to the flat.

He was conscious, in a lot of pain but not injured except his legs. The right one was crushed between the knee and the ankle, almost severed. The left femur was broken, the thigh so tightly swollen that it felt rock-hard through most of its length - meaning that already a quart or more of blood had leaked into the muscles from a torn artery. His blood pressure at this time was only slightly low and his pulse moderately fast.

We loaded him into the vehicle. I started an IV of saline, ran it as fast as the needle would carry it, and gave him repeated small doses of Demerol through the tubing. By the time we got back onto the main highway and smoother riding he was considerably more comfortable, and his vital signs were staying about the same.

The way back passed our hospital in Prairie City, then another 13 miles to Jerry and Martha Van der Vlugt's hospital in John Day, and here is a part of the event that I've thought about a lot over the years. My partner and I were still trying to work out the tactical details of our "friendly but separate" policy. Part of this had been to avoid the appearance of active competition with the Van der Vlugts, being careful to let patients freely choose which place they wanted to be treated.

Since Freddie seemed fairly stable and only a few minutes more would be required to go one place rather than the other, I asked him where he would rather go.

"Well," he said, grimacing as we rounded a curve and everything tilted a bit to the right, "Dr. Jerry's always been my doctor, and I guess I'd rather go there." His somewhat ambivalent answer makes my reflections more uncomfortable now.

We drove into John Day, and as Freddie was being unloaded I briefed Dr. Jerry on the injuries and on what I had done thus far. He directed the stretcher into his operating room. The second liter of saline solution was nearly finished as we transferred the patient to the operating table. His pulse was still about 100, but his pressure dropped during the move, from 106 to 96 - still not too alarming, but obviously indicating shock from the trauma and bleeding.

"The best way to control his pain will be to give him a spinal anesthetic," said Dr. Jerry.

"He'll be needing some more fluids and some blood," I said.

Jerry said "Yes," and the nurse was already hooking up the next bottle of saline. Jerry and another helper turned Freddie onto his side. I worried that giving a spinal just now would paralyze the automatic blood vessel constriction that was keeping him partly out of shock. I was thinking how, without overstepping my bounds - having now relinquished the responsibility and the control - I might persuade Jerry to hold off for a bit, to wait until things were more stable, and use the time to get some blood replacement and get the operating room ready for whatever surgery was going to be needed.

With this hesitation I was too late; Jerry had deftly injected the Pontocaine, mixed with glucose to weight it and thus give some control over how far up the spinal column the anesthetic would go.

Within less than two minutes Freddie's blood pressure dropped out of sight, his carotid pulse was barely detectable, and he had lost consciousness.

"We've got to tilt the head of the table down," I said, "get some blood to his brain and his heart."

"But if we do that the spinal will go too high and maybe stop his breathing."

"True, but he's going to die now of shock. We may have to breathe for him."

117

Jerry cranked the table into the head-low position. Freddie's breathing was already becoming very shallow, gasping, agonal.

Jerry began mouth-to-mouth breathing. I looked frantically around for oxygen, for anesthesia equipment, a laryngoscope and endotracheal tube. Freddie vomited, filling his airway and Jerry's mouth with lunch. Jerry swung around to the sink, spit and retched, sucked water from the faucet to wash out his mouth. I turned back to Freddie helplessly. Freddie's heart quit and he finished dying.

Jerry and I stood there, not looking at each other, not saying anything.

There are several ways of looking at this. Yes, I fault Jerry for giving the spinal injection too hastily. But there's plenty of blame to go around. I didn't take Freddie to the nearest hospital and take care of him myself. I didn't get aggressive enough with fluid replacement and insist that we get some blood going before doing anything else. I was too hesitant and too late about objecting to the spinal. I didn't know what resuscitation equipment was available and where it was located. Neither of us had ever heard of what trauma specialists now call the Golden Hour, the first hour after severe injuries when opportunities for producing a successful outcome are much the greatest.

If we had stopped at the hospital in Prairie City and I had treated him myself, would he have survived? We shall never know. And the rollover itself - was it caused by bravado and poor judgment? By self-confidence based on skill and experience? By concern for his regular cat-skinner? Just an unpredictable accident? Does it matter?

I can say with certainty that if Freddie had come thirty years later to my emergency department with those injuries, he would have found us all much better trained, more knowledgeable, better equipped, more aggressive in trauma management and circulatory support, and he would have lived to get along with one leg missing below the knee.

A rusted remnant of the caterpillar, with traces of yellow paint, still lies where it came to rest at the foot of the hill by Rail Creek.

Varicose Veins

The old man with a bicycle shop in Augsburg, Germany - old already when I was there in the Army in 1950 - was small, slightly bent, but moved briskly as a sparrow. His thick white hair lay where it chose without the need of a comb. The thin mysterious smile nearly hidden under his bushy Albert Schweitzer mustache reminded me of the Mona Lisa. Did it signify an amused contempt for my whole project, or was it congratulations for having come to the right place?

One of my colleagues at the U.S. Army's 11th Field Hospital had told me that the man would make vein strippers to my specifications, braising an olive-shaped brass head on each end of a length of bicycle brake cable.

"Ja," he said, "Ja!" as I explained in my rudimentary German what I wanted. "Ja-ja! Wie lange?" he asked, holding up a piece of the cable and suggesting a length between his hands.

I took the cable and measured on my leg: ankle to groin plus three inches. "So," I said.

I ordered two different sizes, we agreed on a price, and I would return to pick them up in a week.

At that time, in fact, I had never seen a vein stripper, much less used one. But these appeared to fit the description and the purpose that a surgeon friend had described to me - a fairly new procedure at that time - and over the ensuing years they served me and my patients very well.

Varicose veins are sometimes a problem of cosmetics, sometimes of pain, and can vary from a barely visible blue blemish on the glamorous leg of a vain young woman to the massive bulging ropes, like a tangle of chicken guts, from groin to toes of a baker named Brown, who forty years ago started his tub of doughnuts at three o'clock every morning in the place where the Bird House Cafe now stands.

Varicosities happen because the little valves inside the veins fail, letting the full weight of the column of blood from

119

the heart to the ankle press outward on the fragile walls of the veins, gradually stretching them into tortuous bulges. Presumably genetics separate my kind of veins from those of the doughnut man; but one may also assume that his constant standing through fourteen hours of bread and pastries and cakes and pies six days a week added to the process of vein-stretching. His saphenous veins and their tributaries contained so much blood that at the end of the day, when he finally flopped down on the sagging easy chair in the living quarters behind the bakery, kicked back and propped his aching legs up on a high stool, it was like giving him an instant transfusion of a quart or so of blood. He told me that he felt a rush and a pressure in his head and chest for a minute or two until his circulation adjusted and balanced out.

The long saphenous vein starts at the inner side of the ankle and courses just under the skin, up the leg and inner side of the thigh to the groin, where it dips in to join the deeper vein lying inside and under the muscles. If you have a patient stand, apply rubber tourniquets at several levels on the leg, then watch the distended veins empty as the person lies down quickly with the leg held straight up in the air, you can make sure that there is no blockage of the deeper veins, that they can handle the return blood flow, and that therefore the saphenous vein system can safely be removed.

The method is quite simple: Make a small incision to expose the long saphenous vein at the ankle, and cut and tie it off; repeat this at the other end of the vein, in the hollow just below the groin. Slip the end of the stripper into the vein at the ankle, and slide the cable upward inside the vein until it appears at the groin. (If you try to go from above downward, the stripper hangs up on the valves or the branches.) Now tie a thread securely around vein and cable at the ankle end, and start pulling up on the groin end of the cable, dragging the whole apparatus - with vein attached - up the leg under the skin, breaking off the small branches of vein along the way. The larger branches may require small side incisions to cut and tie them.

The wad of telescoping vein sliding up, briefly puckering the skin and snapping off the tributaries as it moves up the leg, always makes me shudder, appearing so crudely reckless and destructive; but as the whole thing emerges from the groin incision you have removed the consequences of one of natures careless breakdowns. Keeping the leg elevated and wrapped from toes to groin with elastic bandages for a couple of days largely limits bleeding from the small vessels so unceremoniously ripped from their connections. The final result is gratifying to both the victim and the perpetrator.

My friend Bob, a cattle rancher and the husband of my office nurse, had varicose veins in both legs. Coming in from a long day in the saddle or mending fence, he would feel an aching heaviness and mild swelling in both legs, relieved only by lying back with his legs propped up for an hour or so - a routine not easily fitted into the grueling schedule of a one-man ranching operation.

A week after his bilateral vein stripping, Bob was back at work, already rejoicing at how much better his legs felt. They never gave him any more trouble.

Thirty years later, largely retired from ranching, Bob developed heart trouble and needed a coronary bypass operation. But the surgeons could not find any veins in his legs for the graft, and they had to use arteries inside the chest and take some pieces of radial artery from his wrists. This is one complication of vein stripping that had never occurred to me, way back then before the days of open heart surgery.

Last week I called Bonnie Hilliard. At age sixty she's still giving anesthesia at Blue Mountain Hospital.

"Bonnie, do you remember those vein strippers we used to use now and then?"

"Yeah, I do."

"I haven't seen 'em for years, and suddenly got to thinking about them. Do you know whether they're still around?"

"Yeah, I think they're still lying there in the drawer with the spare instruments."

"I was wondering if anybody ever uses them any more."

121

"Dr. Spaulding used them quite a bit. I don't think Dr. Berecz has used them yet; but they're still there."

Feeling a strangely warm glow of relief, I mentally raised a toast, "Ja-ja!" to the only vein strippers I've ever seen, and to the little old Albert Schweitzer Mona Lisa bicycle man.

Coy Johnston

The sawmill at Long Creek is now only a distant memory, obliterated along with some twenty others in Grant County by political change, environmental regulations, and the relentless arithmetic of what now appear as past logging excesses. With this loss, aided by some years of drought and wildfires, economic devastation lies like a pestilence on the land.

But in the green and bustling summer of 1960 the Long Creek mill was operating full bore, and Coy Johnston, one of its stalwart workers, rode the 40 miles to our clinic on an improvised bed in the back of a station wagon. He was understandably anxious but his color, pulse. and blood pressure were surprisingly normal. A dressing of vaseline gauze and pads had been placed over a wound in his left upper chest, and when the edge of the gauze was lifted there was a whoosh of air in and out of the hole with each breath.

He could talk pretty well, and explained that he had been cleaning sawdust out from under a machine with a stick when a cogwheel caught the stick and drove it into his chest.

Howard and I assessed the situation, and decided that one of us could take care of it in the operating room under local anesthetic. Howard followed the station wagon the 13 miles to the hospital in Prairie City and I returned to the office, which was full of waiting patients.

About 45 minutes later an urgent call came to the clinic: Dr. Newton needed Dr. Merrill in surgery right away.

It took me 11 minutes to get there. While I was putting on surgical scrubs Howard briefed me. Everything had seemed stable, and Coy was breathing adequately despite the open chest wound. After infiltrating the tissues with lidocaine Howard had debrided the margins of the wound the size of a silver dollar and was getting ready to close it; but the clavicle had been broken and the piece, a bit more than an inch long, that was attached to the sternum was angled directly backward. When he grasped it with a clamp and pulled it forward the whole area suddenly filled with blood. By putting his finger into the hole and pressing forward against the back side of the joint where the clavicle attached, he could stop the bleeding. With the suction tip he got the wound and the space around the top of the lung cleared of blood, but couldn't see in behind the sternum to see where the blood had come from. This is when he had sent for help.

The two of us had no better success. It was apparent that the internal mammary artery, which runs down just behind the border of the breastbone, had been torn off, and that the piece of clavicle had been jammed in such a way as to compress the artery and prevent bleeding - until the bone was moved to its normal position. Each time one of us would release the pressure slightly to see whether the latest clamp was on the artery, the entire wound again filled rapidly with blood.

At that time we had no blood bank, but had instead a box of file cards with names and blood types of about 40 local residents who had volunteered to donate blood in emergencies. Fortunately Coy's blood type was O-Rh Positive, the most common type. The receptionist started calling in donors, and the lab technician drew blood as fast as possible.

Phyllis McCarthy, the hospital administrator, was also our anesthetist. She was sitting at the head of the table reporting on the patient's blood pressure, which had fallen significantly. She called another nurse to take her place, and was the first donor to lie down and put out her arm. The second was Mary Chapman, the patient's mother-in-law, who had just arrived. Then came a forest supervisor, an accountant, two teachers - one after another they came.

Howard and I continued to struggle, working through the two-inch hole, to secure the hidden artery. As we continued working, trying to see or feel or blindly clamp that vessel about the size of a matchstick without damaging something else, from time to time one of us would lean over the anesthesia screen and say, "How're you doin' Coy?"

"Pretty good, Doc."

A few minutes later Coy's feeble voice would come from behind the screen, "How ya doin' Doc?"

"Pretty good, Coy."

He received seven pints of blood to replace most of what we had sucked out of the chest wound.

Finally, by feel and by blind dissection we freed up the torn end of the artery and ligated it. To our relief the bleeding decreased drastically. We could then see that there was a small, quarter-inch tear in the innominate vein, a vessel the size of one's thumb leading down into the chest. A couple of small stitches closed this without much trouble, and everything seemed to be wonderfully under control.

Then we noticed, coming from under the outer edge of the wound, a steady drip, drip, drip of thin milky fluid falling down into the chest cavity. The thoracic duct was torn off, the end of it hanging there.

Throughout the body there are lymphatic ducts - very tiny channels that carry lymph, the thin watery fluid outside of the blood vessels and between the cells. The lymph channels converge like tributaries of a river so that most of the lymph from the whole body ends up at the thoracic duct and trickles back into the left subclavian vein. I had found the thoracic duct in our cadaver in medical school 16 years before, but never had occasion to see it since. Neither of us knew what to do with a torn thoracic duct. Tie it off? Attempt to patch it back into the vein? (This would be impossible - a tiny tubular shred of tissue the size of a toothpick.) Bring it to the outside?

Howard prepared to close the wound while I went out, removed my gloves, and called Dr. Marvin Lacey, a surgeon of our acquaintance in Portland.

"Tie it off," he said. "Just tie it off and don't worry about it. It'll be fine."

And so it proved. Coy was back working in the mill just under four weeks later.

In the spring of the year 2000, having retired and returned to John Day to live, I met a couple in the produce aisle of the grocery store.

"Dr. Merrill, isn't it?" the man said. "Do you remember me?"

125

I looked at him and stammered some evasive reply.

"Remember this?" he said, unbuttoning the top two buttons of his shirt.

"Coy Johnston! How the heck are you!" And we spent the next half hour, between the squash bin and the tropical fruits, reprising the whole adventure, board by board, pint by pint, stitch by stitch. His wife stood smiling, nodding, filling in 40-year-old details.

The Lady from Jordan Valley

I never knew why she came all the way from Jordan Valley, two hundred miles to our little hospital in Prairie City; there were several larger ones closer. I only saw her twice during her pregnancy, and advised her against it.

When her labor began, though, the trip went smoothly and she arrived in time, an hour before her water broke.

The baby, too, made his trip uneventfully - a fine looking boy close to eight pounds, who honored us with a prompt cry. As always, I used a suction bulb to clear mucus from his nose and throat, laid him in the bassinet, and turned my attention back to his mother.

A couple of minutes later I glanced at the baby and saw that his color had changed from pink to faintly dusky. He wasn't choking or gurgling, and was breathing easily. I picked him up, slightly head-down, and suctioned him again. His color promptly returned to normal.

During the next 15 minutes or so, while the placenta delivered and her scant bleeding subsided and the mother returned to her room, about every two minutes or so the baby's slight bluish tinge reappeared and I resorted to the suction bulb. Clearly something was amiss.

His heart and lungs sounded normal. It did not seem that mucus or fluid was blocking his throat, and his swallowing reflex was obviously working, yet frequent suctioning was needed to to keep him pink. A chest x-ray showed nothing abnormal.

I had never seen a case of tracheo-esophageal fistula, but from what I remembered from reading, that possibility began to seem likely. The esophagus lies just behind the trachea; the one tube carries fluids and food to the stomach and the other takes air to and from the lungs. As the baby's organs are developing, sometimes the trachea and esophagus - each one barely the size of a pencil - don't completely separate, leaving a blockage partway down the esophagus and a small opening from it into the trachea. Thus swallowed fluid goes into the lungs instead of the stomach.

Carrying the patient around in a warm blanket, suctioning his mouth and pharynx frequently, I made a one-handed phone call to the pediatric resident at Doernbecher Children's Hospital in Portland. He agreed that the baby should come there immediately for evaluation. I explained the situation to the mother, and between suctionings I called Phil Boyer, a local pilot and owner of a small plane.

Throughout the 90-minute flight and the 30-minute ambulance ride from the airport, the baby seemed only mildly disturbed by the regular slurp of my suction bulb.

A few minutes was enough for the pediatric doctors to see the problem. After taking an x-ray with a small amount of radiopaque dye in his esophagus, they called the surgeon, and I was allowed to watch the operation over his shoulder. I had never seen surgery inside the chest of a newborn, but the surgeon, his assistant, and the anesthetist made it look almost easy. Separating the esophagus from the trachea, closing the small opening in the side of the trachea, removing the blocked segment of the esophagus (which luckily was very short) and splicing the cut ends of the esophagus back together went without a hitch, and when it was over the baby's color remained a lovely pink. He had been just six hours old when the operation began.

"That's pretty good," said the resident. "There's another baby in Doernbecher that had the same operation three days ago. He was born right here in the University Hospital next door, and he was already 18 hours old before he got diagnosed and onto the operating table."

Bandy Sintay

Miners are burrowing animals. They are drawn to holes, to dismal claustrophobic places of darkness and seeping water and bad air, with uncounted tons of dirt and rock poised overhead.

Such people have pursued minerals in Grant County for 150 years, more or less. At Canyon City's annual '62 Days Celebration we commemorate the discovery of gold in Whiskey Gulch in 1862 (and, now, the blind date on which I met my second wife 20 years ago). The yearly Cinnabar Roundup in Mt. Vernon refers to the reddish brown ore that contains mercury. There is also silver, lead, and chromium. I've even heard of an asbestos deposit on Little Canyon Mountain. Mining continues, though on a much reduced scale, in modern times.

I got a call one afternoon from Carl Driskill. A man had fallen down a mine shaft and was injured. I grabbed the things I thought we might need and hurried down to Driskill's Mortuary, and rode with Carl out to the scene of the mishap.

Bandy Sintay was a big man, square-built, around fifty, hair beginning to thin a little; a good Christian and an avid seeker of cinnabar. He and his partner worked for a group that had leased the beginning of a mine out in Bear Valley.

Bandy's mine shaft was a square hole about seven by seven feet and forty feet deep. Its crumbly-appearing sides were shored with timbers the size of railroad ties, a line of pieces up each corner and a horizontal piece every six feet across each earthen face. Ladders were nailed to the timbers. Bandy, with a young helper named John, had been cleaning out the shaft with a shovel and a bucket on a rope, and was starting to replace a couple of the timbers that showed some dry rot. As he stood on a timber halfway down it broke loose and fell with him to the bottom of the pit.

John drove to a nearby ranch, made the phone call, and hurried back to the mine with the two ranch hands..

John and I climbed down, stepping sideways to the next ladder every six feet. I could see the place where the timber that

Bandy stood on had crumbled away, a few inches from my face as I moved downward into the shadows. The ladders felt solid but they, too, had been there a good many years; my knuckles were white and my feet mistrusted every step. The air felt heavy, damp, and inhospitable. That little square of blue sky up there, with the silhouetted heads, seemed very far away.

Bandy was lying in the cramped space on the uneven floor of the pit. "I'm awful glad to see you, Doc!" he said. He had pain in his lower back, his left ankle, and his right leg. He could move his toes and didn't notice any numbness anywhere.

His pulse was a little fast but his blood pressure was normal. Carefully removing his right boot, I could tell that both bones were broken above the ankle. I slid my hand under his back, and found a slight prominence that shouldn't be there and that was definitely tender to pressure. I could visualize what the x-ray would look like: a compression fracture of one of the lumbar vertebrae.

Someone up topside untied the rope from the bucket and used it to lower my medical bag down to me.

How to get Bandy out of the hole? I called up to the two men from the ranch. "If we get him rigged up and stable here, can you lift him out with the rope?" They promptly answered "Yes."

In the hearse that doubled as an ambulance Carl had, along with his wheeled cart, a folding stretcher of canvas on a steel frame hinged in the middle, and he lowered it down with the rope. When it was right side up, the fold locked so that it was full length and rigid; but it was apparent at once that the extended stretcher was too long to fit the hole and clear the timbers, even on the diagonal. I worried that lifting him vertically would put him into shock, as well as making stabilizing his back more difficult when he got to the top. Turned upside down, however, with Bandy secured to it, the stretcher should fold in the middle somewhat like a chair and would adequately splint the spine. I had an air splint that nicely took care of the broken leg. Whatever was wrong wih the left ankle could wait inside the boot for now. From Carl's rig came several lengths of webbing with buckles.

The people above tied the rope - five-eighths inch hemp rope; nobody knew how old it was - to a thick pole laid across the top of the hole. As this was being accomplished, some pebbles and bits of dirt came dribbling down. John removed his hard hat, reached across Bandy and set the hat on my head. I looked at him a moment and said, "Thank you!" He and I together hung on the rope briefly to try its strength. Fortunately there was extra length. I cut off a piece and tied it diagonally from one end of the stretcher to the other, like the bail of a bucket. With Bandy snugly fastened with straps across his chest, pelvis, and knees, I signaled to the lifters to test the load. The stretcher folded at his hips and the whole package was solid, just as I had hoped.

At this point a few more, slightly larger stones dropped from the edge of the pit and landed beside us. John reached over, took the hard hat from my head and put it back on his own. We did not speak nor look at each other. I signaled to the men on the rope to haul away.

This adventure had started early enough so that daylight made its way to the bottom of the chamber, but by now it was fairly dark down there. As the bizarre load moved slowly upward I climbed along beside it, keeping it lined up diagonally so it didn't catch on the timbers, and we emerged gradually into the light. John came behind me, bringing my bag. At the top, with me pushing and someone above pulling, the load was landed on solid ground and the stretcher relaxed onto the flat.

I climbed out and heaved a sigh of tremendous relief. Turning to thank the two men who had done the lifting, suddenly I was more frightened than I had been at any time during the process - frightened at how it could have ended. The two fellows were collapsed at the edge of the hole, gasping, their faces ashen and dripping sweat. Their palms were blistered and raw. One of them, the older one, coughed, then retched once, then got himself under control.

Both they and I had greatly underestimated what I had asked of them. Obviously they had used every ounce of their strength and endurance to lift this load to safety. I shuddered at what might have happened if either of them had given out in the process.

Bandy spent a few days in the hospital and a few weeks in leg and body casts, and recovered nicely. I never did know who the levitators were. Neither Bandy nor I would ever be able to give them enough thanks for that day's work.

Hearts and Minds
A Quick Dip Into a Polite War

As we left the badminton court the motionless air held a gentle scent of mud and slow-moving water. Through the trees the river glowed red-orange with the rising sun.

It was a three-minute walk back to the house. I was wiping sweat, but Romeo Gloriani didn't seem bothered by the exertion or the sodden heat. "This afternoon," he said, "we'll go to the market and get some of those eggs with the duckling growing inside. I like the twelve-day stage. In my country they are a great delicacy."

Miss Nga appears with a shy smile, and glides along like a shadow as we leave the house. At seventeen she quit school to study English and become an interpreter for Americans. She is assigned to me for my two-month tour.

Six long, low, stucco buildings make up Long An Hospital, built by the French thirty years ago. I make a courtesy call on Dr. Ca, hospital administrator. Then Dr. Lowe, a surgeon from Salt Lake City whom I'm replacing, shows me around.

In 1965 the U.S. had set up this program for American doctors to volunteer for a two-month period, treating Vietnamese civilian patients. I received a round-the-world air ticket, and $10 for each day in Vietnam. About 32 doctors were in the program at any one time. My tour was in February and March, 1966.

The American military buildup in Vietnam was just beginning, and the 20,000 or so combat troops "in country" were up near the 17th parallel; the 36 U.S. soldiers in Long An Province were non-combatants, advisors to the Vietnamese in the six districts, and were vaguely responsible for the safety of us civilians. Except for air support flown by Americans, all of the fighting there was done by the Vietnamese, mostly by the ARVN (Army of the Republic of Viet Nam). The Regional

133

Forces were troops briefly trained, armed, and sent back to defend their own villages.

Dr. Lowe and Miss Nga and I make rounds in the post-operative ward. Two patients lie foot-to-head in each bed on a thin woven mat of straw.

Patients are waiting in front of the surgery building on stretchers or sitting on the steps, and we begin the day's work. They keep trickling in:

Hamlet chief, gunshot wounds of thigh and chest.
Woman, mortar fragments in leg, thigh, and abdomen.
Old man, bowel obstruction and peritonitis.
Child, burns of back and buttocks from hot soup.
Rice farmer, stepped on mine in his field; chest, abdomen, and face sprayed with fragments; part of right hand gone.

And so on through the day.

As we get ready for bed, Dr. Lowe calls me out onto the screened second-floor porch to point out "the typical tropical evening": a full moon, banana trees waving gently in the faint breeze, the sound of singing insects, and occasionally the dull deep thump of far-off bombs or mortars.

I had gotten briefing and assignment three days earlier in Saigon.

"Tan An. Yeah, pretty quiet, not much going on down there," said Hudson, our shepherd and logistics master, handing me my papers. "Second most pacified province in the country." I exhaled gratefully.

That rumbling and shaking?

"That's B52's dropping bombs on The Iron Triangle, ten miles north. VC are pretty thick up there but they're dug into caves and bunkers and hard to find, so the bombers try to keep 'em hunkered down."

The others were assigned their posts around the country, and we asked questions.

"Everybody knows it's a civil war," Hudson said. "The VC's appeal to the people isn't communism, it's anti-colonialism. In their view, we've taken over where the French left off 12 years ago."

We headed across town to the General's house at six p.m. through a prodigious jam of motorcycles, bicycles, pedicabs, trucks, buses, and taxis. "Keep the windows rolled up," Hudson warned. "Some folks like to drop a grenade into a car full of Americans."

General Humphries shook our hands cordially.

"You doctors are greatly appreciated here," he said. "These people have never encountered modern medical treatment. Their doctors have all been drafted into the army." He waved us into seats around the room.

"Our main mission here," he went on, "is to secure the country so the people don't have to live in fear."

I had Hudson's view, but wanted a second opinion.

"Sure," the General said, "it's a combination of invasion by the North and internal, civil conflict. You'll never see a situation where the issues are so confused and unclear. Part of what you'll help to do is to win the hearts and minds of the people."

The phrase stuck like gravel in my mind. Where are their hearts and minds now?

Feb 4, 1966

Sgt. James took me to Tan An in his jeep, an hour down Highway 4.

"Would you stop here so I can take a picture?" I asked.

"You don't stop around here," he said, grinning. "It's a good bet there's a bunch of VC hangin' out in those banana trees."

I tried to sound casual. "I thought this was a quiet and secure area."

"It is. They won't bother us as long as we stay on the road and keep movin'. They take over at five o'clock; you don't want to get caught out on the road at night."

In our house are several other American civilians with improvised government titles and functions:

Travis King is chief Civilian Advisor in the province.

Romeo Gloriani, from the Philippines, is on contract as a Civic Action Worker.

Harlan Grosz, Agricultural Advisor, teaches sixth-generation rice farmers how to grow rice.

Don Besom is from JUSPAO (Joint U. S. Public Administration Office), whose business is psychological warfare, education, community organizing - meaning, I presume, winning the hearts and minds of the people. He says he's here "to stick a thermometer up the rectum of the body politic."

Sam Adams, from the embassy in Saigon, is here to interview some VC defectors in a camp nearby.

I am a general practitioner from rural Oregon.

None of us can speak Vietnamese.

February 8, 1966

Dr. Lowe left yesterday. There are now only two doctors for the 140-bed hospital: myself for the surgery, and Dave Brown for the medicine and pediatrics.

Mr. Ba, surgical assistant, is tall and thin, with an open smile and elegant hands. He speaks just a little English.

Miss Phuoc gives primitive anesthesia quite well, but we do as much as possible with local anesthetic.

It's rather daunting to be entirely without blood transfusions.

The lab technician's equipment and methods are useless and I don't use the lab at all.

February 10

> *Boy, bullet through left scapula down into abdomen.*
> *Man stabbed in chest by friend last night after drinking and insults.*
> *Three-year-old girl, missile ripped two-inch gash in chest.*

Man with missile wounds of chest wall, buttocks,
thigh.
Woman, mortar fragment into abdomen, perforated
small intestine.

We are in the operating room all day, every day.

My understanding of "quiet, not much going on down there" is being sharply altered. My patients are children, women, or old men; the young men are all out fighting on one side or the other. Three fourths are wounded by some sort of missiles, and it makes little difference to the victim whether the chunk of metal was from a VC mine or mortar, an ARVN artillery round, or a bullet from an American plane.

Dave Brown has been here eleven months.

"Why are we here?" I ask. "Are we guests, or advisors, or invaders? Should we just be taking care of the sick and injured the best we can, or are we supposed to change things, teach people things, upgrade the system, or what?"

"I've been asking myself that for a year," he says. "Dr. Ca has been a challenge to work with - suspicious, intimidated by Americans. My first two months here I was really miserable and frustrated. But now we get along pretty well; he knows I'm not trying to take control of the place."

One afternoon Travis and I drove up to Saigon to shop at the commissary. On our way back, against a lovely sunset, we watched four Skyraiders making an air strike a couple of kilometers away, strafing and dropping napalm. It was a beautiful sight, seeing them circle, dive down like dragon flies almost to the tree tops, lay a barely visible strip of fire, then pull up and climb gracefully back to the sky. Surely something so small and delicate and far away couldn't possibly hurt anyone! (I'd be on call at the hospital tonight and tomorrow.)

February 20

Mr. Mohammed Ibrahim Nam is the biggest contractor

and the richest man in town, is half Indian, and lives across the alley. He invited us to dinner.

Mr. Nam is pleasant, short and solid, casual, and barefoot. I ask, "What percent of the people here in the countryside are pro-VC? Fifty percent?"

"Sixty percent," he says. "Make big war, can finish in one year. Continue little war, no finish in ten years."

March 4

The 105 mm. howitzers across the bridge are banging away tonight, as they do every day or two, firing at a specific target or "just stirring up a rice paddy" a few miles away. Business at the hospital should be brisk tomorrow.

> *Boy 7 years old, bullet in leg.*
> *Boy aged 10, compound fracture of femur.*
> *Man with femur fracture from yesterday's bus*
>   *accident.*
> *15-year-old girl, grenade fragments in neck, leg,*
>   *and ankle.*
> *Boy 19 years old, fell from little three-wheeled bus*
>   *and ruptured small intestine.*
> *Little girl with grenade fragments, one in the side*
>   *of her neck; can't move hands nor legs - and never*
>   *will.*
> *Infant boy in emergency room, moribund with*
>   *cholera. Three more cases of cholera admitted*
>   *today.*

Make rounds, check some X-rays. Just a routine day.

March 20

Last night the VC hit five of the six districts in the province, overran the outpost at My Binh, and laid a few mortar rounds at the edge of town. The nearest hit raised a cloud of smoke visible through the banana trees, illuminated by a flare plane circling above. The 81-mm. mortars in front of Col. Anh's mansion across the soccer field were returning the fire. We heard small-arms fire, and once an armed helicopter plowing a furrow with its rockets.

Travis, our leader, had on flak jacket, helmet, cowboy boots, and carbine at the ready. Romeo and Harlan knew where the grenades and 12-gauge shotgun were stored upstairs. I was armed with my stethoscope and my honest, friendly smile.

After two hours things quieted down and we all went back to bed. At 7 am I was called to see three civilian casualties, and they came pretty fast after that. Don't know how many I've seen, but included were:

> *Compound fracture of leg and ankle - old woman.*
> *Compound fracture of foot - old man.*
> *Soldier, wife, and two infants, all with metal*
> *fragments in them.*
> *Fragment completely through thigh of 12-year-old*
> *girl.*
> *A captured VC brought in by chopper; injured by*
> *explosions, then stabbed in chest.*

The Chieu Hoi (Open Arms) program illustrates the bizarre and almost comic aspects of this whole situation. Defectors from the Viet Cong are interrogated at local reception centers, confined for one to three months for "indoctrination" with anti-communist and pro-Saigon views, and some vocational training. Having thus become loyal and dedicated citizens of the South Vietnamese government, they have a graduation ceremony and are released.

The Viet Cong have a similar program for defectors to their side.

In my childhood we played Cops and Robbers. A Cop, once fairly captured, became a loyal and dedicated Robber, and vice versa. The depth of loyalty there was probably comparable to that of the Chieu Hoi graduates.

I'm trying to get clear, to find a pattern. A physician is always trying to see a pattern in the symptoms - skin temperature, pulse, breath sounds, feel of the abdomen, the subtle look about the eyes. Where is the pattern here? What is war? What is this war? It still eludes me.

March 22

Sgt. Loucell is a fine and capable medic. As we loaded up for the MedCAP (Medical Civic Action Program) trip to Thu Thua I asked him about medics carrying weapons.

"I'm not a violent man," he said. "But I've got a wife and children, and we get shot at sometimes, so I keep a carbine in my jeep."

The possibility of intentionally killing someone is a psychological barrier I would dread to cross, a prospect that terrifies me even beyond concern for personal safety.

At forty-three I am a child-doctor: innocent, eager, dedicated. In World War II the Navy put me through medical school; in the Korean episode the Army sent me to Germany. My third war now, and still I have never seen combat; I just play my one-on-one game of doctoring.

Am I different from Sgt. Loucell? Is committing violence something I could learn, or could be taught? So far I've avoided facing this. I eagerly cling to my sense of being part of the hospital: benign, beneficent, safe - and non-violent.

In the hamlet a half mile from Thu Thua village, the road is lined with houses of bamboo and thatch. Pigs, dogs, and chickens trot purposefully about. Children run alongside or jump up and down shouting "Okay!"

At one of the larger houses we set up our clinic. The elderly couple who own it are smiling and friendly, and the man serves us little cups of tea as we work. The Vietnamese medics take down names and examine patients, and refer some to me. I open an abscess; send a dehydrated baby hastening to the hospital; treat respiratory infections (with sulfadiazine, which is all we have); examine a boy with paralysis of both legs, probably polio; and numerous adults complaining of "pain in chest and can't sleep, two months" (diagnosis: they like the Americans' colored vitamin pills). About 260 people go through the line in four hours.

I am ambivalent and uncomfortable. In such a situation I can rarely make a certain diagnosis, and can give little more than placebo treatment.

Thu Thua seems friendly and hospitable indeed; yet we are told that most of the young people are with the Viet Cong. Two days earlier the hamlet chief and leading citizens were scheduled to meet with the American advisor and a Vietnamese district official, to discuss school construction and other improvements. The night before the meeting a Viet Cong delegation came to the hamlet and said, "Don't go to the meeting tomorrow. If you go and talk with the Americans, we will come back and burn four houses in your hamlet." The meeting, of course, didn't happen.

After a delightful, frustrating, sweaty, discouraging, and intriguing day, the Regional Forces troops hurry us away from the place about 4:15 because "VC come soon."

As we leave the place in our jeep, with a hundred kids loudly dancing "Okay, okay!" and most of the adults smiling and waving, I wonder: Even if I could speak Vietnamese perfectly, how could I - or any American - know where these people's sympathies lie? How do I recognize an enemy, whose home perhaps is where I drank tea this morning? When the VC drift into the village streets this evening, will they be seen as enemy, or as hometown boys coming in from a day's work?

General MacArthur told President Eisenhower, "Son, don't ever get bogged down in a land war in Asia."

I would add, "Don't count on the hearts and minds of a people whose language and culture you don't understand."

It is such a polite war. The VC have lunch and a nap while we use Highway 4 by day. We hurry away from the hamlet at 4:30 p.m. so the VC can come home, visit their families, do their own MedCAP and other good works, make their threats, fill their rice bags, and head back to the trees at dawn. The Regional Forces in Thu Thua were there two whole years before they killed a VC.

March 26

This team—Ba, Phuoc, Nga, and I—work wonderfully well together. I am delighted to see them each day. The wounds, the variety, the challenges, successes and failures, the feelings and efforts, empathizing and improvising, teaching and learning: they have become the center of my world. I love these people! It's frightening to think that this must soon end.

March 30

General Humphries came to visit Long An Hospital to discuss a MilPHAP team (Military Province Hospital Augmentation Program) scheduled to arrive at our hospital in June. Three doctors, three nurses, and six corpsmen (all U. S. military) would upgrade the quality of medical care.

Bac Si Ca, the hospital director, however, was not happy, and Dave and I shared his apprehension. The working relationship we had achieved with Bac Si Ca and the nurses and technicians, built up gradually and laboriously, could easily be demolished by a gung-ho group of uniformed Americans descending on the hospital determined to get things done right for a change.

General Humphries turned a deaf ear to our concerns, reassuring us that most of the team would not stay in the hospital, but probably "in the field" or wherever they were most needed, and that furthermore these people were thoroughly briefed on how to work with the Vietnamese. But we knew about Pleiku Hospital, in the Montagnard country. There a MilPHAP team arrived; their American methods and attitudes proved incompatible with the Vietnamese ways.

"If you can't join 'em, whip 'em." The MilPHAP people ended up running the hospital, while the Vietnamese doctor and nurses ran a separate operation off in a corner.

I'm glad I'll be gone before the MilPHAP team arrives.

One hot afternoon I heard murmuring outside the operating room window. As I went out an old woman in black and a young one in a white *au dai* got out of a pickup. They walked slowly toward the morgue beyond the fence, unmindful of the handful of people who stood awkwardly around. Each moved alone, as if unseeing and unnoticed by me or the others, and went inside. Then they came away, shuffling along. The old one wept softly, almost inaudibly; but the young one leaned against the truck and slowly cried "Ai-ee! Ai-ee!"

I went inside the morgue, pretending invisibility, wondering what these dead and these living were saying to each other and which would be more offended by my presence.

The action had taken place two nights before. The body count of VC, I was told, was over a hundred, and here were only nineteen of ours. Pretty good, yes? And they're not Americans; we could be thankful for that, couldn't we? Four platoons were pinned down all night without food or ammunition. They went back for the bodies after air strikes had driven the VC away.

I felt that if I spoke to these men they wouldn't answer me, not so much because they were dead as because I couldn't speak their language. There was something I wanted to tell them but I didn't know what it was.

Dead soldiers don't look as if they're sleeping - not after two days under the tropical sun, they don't. They had names sewed above the right shirt pockets, but the names seemed unimportant now. You only knew that these men all belonged to each other. They all wore the same uniforms, complete with the seeping brown fluid and stifling odor. Even the one missing from the collar bones up was obviously part of the team. The one beside him, whose face looked calm and peaceful, had such a small innocent hole in his belly; his aspirations for the future lay black and clotted in his mouth. They had all died together for the cause.

What cause?

I faded back through the little crowd to the operating room, suddenly desperate to find people who could still use my services.

Charlie Shafer

Coming down Dixie Mountain, the car swept around a curve, came upon a patch of black ice, made a graceful 360 degree pirouette, and dashed itself against a tree. Seatbelts were not yet compulsory nor even common, and Charlie Schafer's 180 pounds continued moving forward as the vehicle abruptly stopped. His head struck the frame above the windshield, his chest struck the steering wheel, and his legs tangled with something down under the panel.

On arrival at the Blue Mountain Hospital about an hour later, Charlie had regained consciousness and complained of pain in his chest and right leg. He vaguely remembered what had happened just before the crash.

There was a bruise across his forehead. His lungs sounded clear, but with every breath there were audible clicks and snaps, and his chest showed "paradoxical" movement: as he breathed in - with obvious effort - the front of his chest sank inward, and on exhalation it moved outward. There was an area of tenderness down each side of his chest. His right leg was angulated below the knee and a sharp point of bone protruded through the skin.

We had no method in those days for measuring the level of oxygen in the blood; the color of the skin was the main guide. Charlie's lips and nailbeds showed a faintly bluish tinge, but not too alarming.

After viewing the x-rays and while preparations were being made for surgery I made notes in the chart:

"1. Cerebral concussion, mild, resolving. 2. Multiple bilateral rib fractures, flail chest, with marginally adequate ventilation. 3. Compound fracture, right tibia and fibula."

The flail chest was worrisome. The few times I had seen this in the past it had usually been fatal. Charlie was working too hard at breathing, and wouldn't be able to cough well enough to keep his lungs cleared over the next few days.

Now, forty years later, the first and obvious step would be to sedate the patient, insert an endotracheal tube and connect him to a positive-pressure ventilator which would keep the ribs from flopping and the lungs from collapsing for a few days until the rib fractures had stabilized. But then we had no such machine. In any case, his ability to tolerate an anesthetic was not going to get better. We needed at least to fix the broken leg, since it was an open fracture and any delay would guarantee infection.

Once Charlie was asleep Bonnie inserted the tube into his trachea and was able to do the breathing for him by squeezing the bag on the anesthesia machine. With this, Charlie's color improved noticeably.

An hour and a half later the work on the leg was completed and a cast had been applied from toes to upper thigh. Bonnie discontinued the flow of anesthetic and switched Charlie over to room air. He began to stir slightly. But when she tried to stop squeezing the bag and let him breathe on his own, the ominous blue tinge returned. It was obvious that this was not going to work, and there's no good way to splint a bundle of broken ribs.

If only one could somehow figure out a way to lift up on the sternum . . .

I told Bonnie to keep Charlie lightly asleep and ventilated. We shaved and scrubbed an area over his sternum. After making a small incision in the midline down to the bone I drilled a hole just through the outer hard layer of the sternum, into the shallow marrow cavity. With pliers and a Kirschner wire I fashioned a short hook with a round eye at the other end. By inserting the hook into the hole one could lift up on the sternum. The hook's grip on the bone was not secure, however, and any small tilt of the wire made it slip out.

I drilled a second hole three inches farther toward his head, inserted a second hook pointing in the opposite direction, and connected the two by an improvised wire yoke-like spacer. This arrangement seemed quite secure.

With Charlie's bed wheeled into the OR it was only a matter of a few minutes to rig a traction frame over the bed, with appropriate pulleys and cord. With Charlie settled onto the bed and four pounds of traction lifting up his sternum, he remained pink and breathing nicely without assistance.

I hadn't known Charlie before. We soon learned that he was a nice enough fellow but sometimes irritable and inclined to ignore instructions or advice. On the second day he fiddled with the traction device and dislodged one of the hooks. By the time I got there the other hook had come loose also, and he was anxious and struggling to get his breath. We gave him some oxygen by mask while the wire gadgets were being sterilized and reinstalled.

We gave him further lectures, and put some loose restraints on his wrists at night. On the fourth day he again got impatient, again decided that the ropes and wires were confining him too much, and deliberately worked the hooks loose. But by then his rib fractures had glued themselves together enough, and the tissues around them congealed enough, so that he was able to continue breathing well on his own. Within a few months he was back driving a log truck again.

The Potato Patch

It was the shortest day of the year. No snow but it had been bitterly cold all week. I had to scrape frost from the windshield in the dark when I left the office.

I visited with my wife and played with the children for a bit after a late dinner. We had just gotten settled in bed when the phone rang.

It was John calling. His voice was kind of whiny as usual. Evelyn was bleeding, started in the afternoon but getting heavier now. Yes, she was having some cramps off and on. Well, no, she hadn't had her period for a couple or three months, he wasn't quite sure. OK, he'd go and ask her . . . No, she didn't know exactly either, but it had been a while.

All right, I'd be down in about a half hour.

John opened the door after my second knocking. He was in his late fifties, about twenty years older than Evelyn, but looked another ten years. Hard times, and smoking a lot, and drinking a good bit, and wandering from place to place and job to job had wrung the juice out of him; he was thin, leathery, neck wrinkly, never seemed to stand straight up. What hair he had was aimless and the color of an over-used dish rag.

He stood aside and I stepped into the living room. He pointed and then led me past a crackling wood stove into a small cluttered bedroom, where Evelyn lay on the double bed between thin grey blankets. She smiled cheerily when she saw me, and showed me that she had tucked a couple of tattered blue towels between her legs, and there was some blood soaked into them.

She heaved her bulk over on her side so we could face each other, and said anxiously, "I think maybe I'm pregnant again. Can you tell me if I've lost it?"

I set my bag down, and took off my coat and laid it aside. "Well, I can't just yet," I said - but I fervently hoped she had. She barely had the mental capacity to take care of herself. I always cringed at the thought of Evelyn having a baby to deal

147

with. She was determined that she wanted a baby, and in the previous four years had miscarried twice. She did not want any contraceptives - nor did she show interest in taking care of her diabetes or her high blood pressure. John didn't care much one way or the other. I had explained to John the high risk both to Evelyn and to the baby if she ever carried one close to term, and repeatedly had urged him to have a vasectomy, but he never quite made up his mind.

"Have you passed anything besides blood?" I asked. "Any solid pieces of anything?"

"I don't know," she said.

"Have you used the toilet?"

John pointed out a white enameled bucket with a bail and a flared rim, standing near the foot of the bed.. "She used that a while ago. We just have an outhouse, and seemed like she was bleedin' too much to go out. It's cut down a good bit now from what it was when I called."

I looked in the bucket. There was a small amount of faintly bloody water in the bottom.

I put on a glove, had her roll onto her back, and did a vaginal exam as best I could. Because of her obesity I could barely reach her cervix. I couldn't feel any tissue protruding from it.

"What was in the bucket when you emptied it?" I asked John.

"I don't know. It was kinda' dark. There was some blood, and a piece of something, but I don't know whether it was some shit in there or what, I couldn't tell."

"I'd really like to see what it was. If it was a chunk of afterbirth, then the miscarriage has probably completed itself and the bleeding will be stopping. If not, it may get heavier again, and we might have to take her in and clean out the uterus. Where did you empty it?"

"Out there in the field. Didn't want to fill up the outhouse any more'n we have to."

"I've got a flashlight in the car," I said, and reached for my coat. "Let's go and see where you dumped it."

148

John hesitated only for a moment, then pulled on a thin jacket, and we stepped outside.

Our breaths curled away in heavy white clouds. His "field" was a fenced area maybe twenty or thirty yards square. The feeble little circle of yellow light dancing ahead of us cast more shadows than illumination on the rough, irregular ground. The potatoes had been harvested a few weeks before, and the shriveled remains of dug-up plants lay helter-skelter among hard-frozen pits and clods and furrows.

John led me to where he thought the bucket had been taken. I swung my beacon back and forth, searching hopefully for a wisp of steam, but saw only shadow. A thin fragment of moon cast just enough light to distort the appearance of the ragged ground.

"John," I said, "you stand about where you think you put it, and I'll search around you." I tried to walk a systematic pattern, back and forth, stumbling over the rock-hard ups and downs, trying to cover every square foot of the area. I widened the perimeter, but still to no avail.

Suddenly my mind's eye stepped back - way back - and surveyed this bizarre scene. Is this a clinical procedure, or what? Two otherwise sensible men roaming aimlessly about in the middle of the night in a frozen potato patch, looking for a discarded placenta or bloody turd or whatever.

"Let's forget it, John," I said abruptly. "If the bleeding gets heavier again, bring Evelyn in to the hospital tonight. If not, call the office tomorrow to let me know how she's doing."

I said goodbye to Evelyn, collected my bag, turned up the heater and drove back toward a nice warm home and bed.

The Inner Sanctum

"Good morning, Ardith. Did you get some sleep last night?"

"Yes, thank you, Doctor." She had to try twice to answer, and her words were slurred. "My mouth feels like cotton."

"That's from the shot you had a while ago; it's medicine to make the anesthetic work better. I'd like to check your tummy once more."

I turned the covers down and she pulled up the edge of her gown. My hand on her abdomen and fingers probing gently confirmed that it was still flat and soft. "Take a deep breath, please." This brought her liver down to where I could just feel it, and she winced.

"It will be good to get that gall bladder out now before it gets more inflamed. The anesthetist will come in a few minutes to wheel you into the operating room. I just met Deena outside; she'll be here to see you before you take off down the hall."

She nodded, we squeezed each other's hand, and her eyelids sagged again as I headed for the door.

The evening before, Deena had been waiting for me, slumped in the lobby. She had stubbed out her cigarette and stood up quickly, pushing back a straggling wisp of hair. She leaned forward, face taut, almost contorted.

"Doctor," she said, reaching out to press my arm, "if you find cancer tomorrow, don't tell Mom. She wouldn't be able to take it. She'd go all to pieces."

"Come and sit down a minute." I motioned her to a chair by the window and took a seat next to her. "I haven't any reason to expect to find cancer. I expect to find just a thickened gall bladder full of stones. But we never know for sure what we'll find until we get in there. If we did find cancer, would you really want me to lie to your mother?"

"Well, but . . .?"

"I think maybe what you're saying is that you wouldn't be able to handle talking to her, knowing that she knew that you

150

knew that she had cancer, and you wouldn't know what to say. But when there's bad news, it's very important that you be able to share it with the people you love. She'd soon realize it anyway, and if those around her were afraid to face the truth, then she'd have to pretend and live a lie too, for your sake, and then she'd be totally alone in facing it. If she knew, and asked me not to tell you, I'd try to talk her out of that too. So if we find cancer I'll tell you, and I'll tell her, and then we can all deal with it together."

Her eyes filled with tears, but she smiled. "OK, I guess so," she said.

In the cramped little doctor's lounge, I change from street clothes. The familiar clank and shimmer of the locker door on its hinges offers a subtle exciting signal, drawing me into that elegant world behind the wide heavy door of the operating room.

A century and a half ago Ignatz Semmelweis in Hungary discovered that if a doctor washed his hands before delivering a baby it could prevent the mother's death from "childbed fever"; Louis Pasteur in France was developing his theory of germs as a cause of disease; and Joseph Lister in England started using carbolic acid to wash instruments and as a spray in the operating room to prevent infection. Boiling or steam sterilizing of instruments replaced carbolic acid, and continues to be used now.

In the surgical mind's eye there are germs contaminating every surface except those that have been specifically sterilized; anything that touches a contaminated surface transfers contamination to anything else it touches. Bacteria that are harmless on the skin may be a serious threat beneath the skin. Asepsis, the mantra and ritual of the surgical suite, is <u>avoidance</u> of transferring contamination, to avoid carrying any bacteria into an open wound - an instinctive surgical choreography of thought and movement as one reaches to push open that door.

The pale green scrub suit, disposable paper shoe covers, white cloth cap and surgical mask are the uniform of the team: Bonnie, the anesthetist, who has been doing this for years, checking her tanks of oxygen and anesthetic gases; Marge,

151

another old-timer, setting up a second instrument stand and adjusting the table; Izetta, time-tested scrub nurse and head honcho, already gowned and gloved, laying out the tools and counting sponges and needles on her tray.

Ardith lies on the operating table. A needle has been placed in a vein in her hand, and saline solution is dripping slowly from the inverted bottle hanging above. At about the time Pasteur and Lister were reducing the hazards of infection, John Snow in England was furthering the new art of using ether for anesthesia. For today's operation Bonnie will carry on that art: the jar on the side of the anesthesia machine has been filled with ether. This will be added to the mixture of nitrous oxide and oxygen which Ardith will breathe throughout the operation.

Ardith signed a piece of paper yesterday which says she understands what will be done to her today, and she voluntarily gives her consent. In full understanding she chooses to do this. This, of course, is totally untrue. Ardith does not understand how the anesthesia machine works, nor how skillfully Bonnie operates it, nor how the inhaled substances get from the black rubber breathing bag to her lungs to her blood stream to her brain, nor how delicately Bonnie will judge from moment to moment Ardith's breathing and heart rate and blood pressure and muscle tone and the color of her blood in lips and nail beds and in the incision viewed over the top of the screen in order to keep her gaseous recipe adjusted precisely, or whether Bonnie has made sure there is enough oxygen in the tank to keep Ardith's heart and brain alive while she sleeps. Ardith has never seen a gall bladder, much less watched me remove one. Will I cut the right things? Will I accidentally clamp the hepatic artery, or constrict the common bile duct when I ligate the cystic duct? Will my knots be secure? She also depends on me (without knowing it) to assure that Marge has properly sterilized the instruments, and that Izetta hasn't contaminated them as she lays them out on her tray; and that the x-ray images do indeed show stones in the gall bladder as I have claimed.

No, Ardith could not possibly give truly "informed" consent for us to render her helpless, put her unconscious, keep her brain oxygenated, cut her open, then restore her to life, improved but temporarily in pain.

This is trust, pure and simple. The entire system rests on deep and mutual trust. Surgery is surely the most intimate act one can imagine: to enter, with a blade, into hidden depths and secret places of someone - even a perfect stranger - who willingly lies down and consents.

Where does the trust come from? How does it form? Bit by bit, event by event, in the appearance of good intent, repeated acts and voice and body language of openness, of honesty and kindness. By all of us. By almost everyone in the entire system, even those far from here, assumed even in strangers.

Kindness is the indispensable part. Kindness even in the cutting, in the tender respect for the skin as it parts under the knife; love for the startled, astonished muscle as it separates before my tools and quivers, recoils, and bleeds; awe at the structures that confine and support and defend the gallbladder and that must be gently violated and persuaded to relinquish the offending organ at last into my hand; and remembering always that it is Ardith lying here appearing so anonymous under the sheets.

Dr. Howard Newton, the assistant - himself also a competent surgeon - today holds retractors, dabs with sponges behind my cutting and snipping, clamps small bleeders, holds and turns the hemostats as I tie off the clamped bits of tissue, and he clips the ends of the ligatures close - but not too close - to the knots.

When it comes to the crucial clamping and tying - the two ties on the cystic artery for good measure, and one on the cystic duct, deep down in the shadows - I tie them myself, and even take the long slender scissors to clip the ends. Not that I don't trust Howard's touch with the scissors. I would trust his hands inside myself - have in fact done so. But this part is the responsibility of the surgeon. If these knots are not properly laid and tightened, if these ligatures slip off later, disaster follows. Let him who bears the burden of success or failure tie and trim the critical knots.

"Why do you always seem anxious?" people have asked me. "What are you worrying about?"

It's true, I suppose, that I'm always anxious. A proper level of anxiety, well modulated and controlled, is necessary, is the force that drives the care, the attention to detail, the power to make the difficult decisions. Anxiety, however, is a positive force only when fully balanced by confidence based on knowledge and skill.

The beat goes on: the learning, the research, the advances in technology, even in my short span, a mere half-century of practice. Other inhaled gases have now replaced ether for anesthesia. Gallbladders now are usually removed by laparoscope - instruments inserted through three tiny incisions in the abdomen - so that recovery is a matter of hours and days rather than days and weeks. Now the patient is monitored routinely by electronic devices: heart rate and rhythm, blood pressure, oxygen content of the blood. But the essence is still the same: honesty and good will, and kindness, and trust, and anxiety, and knowledge and skill and confidence, and humility, knowing your limits and when to call for help - and knowing how to face failure and even error, to accept responsibility.

Why, I ask myself, is surgery the best part, the most consistently rewarding? There is no single neat, clean, sufficient answer. Anatomy, gross and microscopic, was always my favorite study in school, the most awe-inspiring thing to learn; and surgery is just anatomy brought to life. This and craftsmanship, the ability to perform fine small acts and thereby build fine solid structures, things for the magical healing powers of the body to finish off.

It goes, though, beyond that, to a feeling, striding with confidence through the doors marked "NO ADMITTANCE," knowing that this rarified air of place and action is home. And then on past the second "NO ADMITTANCE" sign stamped invisibly on the belly of the trusting client.

This is not a vanity, I tell you, but a grateful sense of privilege, this access. It feeds the self, to be sure: after the long rites of passage, now a privilege and empowerment. But not an end point, certainly, just the unbroken continuation of a process that started back at the beginning of my time.

I am left now, long after, with a diffuse memory, a fusion of all the times I've been in the OR at Blue Mountain Hospital, a pale green memory in that circle of sterile bright light, heads leaning to the glistening red of life and diseased tissue or broken parts, anxious glance at the anesthetist behind the screen, the black bag filling and emptying, filling and emptying, more sponges, adjust the light, suction . . . the shifts of tension, of light talk between minor crises, oh shit a bleeder loose, suction, more large sponges . . . and old Bill back for the third and last and still thinly hopeful attempt to relieve his bowel obstruction, riddled with adhesions, getting peritonitis because neither of us saw the needle dip a little too deep on that last stitch trying to pull the thin, fragile fascia together, nicking the intestine, and next morning the bile-stained fluid from the wound so that suddenly you know it is all over but a day or two of helpless watching and morphine and fiddling with the Miller-Abbott tube . . . and the logger with compound fractured tibia and flail chest who lived to drive truck again because of the skeletal traction we invented and hooked to his sternum so he could breathe . . . and the gangrenous half of a 70-year-old diabetic foot and knowing reluctantly that you must take it off above the knee, the always shocking sound of saw on bone, the visceral protest you feel and the pallor visible above the mask of the nurse as you hand her the disembodied leg . . . and the caesareans when the nurses swore I always tilted the gush of fluid into the other guy's shoes as the miraculous package of new life was lifted gasping and crying from the bloody hole. Always that atmosphere, a familiar and reassuring and supportive team all focused on one goal: the sponge and needle count and getting off the bag and breathing well and the BP coming back up and the victim starting to move, to respond, alive again. That embracing circle of light, the successes and the failures, the challenges, the improvisations demanded by our remoteness in time and space bound all our lives together in so sweet a manner, oh yes!

That was a very good set of years for all of us in Blue Mountain Hospital. Remember Izetta, and Phyllis, and Pauline, and Bonnie and her sister Theresa, and Wilma, and my partner for eleven years, Howard Newton, and all the succession of faces that furtively replaced each other behind the half-mask through the years.

I am bonded to a great human throng by their scars. The patient owns my soul, but it's still a fantastic dance.

Sabbatical

> "Identity would seem to be the garment with which one covers the nakedness of the self, in which case, it is best that the garment be loose, a little like the robes of the desert, through which one's nakedness can always be felt, and, sometimes, discerned. This trust in one's nakedness is all that gives one the power to change one's robes."
>
> *James Baldwin, "The Devil Finds Work" (1976)*

The garment of Medical General Practitioner had suited me well; but after eighteen years, and living in a remote village in eastern Oregon, I found myself looking for my nakedness and thinking about other possible robes. Is there anything left of me, I wondered, outside of this M.D. stereotype?

Maybe, after all, I should take a break for a while from other people's pains and anxieties, injuries and illnesses, dying and being born—take a sort of sabbatical.

Teaching, I thought, seemed a likely robe to try on. I started to make inquiries.

At one university they said they could find me a part-time job teaching nutrition. At another, there might be a position available in two years as assistant in the biology department.

That robe wasn't going to fit.

I had heard of a small, private, "experimental" college in Vermont, and flew to San Francisco to meet Tim Pitkin, the founder and president of the 25-year-old college, who was there on a speaking engagement. We spent an intense and intriguing couple of hours in his hotel room.

After we had returned to our respective homes, Tim wrote to me: "What four subjects would you offer to teach, two each semester, that could justify my hiring you?"

I heaped together most of my major interests, cut them like a pie into quarters, and visited Goddard College with my proposal.

My first reaction to the place was to laugh. My second, after talking to people for a day and a half, beginning to understand better Tim's educational philosophy, was to want very much to teach there.

This old family farm in Plainfield, renovated and converted into a college, was not a baby-sitting institution. It had become the hippie capital of New England. It was common for a student just out of high school to enroll for what I perceived as negative reasons—to evade the draft and a trip to Viet Nam, or for a pretense at education without accountability; to waste his time and his parents' money. But for a student a little more mature, in school with serious intent, it offered an excellent learning challenge and opportunity.

The college was divided into two campuses separated by a ten-minute stroll through the woods. Northwood was three low dormitories around a pond. Greatwood had the farm buildings: the Silo, converted to administrative offices; the Hay Barn, now an auditorium, stage, and dressing room; Martin Manor, with conference and classrooms; a former extra residence with Physics in the basement and Chemistry on the first floor; and the herbarium-turned-library which I was to dismantle and remodel into a biology lab because a wealthy alumnus had donated a fine new library - incongruous in this setting, but fine nevertheless.

Northwood featured nude sunbathing around the pond. On Greatwood, when the students played volleyball, they kept score.

My subjects would be Anatomy and Physiology - to be taught each semester - and a few eccentric smaller courses like Homeostasis, Principles of Ecology, and Some aspects of Life, Death, and Dying.

Somewhere along here I had to face a fact: the salary for teaching at Goddard College was just half of my current very modest annual income. After some discussion, Betsy and I agreed to believe - or at least to pretend and optimistically hope

158

- that, beyond subsistence level, the quality of life does not depend on the size of one's income. We figured that there are two ways to get by or to get ahead: get more, or need less.

In December 1968 I signed a contract to start teaching when school opened the following August. That would give me plenty of time to recruit a doctor replacement.

There were six doctors in John Day: my partner, Howard Newton, and myself; Craig Bennett, who had started as our partner but later moved to his own separate practice; Drs. Jerry and Martha Van der Vlugt, with their own private hospital; and Brian King, a surgeon who worked with the Van der Vlugts.

My recruitment efforts, launched so confidently and pursued with increasing intensity and finally desperation, did not bear fruit. Meanwhile Dr. King - a British citizen - completed the two-year "service in an area of need" which exempted him from military draft or deportation, and he departed abruptly to a large surgical clinic in the Midwest. Dr. Jerry became ill and died. Dr. Martha closed their hospital and took a job with the Public Health Service in Washington, D.C. Dr. Bennett did not get along well with Dr. Newton and did not want to be left practicing in town alone with him, so he moved to southern Oregon. So on a warm and sunny morning in mid-July, drowning in guilt, I loaded Betsy and our five children and two cats into our red Greenbrier bus and pulled out of town, and poor Howard Newton, my partner of eleven years and now abandoned, the only doctor remaining in the county, stood and watched us disappear in the distance. I could only guess what he was feeling.

Thus in my late forties I lived in Vermont in a small college town, a village, amid a wealth of hardwood forests such as I had never seen. Here the people and the wood seem in some way to be part of each other. The history and traditions, industries, house and furniture construction, hand tools, the culture and style of New England are largely the result of interactions of man, wood, and weather. I hardly knew which prospect was more exciting - the new challenges of teaching, or the glorious possibilities for wood carving and sculpture.

Almost the last official act of Tim Pitkin before he retired was to hire me. As I arrived at Goddard, so did Jerry Witherspoon, the new president of the college. Formerly the state's tax commissioner, he seemed to have a different vision for the college - somehow more focused on programs and finances and growth than on students and education. On my fourth day in town, before the opening of the school year, I attended a faculty meeting and found myself, a total newcomer, already digging in my heels and defending the intentions and principles of Tim Pitkin and the "old" Goddard. My new career was off to a stimulating start!

For students of the '60s and '70s whose attitudes were largely anti-authority and anti-science, Anatomy and Physiology seemed too forbidding a title, so I played at their own game and called the course "Human Form and Function as a Basis for Identity." What caught me by surprise, as we got well started, was that this was exactly the right title; this is what I wanted the course to be, the reason I wanted to teach it in the first place. Maybe you are what you eat, or you are what you do, but before all else you are what is contained in your skin.

It worked. The students came, and they and I had a good time. I scrounged at a small local slaughterhouse for cows' eyes, pig's heart and stomach and kidney as specimens for anatomy lab; showed a movie on childbirth; showed x-rays of normal and abnormal subjects; did ECGs on the students. (This was when a student asked in class, "Ted, are you a doctor?")

For the final assignment, I mounted three full-length mirrors backstage in the Hay Barn Theater (sharing the cost with the drama teacher) so that each student could strip down, examine his or her actual self in the mirrors from all sides at once, and write an essay about the "basis for identity."

The whole course was great fun.

Rights and Choices

The eggs were sensuously warm, smooth, and white as they came out of the incubator. Pencil marks on them said "36 hours," "48 hours," "72 hours," and so on up to one week. I had gone to the lab every few hours, day and night, to turn them, check the temperature, and add more fertilized eggs to the racks.

The class of nine women had studied the bones, muscles, heart and lungs, digestive system, then the reproductive system, with a movie on childbirth. I happened to have a vaginal speculum, and they eagerly seized on my suggestion that they could inspect an actual cervix and have a better idea of what a birth - or an abortion - involved.

"Wow!" they said. "Cool!" They had stayed an hour after class to take turns checking each other's hidden anatomy.

Today's topic was embryology. I pointed out to the students how closely all vertebrates, including humans, resemble each other in the very early stages of development. An easy vertebrate to inspect at this stage is a chicken.

As the students settled at their microscopes and I prepared to pass out the eggs I thought of the previous class period, in which pictures of the uterus had raised questions about abortion: how soon can you tell you are pregnant, how is the procedure done, what about some of the methods of self-induced abortion they've heard of.

"It's our body," they said. "Why is it somebody else's business if I don't want to be pregnant?" "A woman should have a right to do what she wants with her body." "A right to choose should be in the Constitution just like the other Bill of Rights!" And so on.

After 36 hours of incubation there is a pale spot about the size of a small fingernail on the side of an egg's yolk. If you clip around and float that bit of membrane into saline solution and onto a microscope slide, you can see the first silly rudiments of an embryo. Somewhere in the middle is a crude tubular structure that twitches rhythmically. At 48 hours you see

161

an elementary but definitely formed heart, pumping real little blood cells around through a looped network of tubes, and a recognizable eye is there. In another day there are limbs, a face, a brain like three link sausages, all sorts of confusing things forming inside, and a caricature of a chicken develops fast from there on.

As the young women looked at these early stages and watched the amazing little heart beating, one asked, "If we closed up the egg and put it back in the incubator, could it still grow?" Another said, "It's going to die in a little while, here under the microscope, isn't it?" A third said, "I don't think we should be doing this!" Some of the women were very excited and hurried on to the later stages to see how the pattern blossomed and unfurled. Others refused to open any more eggs, and became quite upset.

I brought the talk around to abortion again, and this time it was a different talk.

"Yes," said one, "I still believe a woman has that right . . ." The others nodded agreement.

"But this is just a chicken."

"I'm going to have to think about this," said another.

"When does the heart start beating in a human?" one asked.

"Sometime near the end of the third week after the egg and sperm meet," I said. "Right around the time you suspect you may be pregnant."

They stuck with their conviction that abortion was their right; but it was no longer a clear-cut, yes-or-no, coldly political question. A new dimension had been added.

When I later described the chicken-egg incident to a group of educators, one person became incensed. She said accusingly, "You're against abortion, aren't you!"

She had completely missed my point: informed choice. As a general practitioner I have performed - reluctantly - a small number of abortions myself, and have referred a few patients elsewhere for abortions. But I have never felt glibly satisfied with this option, and the decision has always been preceded by

162

discussion, counseling, and explorations of all the available options - for both the patient and myself - as best I could discover them.

The point of the egg story - the point that the lady so glibly missed or evaded - is simply this: If one is going to make a choice about something, it is only reasonable and prudent - sometimes crucial - to understand clearly the reality of <u>what</u> one is choosing - in this case choosing on the one hand to terminate a life with its beating heart within the mother's body, or choosing on the other hand not merely to have a baby but to accept responsibility for the future welfare of a child for all the years until it is able to take care of itself. Properly understood, it should be a daunting choice either way.

Yes, human life is sacred. In fact, I would hold that <u>all</u> life is sacred. The life of all organisms is based on almost exactly the same chemical reactions, from very simple creatures to the most complex, including ourselves. Though the ameba - or even the chimpanzee - can't speak and write down a complex language and accumulate knowledge over many generations and philosophize and worship and wonder, the similarities between them and us are profound. Furthermore, my life is totally dependent upon and intertwined with other life, both human and non-human. For me, as well as for the ameba, the energy which keeps the cooker of life cooking comes from the sun, <u>exclusively</u> through the chlorophyll molecules in green plants, even though the supermarket gets the credit. I would argue that the entire life-system is sacred.

If this be true, then as a practical matter - the necessity of making choices - I am forced to the view that sacredness of life is relative, that some lives are more sacred than others. I murmur "excuse me" when I swat a fly, but swat it nevertheless; I apologize and meditate when I butcher a chicken; I grieve when I run over a dog. In fact, for want of a better yardstick, I offer my degree of intuitive pain as the best measure of the degree of sacredness: I feel bad if I see a miscarriage; much worse when I see the stillbirth of a full-term baby; and much worse yet to see a young child killed by accident or by abuse. A child unwanted by its parents is definitely an endangered person.

There is a hollowness in the argument of a protagonist, on either side of the abortion issue, who doesn't feel some ambivalence in the matter. Someone who is convinced of the absolute rightness of either side just doesn't fully understand the situation.

Like any really worthwhile question, it should be a matter of seeking reality and truth; assigning relative degrees of sacredness; working out a resolution of conflicting values; and humbly accepting responsibility for one's best shot as a human organism making a choice.

Full Circle

In the hours I could pry loose from teaching I began to make the acquaintance of some of Vermont's trees and their fabric, and bought my first chain saw, for wood sculpture as well as cutting firewood. I felt shock at stacking sugar maple and beech and yellow birch and - heaven help us! - cherry and apple cordwood for the fire. To burn such treasure seemed a sacrilege, even though I knew that burning hardwood is safer and more economical than burning fir and pine. Wood carving and sculpture took much of my spare time, and I became a compulsive wood collector and admirer. I would rob the firewood pile and put away all of the better pieces, until I had nothing left to burn and had to haul it all back out of the shed.

I went every month to Burlington to visit the University of Vermont Medical School, to talk with teachers and go on Grand Rounds with the professors of internal medicine, just to keep a little of the touch and feel of it.

Like a handful of the other Goddard College faculty members, I remained one of the few straight folks in a hippie enclave. By this I mean that, although I dressed very casually in lumberjack shirt and leather boots with pant legs tucked into them for convenience in walking through two feet of snow to classes, and, like the students, called everyone by first names, I didn't wear a beard, didn't smoke pot, and when others were out blocking the highway and passing out anti-war leaflets to motorists, I was in the lab with a couple of extra typewriters offering to help students write letters to their congressmen. When I did join in a protest march against the Vietnam war, I carried a big American flag to make clear that I was not marching against my country nor against the troops, but specifically against the misguided policies of my government.

Teaching at Goddard for two and a half years was one of the best experiences of my life; but I knew that if I didn't get back into medicine soon I would get hopelessly behind and out of the flow. I felt satisfied that I had largely achieved my purpose of rehabilitation and self-rediscovery.

About this time Dr. Paul Michlin arrived in town, and together we persuaded the Central Vermont Hospital in Barre that we should staff their Emergency Room from 7 am to 7 pm so the local practitioners would be spared the frustration of being called from their busy offices during the day. The medical staff was enthusiastic, and not much persuasion was needed. Paul and I were later joined by Dr. Paul Laffal, and we formed our own corporation. With some regret I left the teaching job at Goddard. I went to Boston to take the American Board of Family Practice exam and become certified by this new specialty board.

Teaching had been an open-ended pursuit that swallowed me up. Like my former medical practice, it had no clear boundaries, the obligations and opportunities never completed. Now, working the limited hours of the ER only three days a week, I had even more time for playing with wood. On a lovely rough pine board I carved a sign for the front of our house: WOOD, SILVER, AND STRING. Betsy did weaving, our daughter Kathie did silver jewelry, and I entered into commercial wood carving.

By that I mean that I sawed, chiseled, rasped, whittled, and sanded much of the time, and occasionally finished a piece that I considered "for sale." No two pieces alike; what would be the fun in that? My wages - omitting any costs of materials, tools, utilities, or keeping the house warm, and counting only my time spent in the shop - figured to about eight cents an hour. The other two craftspersons in the house fared much the same. But it really was a nice sign over the door.

After six years in Vermont we decided to move back to Oregon - because for Betsy the Vermont winters were hard and long, and because, after all, Oregon was home. And besides, Vermont has no lava rock nor sagebrush, and that just goes against nature.

I took the first ER job I could find in Oregon, at Good Samaritan Hospital in Corvallis - another college town, which gives a place a special flavor. And I brought west in a U-Haul truck more than a ton of nicely seasoned carving wood.

Another chapter had begun.

The Tensor Tympani

Go early to the symphony, before the strings, before the woodwinds, before even the horns come in, when the stage is still empty. The tympanist, a man with receding hair and a mouth shaped like an O and cheeks that flutter with the movements of his head and hands, furtively appears and pretends invisibility as he approaches his big kettledrums. He tests the heads with his fingers, then very lightly with his padded drumstick. He makes delicate adjustments, turning brass thumbscrews to tighten or loosen the parchment-like leather, raising or lowering the tone to match his pitch pipe as he repeatedly caresses the tympanum with his stick.

Inside the human head, something similar goes on.

If you picture all the other bones of the skull removed, the right and left temporal bones support the brain like two uplifted hands holding aloft a crystal ball; and deep inside the temporal bone are the tiny mechanisms of the ear.

After we had studied the muscles of the head in *Grant's Atlas of Anatomy*, then in the cadaver, then observed them in life by touch and by viewing ourselves in a mirror, we stripped it all away from the outer surface of the temporal bone and could investigate the mysteries of the ear.

Not everyone cared to do this part of the dissection, exploring the depths with chisel and hammer, and instead retreated to books and illustrations and some prepared specimens in glass cabinets that lined the walls. But I, along with a few others, was eager to proceed. I found a carborundum stone and sharpened the chisel - unused until now - that had come with the dissection kit.

Following the illustrations in the book, we carefully removed the bone in tiny chips. Down inside the bone, next to the semi-circular canals that lie in three planes at right angles to each other like the gyroscopic guidance system of a space vehicle, was the cavity of the middle ear, separated from the outside world by the tympanic membrane, the ear drum.

168

Bridging the space from the drum to the inner ear is a chain of three tiny bones that carry the vibrations of sound to the nerve endings of the cochlea.

The range of sound intensity in the world is so great that many people gradually lose part of their hearing ability through exposure to loud sounds: gunfire, factory machinery, chain saws and leaf blowers, or super-amplified rock music.

Hence the body's defense. There in the depths of the temporal bone we found not brass thumbscrews but an ingenious little muscle, the tensor tympani - "tightener of the tympanum." In quiet times this muscle is relaxed; but if a loud sound strikes the drum the muscle instantly tightens, impeding the vibrations of the drum and thus of the chain of little bones so they don't rattle themselves too violently and maybe damage the nerve endings. Our instructor, Dr. Truax, challenged us to find not only the tensor tympani, but also the even smaller muscle to the stapedius bone. In fact, he offered to buy a beer for anyone who could find the nerve to the stapedius muscle. No one qualified for the beer, but the tensor tympani was not too hard to find, a short flat muscle about the width of a matchstick.

There was a problem here. With the biceps or many other muscles I could readily demonstrate the action and feel a firm contraction through the skin. But I could find no way really to experience the action of the tensor tympani. I had to take its function on faith, from hearsay and from the textbook.

Almost exactly 30 years later I was standing in the yard, putting the last touches on a sculpture carved from a piece of elm log taller than myself. Boldly colored leaves from autumn-kissed maples drifted down around me. Across the road, the faint trickling of Great Brook and the sigh of a Vermont breeze through fir trees made a gentle backdrop of sound to the ringing of the mallet as the curved gouge spooned away chips of elm.

Suddenly I was aware of a new sensory rhythm matching that of my arm. With each impact of the mallet, for about a half second after the musical sound of the wood, the whisper of wind and water vanished. The effect was something like "boink . . . . sh-h-h-h-boink . . . . sh-h-h-boink . . . . sh-h-h-h-h."

Here at last the tensor tympani had revealed and proclaimed itself! Just too late but faithfully trying, it contracted with the arrival of each "boink," and a half-second later relaxed because the emergency was past, only to be summoned to action again and again.

A mallet of black locust, an elm log, and the murmur of Great Brook had at long last combined to complete my lesson in anatomy!

Sacrifice

A young man walked into the Emergency Room and said, "I need some help. I can't get the bleeding to stop."

His fair hair was neatly trimmed, his short-sleeved white shirt fresh and open at the collar. He walked stiffly, not quite hobbling. He unfastened his trousers and showed me that the towel tucked inside his underpants was half saturated with blood. A two-inch wound on his scrotum was oozing briskly.

"What happened?" I asked, as I motioned him to lie on the table.

"I castrated myself with a razor blade, but it keeps bleeding, and I got afraid to bleed so much."

"You what? Castrated yourself?" I could hardly believe it. "How could you do that? Are you sure?"

I applied a sterile pad and some gentle pressure; the oozing blood ignored my gestures.

"Yes, I'm sure." His voice cool, confident. "I flushed them down the toilet."

"For heaven's sake, why?"

"Yes, that's the reason. For heaven's sake. I know that masturbating is a bad thing, a wicked thing. But I just couldn't stop doing it." He was tense now, his face tightened. "I tried. I tried so hard, but it would just keep happening. I knew that whenever I did that, Jesus cried. So I figured this would be the best way."

Speechless, I put down the gauze pads and turned to face him.

Our eyes met, locked on. I fancied that for an instant a merciless force flowed between us, that we hung suspended in space with no place to hide.

I looked away, back to the wound, and added more sponges. I wanted to curse him, or to embrace him, or to cry. Instead, in silence, I reached for the phone.

The surgeon came promptly with his colleague the urologist. They examined the patient briefly. There was still a

171

steady trickle of bleeding, and the loose, soft tissue of the scrotum was greatly swollen and infiltrated with blood so one couldn't see the bleeding source nor confirm whether the testicles were actually gone. They decided to take him to the operating room and explore and suture the wound under general anesthesia.

The surgeon came by later, visibly shaken. It was true. The boy had accomplished his mission. The doctor admonished me not to talk about it to anyone.

I never saw the young man again. But now and then I think about him, and feel a churning somewhere inside.

Just Do It

I was in the x-ray department looking at some films of an injured wrist when the pediatrician approached me. He, too, had been looking at an x-ray - a chest film on a baby just a few hours old.

"As you can see on the film," he said, "this baby's got a pneumothorax - a pretty significant collapse of that right lung. He's fine otherwise, and there's no history of trauma. We just noticed he was breathing a little fast. Would you be able to take that air out of his chest?"

"Well, yes, I could aspirate most of it. I don't suppose you'd want to put in a regular chest tube with a water trap and all that, in a newborn. But how do we know it won't just come right back?"

"Really we don't," he said, "but it usually doesn't in this situation - unlike an adult. You just have to watch it closely, in case it does."

"OK," I said, "I'll do it as soon as I tell this lady with the hurt wrist the good news."

"The baby's right over there. Where do you want him?"

"Right there will be fine. I'll get the gear."

The "gear" actually was nothing but a 10 cc. syringe fitted with a small-gauge IV needle, the standard kind with a teflon sleeve over the outside of the needle.

After listening to the baby's breath sounds with a stethoscope (and making sure the baby and the x-ray had the same name) I selected a spot on the chest, swabbed it with antiseptic, pushed the sterile needle just over the top of a rib (the artery and nerve are at the bottom of the rib) until air could be drawn into the syringe. I then held the hub of the cannula in position and withdrew the needle. With the syringe reattached to the hub of the teflon cannula - which was flexible and had a blunt end - I could now draw out the air until the lung was expanded almost all the way out to the chest wall, with little danger of injury to the lung.

173

The whole procedure took about three minutes. The baby was fine, his lungs sounded normal, and he was ready to go back up to the ward for his doctor to check him again.

As he was leaving and I was about to return to the ER, the nurse pushing the bassinet stopped and asked me, "Were you in 'Nam?"

"Yes, I was. Not in combat, just a volunteer treating Vietnamese civilians for a couple of months. Why do you ask?"

"There was something about that, the way you did it - no fiddling around, or hemming and hawing and hesitating. You just <u>did</u> it. I saw that over there, no time for formalities or goofing around, just get it done. You made it look so easy."

"It was," I said.

There was no need to tell them that I'd never done that before in a newborn.

Night School

Sometimes quick access to the blood stream via a needle or plastic tube, to replace fluid volume quickly, may be the only way to preserve life. Often the more urgently a patient needs an IV, the harder it is to get a needle into a vein, especially a needle large enough to handle a lot of fluid fast. One alternative to a standard needle stick is to insert a plastic catheter directly into a large vein close to the heart. In the late 1970s the insertion of a "central venous line," usually into the subclavian vein or internal jugular, was becoming more common. Neither of these large veins can be seen or felt, so inserting a catheter requires using a large needle and navigating entirely from external landmarks, with hazard of serious consequence if you miss the mark.

I had never done this procedure, but had read the instructions: "At the junction of the outer one-third and the inner two-thirds of the clavicle, insert a 3-inch, 14 gauge needle [the size of a wooden match] at the lower edge of the clavicle. Staying close to the bone, move the tip of the needle under the clavicle and advance it, aiming directly at the suprasternal notch. When a free flow of blood is obtained, stabilize the needle, remove the syringe and insert the catheter through the needle." Simple enough. Among the possible complications are puncturing the top of the lung, or puncturing or tearing the subclavian artery instead of the vein (under there where you can't apply pressure on it), or putting the needle on through the back side of the vein, or allowing air to be sucked in through the needle into the vein and causing an air embolism, or accidentally pulling back a bit on the catheter so the sharp edge of the needle cuts off a piece of the catheter down inside the vein.

It would be a scary thing to try.

At Good Samaritan Hospital in Corvallis the Emergency Room doctors had agreed with the other doctors on the medical staff: If a staff doctor had a patient who was expected to die, and if this should happen at night or when the doctor was too busy to come immediately, the ER doctor would go to the ward and officially verify the death. Working the night shift, I was quite often asked to "go upstairs to 3-B and pronounce Mr. Smith dead."

On one of my midnight pronouncements I took a subclavian catheter kit from the ER. I found Mrs. McDougal, a frail elderly lady, lying quietly in bed, deceased from long-standing lung disease caused by even longer-standing dedication to cigarettes.

I made the ritual examination. There was no sign of breathing or heartbeat, either to my fingers or my stethoscope. Her pupils were dilated, the color draining from her cheeks, her lips and nailbeds blue. Her limbs were beginning to feel cool to the touch.

After entering my note in the chart, "Pronounced dead at 1:43 am," I returned to Mrs. McDougal's bedside. I brushed back a wisp of fine silvery hair from her brow, and explained to her that I needed to practice an important skill; I requested permission to perform the procedure on her. She didn't object. I untied the gown from around her neck and laid it back to expose her upper chest, and opened the kit.

On my first try I started too high on the right clavicle and had trouble bringing the needle into proper alignment. I moved to the left side and tried again. This time I got a return of blood, but wasn't sure how far to advance the needle; it probably went on through the back side of the vein, and the flow stopped.

I had now used both of Mrs. McDougal's subclavian veins. I thanked her, and left her in peace. At least I now had a better feel for what I was trying to do.

After two more late night pronouncements, whom I choose to call Mr. O'Malley (impressively obese) and Mrs. Ryan, I had succeeded increasingly smoothly on three more subclavian veins.

Scarcely a week later in the x-ray department I found Dr. Craig Lehman, surgeon, supervising a technician as he took chest and abdominal x-rays on a young victim of a motor vehicle crash.

"This man's going to need a lot of blood and fluid replacement," he said. "Can you put in a subclavian line?"

With less than four heartbeats of hesitation I said, "Yes." In ten minutes it was done, without a hitch, the plastic catheter taped in place and delivering a rapid drip of saline solution.

As the patient was being wheeled back to the ICU, Dr. Lehman said, "Boy, a central line like that sure is a great aid to treatment."

I nodded, and returned to the ER. Not until two years later did I tell him that that was the first one I'd done on a live patient.

Manipulating Materials

Roy Robinson came one evening to the ER at Good Sam Hospital. I had seen him a couple of months earlier for some non-specific stomach symptoms, which had gone away but now had returned. It didn't sound like anything organic. Luckily we had a lull between patients so I had time to talk with him.

Until his late forties Roy had been an art teacher in high school, but he felt bored and dissatisfied. He had quit that job and now was selling used cars, but the change had not made him feel better. A former marriage had deteriorated and vanished in the not-too-distant past, and he had no children. His hobby was making knives - really upscale knives, hand-formed steel blades and laminated leather handles beautifully finished. He showed me one of the smaller versions. The satisfaction he felt from the care and meticulous craftsmanship he put into the knives seemed just now to be the only source of fulfillment in his life.

I explained to him the physiology, the "psychosomatic" mechanisms by which covert emotional stresses can affect the smooth muscle cells in the digestive tract and blood vessels, and can produce symptoms such as his. We hit it off well, a reciprocal sort of empathy. He appreciated the unusual time and concern he received in an ER, and our talk started drifting away from stomachs and stresses.

Suddenly he said, "Doctor, I was wondering, with all the time you spend thinking and dealing with other people's problems, you must have a lot of stress in your life. Do you ever get a chance to put time and energy into manipulating materials?" He considered this to be an important and integrative part of life dynamics, and figured some sort of a manual craft would do a doctor good.

I felt the 180-degree shift in our roles: he was now offering me the same nurture and therapy that I had been trying to present to him.

178

Yes, I said, I agreed completely with both his diagnosis and his suggested treatment. And yes, I did indeed manipulate materials extensively in my business - stitching, dressing, looking with various scopes into various orifices, setting bones - but also my main diversion at home was wood carving and sculpture.

He seemed relieved to hear this, and went away to wrestle dutifully with his psycho-somatic interface.

A Good Sharp Blade

I have carried a pocket knife ever since I was six. When I was seven, John Beckwith showed me how to carve two links of a chain. By age nine I succeeded in doing this - having broken many links in the trying - and became an avid whittler.

In those days I sometimes lost a knife, through a hole in my pocket or from standing on my head or even laying it down and forgetting it. Quite a parade of knives had passed through my hands by the time I entered medical school.

There, in the second year, my classmate and roommate Holmes Yealy gave me a knife. His father was vice president of a steel company in Pennsylvania. The knife - a thin, flat, simple but elegant stainless steel thing whose two blades opened by the twist of a small ring on either side - was a promotional item, and engraved on the side of the larger blade was "Latrobe Electric Steel Co."

In medical school there was little time to play with wood. However, I did come upon a leg that had broken off a pool table, probably tulip wood. I cut off a piece and used the knife to carve a little gnome-like man as a gift. (It's a daunting challenge, in a large metropolitan university and medical center, to find an ordinary hand saw. Don't bother to look on the upper floors; you have to go down, and then down some more.)

I carried that knife in my pocket from 1946 past graduation, two years in the Army in Germany, and two different medical practices, all the way to 1966.

I was getting ready to go for two months to Vietnam, then return via a week in a rural inland part of Kenya. The Latrobe Electric Steel knife seemed rather meager as a survival tool, and furthermore it was getting loose in the joints. It seemed prudent, for moving through the *terra incognita* of a boiling part of Asia and thence into Darkest Africa, to be equipped with a more rugged knife. I bought a simple three-and-a-half inch long "Tree" brand knife by Boker U.S.A.

The new knife saw its first medical duty in the highlands of central Vietnam, opening an abscess on the finger of a little Montagnard girl. Since then it has dressed out two deer, skinned two coyotes (I was forced into this because they raided our chicken flock) and a road-killed raccoon, dressed numerous fish and chickens, and whittled countless objects from wood - chains, balls in cages, animals and people, tree ornaments, and assorted sculptures and doodads. It has seen many hours of quiet whittling in faculty meetings, in the orthodontist's waiting room, and on buses and trains, the shavings dropping into a bag-like denim apron.

It also has trimmed the nails, corns and calluses of many elderly patients. After pulling the knife from my pocket I always made sure the patient watched me wipe the blade with alcohol; and I explained that for such a purpose this knife was a better instrument than the standard disposable scalpel blade. (Recently I was introduced to a nurse. She said, "We've met briefly once before. It was about eight years ago, that last weekend that you had come back to cover the ER at Blue Mountain Hospital. All the elderly folks came in and you did their feet. It was wonderful!")

This knife has been just the thing to integrate and bond together such seemingly disparate countries, cultures, activities, interests, and materials in the world, and it still serves me well after 38 years.

More Birthing

After six years in Vermont and Oregon emergency rooms, I recycled back to John Day and resumed general practice -- surgery, delivering babies, and all the rest of it. One day I received a letter:

.

September 21, 1981
Dear Dr. Merrill,

My name is Holly Porter; I am a midwife and I teach Childbirth Education classes in John Day.

I'd like to meet you and talk to you but I thought a letter first might be more appropriate for my questions. Homebirth can be a rather "touchy" subject, especially in the medical profession.

I'd like to know, in what capacity are you available for emergency back-up for a home birth? I know you cannot go to a home to assist at a birth, but can I call you if I have questions either during the prenatal period or during labor? Would you be on call if we did have to go to the hospital? Would you consider making a home visit to suture a woman if she tears?

Once again, I hope I am not putting you in an awkward position. I look forward to meeting you.

Respectfully yours,
Holly Porter

The drama of birthing is a mix of normal and natural life processes, some important medical elements, and a potential medical disaster.

I once sat by the bed in the labor room, conversing with a woman in the second stage of labor. As we talked and I timed her contractions with a hand on her belly, I heard a dripping sound. I checked the wash basin; no leaks there. I stepped around the bed and was alarmed to see a thin stream of blood trickling from between the sheets and puddling on the floor. She had felt no change at all.

Obviously she had placenta previa - the placenta abnormally located between the baby's head and the exit, now being stripped from the inner wall of the uterus and endangering the lives of both infant and mother. A hasty caesarian section salvaged a healthy infant girl and a relieved mother.

How, I wondered, might a situation like this play out in a home delivery a couple of hours from town? In the past I had talked with a few women who planned to have their babies at home, delivered by a midwife. I hadn't tried to talk anyone out of it, but had sometimes expressed my concern as to whether unexpected complications would be recognized and handled safely at home. Here, now, was my chance to discuss it with the midwife herself.

I answered Holly's note, we talked on the phone, and she invited me to attend her next class on Preparation for Childbirth.

Six women were present. They had been asked to bring a blanket, a pillow, and a husband or "significant other." Holly introduced me, and I retreated to a status of spectator. This session was devoted to a set of exercises, mainly breathing. The ladies breathed slowly and deeply while relaxing totally, and their coaches coached with varying degrees of enthusiasm. It was a good class.

Afterward Holly and I talked about her methods, about potential complications and how she would handle them, about why patients would want to deliver at home instead of at the hospital.

"I'll go this far," I finally said. "If one of your patients has a problem that you're concerned about, and if I'm available, you're welcome to consult me about it. If the patient needs my help I'll see her, admit her to the hospital and take full charge of the situation. You may be an observer, and a consultant, if the patient wishes it, but all decisions as to management - such as medications, or an emergency caesarian - will be made between me and the patient." I made it clear that I was speaking only for myself and not for any of the other doctors; if I was not available she would have to work it out with them however she could.

This arrangement worked well enough. She continued delivering babies, and referred an occasional case to me: a long and difficult labor when she became worried, and a patient with high blood pressure and toxemia of pregnancy, and perhaps one other.

Meanwhile, by talking with these women and with Holly, I became convinced that parts of our usual methods and policies in the hospital were unnecessary. I discontinued routine enemas before delivery, and routine shaving of the vaginal area. I encouraged the fathers to take a more active role in the preparations and during labor.

One day Holly called and asked me to come to a house to check a first-time mother whose baby she had just delivered. She had a small vaginal tear, and Holly wasn't sure whether it should be stitched.

When I arrived an hour and a half after the birth, the mother and baby - a large girl, over eight pounds - were both healthy and happy. The tear was trivial and needed no special treatment; the whole vaginal area seemed fine.

On the way home I thought: If Holly can deliver a baby that big, a first baby, without an episiotomy and without a significant tear, why can't I?

I read a couple of her books. I began giving more time and attention to actively massaging and stretching the tissues around the vaginal opening, a little earlier in the third stage of labor, and found that it actually worked. I seldom did episiotomies after that.

The Hospital Board of Directors and the nurses began openly wondering why so many women were electing not to come to the hospital to have their babies. Three of the nurses organized a meeting between themselves and three women who had delivered at home, or at hospitals where things were done differently. Some of the differences, the contrasts between hospital and home deliveries that the "dissidents" cited were:

· The labor rooms were austere and uninviting.

· Husbands were not encouraged to stay around during labor, and other family members, especially children, were excluded.

· Often you were required to wear a fetal monitor, and whenever the belt holding it onto your belly slipped a little, somebody would come rushing in thinking there was something wrong with the baby. It was rumored that concerns about what the fetal monitor was showing might even get you an emergency caesarian section that wasn't really necessary.

· Just as the peak of the birthing experience approached and you needed to concentrate and try to relax and hold your coach's hand, there would be an upsetting flurry and rushing and uncomfortable transfer on a hard wheeled cart into a strange and scary room and onto an even more uncomfortable delivery table, and then both arms and legs were strapped down as if you were expected to go out of control.

· Then you would most likely be subjected to shots and then cutting and stitches.

· You would barely get a glimpse of the baby before it was snatched away to the nursery, and you couldn't hold it and enjoy the miracle and put it to breast and experience that magical bonding until some later time depending on the convenience of a busy nurse.

· Visiting hours were restricted for somebody else's convenience.

· The doctor usually seemed to be in a hurry and acted as if he were being inconvenienced.

· There just was nothing <u>natural</u> about the whole thing.

The committee went home to think and talk it over. Seriously. Within months the old delivery room was abandoned. The "labor room" was converted into a "birthing center" with a "birthing bed" - a comfortable bed with hidden padded leg supports and a pull-away section at the foot to expose a basin holder and to make room for the attendant. No more frantic trips down the hall. The room had comfortable chairs and carpet and television. The visiting rules were changed to allow brief visits by children, and free access for others at the mother's request.

185

To "deliver a baby" is a pitifully inadequate phrase to cover the rich and varied interactions, relationships, emotions, and experiences of the people involved. After nearly 2,000 babies I never entirely finished learning that. But Blue Mountain Hospital's new birthing center felt like a happy place!

Butterflies

Looking back toward town from the airfield, across the customary fringing parts of a city - dusty lots, bare bones of new construction, a scattering of industrial buildings, a lush field of alfalfa ready for its second cutting -- you could see the hospital. I sat in the car on the shoulder of the road, waiting, and divided my thoughts between the languid buzz of activity just on the other side of the chain link fence and that brick edifice of hope and dread and comfort in the distance.

I had just left my wife there. She has cardiomyopathy, the slow kind of heart trouble, heart muscle gradually dying. She has used up already more than the two years they had given her to live and is still getting around pretty well - can even go shopping for groceries if I'm there to carry the bags for her. Until yesterday.

On the sofa, sitting on her favorite quilt, the wedding ring pattern, she suddenly went quiet and tipped over sideways. I'll never forget that blank stare, how her face blanched, her eyes rolled up and I thought she was gone. But as soon as she fell over on the couch, life returned and she was looking around.

I fetched my portable ECG machine, and it showed atrial fibrillation: her heart had suddenly gone into overdrive, racing so that it didn't pump well. The ambulance took her the 150 miles to the hospital in the city because that's where the cardiologists were. I followed in my car.

The emergency room folks were calm, efficient, and reassuring. After some medications her heart rate began to stabilize and she was moved to the ICU, comfortable and drowsy.

"You'll just be resting here while we wait for the medicine to do its work," I told her.

"You may as well go and find something to do for a couple of hours," the nurse said. Betsy agreed. She felt better now, and safe. The wavy line on the monitor had steadied noticeably. "Go and get something to eat," she murmured, "or go for a walk. I'll be fine."

"In the waiting room downstairs," I said, "there's a notice of an air show this afternoon, with some sky divers. Maybe I'll swing by there for a little while." I patted her hand. She nodded and gave a feeble wave as I turned toward the heavy glass door.

Tickets were $8 but the show was more than half done, the military planes in formation had made their low-level pass over the stands, most of the hot-shot stunt flying was already finished, so I didn't feel like paying that much to get in. A few cars were parked along the side road outside the fence, and I found a place close enough that I could hear the announcer's voice projected through the hot, still afternoon, making intermittent small talk while awaiting the sky divers.

I stepped out and stood sweating in the skimpy shade of the car. The first plane was barely visible - about ten thousand feet, the blurry voice from the speakers said - as three tiny dots detached themselves and fell away. They tumbled, twisted and circled, not close to each other as I had seen on TV but strung out over several hundred yards as their red, white, and blue chutes opened at last and they floated down, swooping and swinging and gliding sideways beyond the stands and out of my view.

There was to be another group of sky divers. I looked at my watch, reached for the car door, then decided to wait for them. Meanwhile, the announcer said, we would watch "a local pilot in his experimental home-built plane" do some maneuvers.

The airfield complex was an open set of bleachers in front of a line of small scrubby trees, beyond which lay some low buildings, two hangars and what I took to be a modest control tower. The runway was barely distinguishable from the surrounding hard-packed and dusty ground which raveled out into sagebrush-studded desert.

A cute little biplane taxied into view, sped down the runway with a snarl and zoomed steeply into the air in front of me. Its colors were a strange combination, green and brown; I thought of some weird tropical insect, the kind scientists tell us they haven't discovered yet. It seemed to me the tail was larger

188

than usual. The pilot in the open cockpit waved at the spectators as he passed.

The plane circled above us and gained altitude rapidly. Sweeping across in a straight pass it rolled 360 degrees and sped on, and I fancied I could faintly hear applause from the stands.

Far out to the north the craft turned, and on the next pass it shot upward abruptly from level flight and did a tight loop, pulling out into the flat again with geometrical grandeur as if riding an invisible track in the air. Though profoundly ignorant in such matters, I would say that this was a highly skilled pilot in a delightfully agile machine.

Next he spiraled sharply upward, higher and higher, until appearing like a tiny toy. At last, nosing over, he began a diving descent, twisting slowly as he fell, obviously under complete control, boring through the cloudless blue sky with vertical precision, a magnificent living power drill.

The announcer had been commenting on the plane's movements, but now was hushed as it came lower, lower, as we waited for the pilot to pull out of the spin.

The machine hurtled on, never flinching from its linear path, and drove straight into the earth two hundred yards from where I stood.

The silence was eerie. No crashing noise, just an instantaneous cessation of motion, a small puff of dust, and the plane's oversize tail projecting upward above the scant curtain of sagebrush. There was no smoke nor flame. No sound came from the announcer.

After what seemed like minutes a woman emerged from the crowd and started walking toward the plane. Two men moved as if to restrain her, then let her go. A vehicle the color of the ground followed her, not an ambulance but what appeared to be an official airport van, moving deliberately, driving in slow motion into the shimmering heat of the desert. Three other men straggled behind the car toward the dust that hung in the motionless air, toward the jaunty green and brown tail fin.

I started toward the gate, to go closer, then turned back to the car. I tried to wrap my mind around what I had just seen, an image too real to be denied, too explicit to be comprehended. The air felt like cotton wool against my skin. The light was different, viscous and heavy.

Back at the hospital my steps felt soggy, as if walking through syrup. I took the Number 2 elevator to the third floor and was admitted to the ICU. She was resting comfortably, they said, and her heart rate was almost normal.

I sat down beside the bed. She looked tired, but her color was good, her greying hair smoothed back, her breathing quiet and easy.

"Hi!" Betsy said. I had to lean forward to hear her. "How were the sky divers?"

"They were fine," I said. "They were great. Looked like big colorful butterflies when they came down and landed."

"That's nice," she said. She squeezed my hand, smiled a wan little smile, and closed her eyes.

Retreat to the Emergency Room

In my first venture to John Day I had a partner from the start, and for 11 years we alternated taking calls on nights and weekends and vacations, assisted each other in surgery, shared what we knew, even operated on each other.

The second time I came, 20 years later, there were doctors who would cover for me if I wanted to leave town, but no one wanted a close and regular reciprocal arrangement. Thus I always expected to be available for daily rounds, and for deliveries or emergencies with my regular patients.

After six years I tired of being constantly on call, and had been thinking again of leaving general practice. About every decade I had made some kind of move or career change, and that time had come once more. Time to phase down again to a hospital Emergency Room.

By "phase down" I mean that the <u>range</u> of medical problems, the kinds of illnesses and injuries, is the same in the practice of a GP as in the ER. True, the proportion of high-intensity cases is greater in the ER. On the other hand, there the hours are clearly set. After my shift ends I am not on call; I need never hang around home to see whether I will be needed in the delivery room; and when I have a severely ill patient I just turn him or her over to another doctor for continuing care.

The other advantage is economic. I have always hated to ask patients for money, especially if I knew it would be difficult for them to pay. In the ER the hospital insulates me from this distasteful matter; I merely check the little boxes on the form to indicate what type of service I provided. I am paid by the hour plus a percentage, and the bookkeepers take care of all the confrontational part.

This, of course, is partly what has corrupted the medical profession: neither the doctor nor the patient has to face the other over the vexing question of fees, because the insurance system stands between them so each is dealing with somebody else's money. Thus both have lost control of the negotiations

191

and neither has an incentive to economize. Dr. Wayne Grodrian, a gruff and revered old GP, told me, "The first doctor who ever accepted a payment directly from an insurance company should have been hung in the public square."

In these times I live in two worlds: the world of work, and the world of home. They are separated geographically. Home is Portland. Work is the ER at Mid-Columbia Medical Center in The Dalles, 75 miles east.

And they are separated contextually. At work I insert myself into the square hole of the Medical Machine, the Health Care Industry, and squeeze the practice of medicine through the filters of medical staff bylaws and rules and regulations, quality assurance and utilization committees, chart reviews, state laws and policies and inspections, continuing education requirements, federal Medicare rules, state Medicaid rules, changing fee schedules and procedure and treatment codes, Area Trauma Advisory Board and American Heart Association treatment protocols, Oregon's new experimental cost-containment program, liability insurance company requirements and "risk-management" reminders, hospital dress code, inter-physician politics and dynamics, before finally getting to the sick or injured or troubled patient, to the heart and the pleasure of the work.

Drained and tired after a pair of 24-hour work shifts plus a few hours of dictating reports, separated by a night's sleep in a motel, I drive home and pour myself through the round hole, back into the real and personal center of my world - warm, soft, fragrant, clean, loving, nourishing and whole.

Boundary Shifts

The mortuary's driver strode jauntily down the hall toward the ER in Central Vermont Hospital, smiling and chewing gum. Behind him, as if he were hauling a load of cabbages, he drew a gurney bearing a body. "Where do you want him?" he asked cheerily.

The young man on the cart was unconscious, snoring loudly through blood in his nose and mouth, his head rolling from side to side as the cart made the turn through the double doors. Other than having been moved, he was no better off than when lying on the roadside an hour earlier after ejection from his tumbling vehicle.

From medieval times until the early 1970s the mission of an ambulance was simply transportation. In large cities, private ambulance services competed, racing their rivals to the scene of an accident. In smaller cities and towns, most ambulance service was provided by mortuaries because they were the folks that had carts and vehicles suitable for carrying human bodies in a horizontal position.

We can give credit to wars in Korea and especially in Vietnam for some of the shifts in the medical culture in the 1970s. The military services had proved that non-physicians trained in the immediate care of injuries could greatly improve the outcomes.

Based on research and training from the Vietnam war, the American College of Surgeons developed an 80-hour course for ambulance attendants, turning them into Emergency Medical Technicians. Economics, changing expectations, and the perception of conflict of interest led most mortuaries by the mid-1970s to give up doubling as ambulances

Had that patient rolling down the hall in Central Vermont Hospital come a mere two years later he would have been brought in an actual ambulance by a crew of EMTs, strapped firmly to a backboard, his neck stabilized with a cervical collar, the blood cleared from his airway with a suction device, oxygen provided by face mask, his pulse and blood pressure and breathing monitored, his injuries assessed and reported by radio to the hospital ER staff before his arrival.

This new breed of people were volunteers, trained at their own expense. You'd have to ask them why they did it. In effect, they had extended the boundaries of hospital care far beyond the front door and out into the countryside.

The boundaries, the difference in expectations between urban and rural medicine have also changed. In any malpractice action against a doctor in 1950, the test was whether his quality of practice was "consistent with that prevailing in his community." But by 1980 the "medical community" for comparison in litigation was the entire system nationwide. If my patient in a remote little town didn't receive "the standard of care" in a critical situation because of time and distance from needed facilities, it could be forgiven; but not so for my failure of knowledge, skill, or diligence.

Mid-Columbia Medical Center is in The Dalles, on the Oregon side of the Columbia Gorge, overlooking Bonnevlle Dam. It stands at a sort of geographical and capability boundary, an intermediary between the scattered rural population and rural medicine of Eastern Oregon and the major metropolitan medical centers in Portland.

Other boundaries too have moved as medical care evolved. In 1950, nurses did simply nursing. They gave intramuscular injections, but were not permitted to draw blood or give an injection into a vein or to start an intravenous drip; those were jobs for a doctor, too difficult and too important for a mere nurse.

How that has changed! Nurses' training has expanded. Constant research in both trauma and cardiac care has brought continually increasing expectations to both doctors and nurses. ER doctors and nurses alike now are recertified every two years by the American Heart Association's course in Advanced Cardiac Life Support, and both take the same course and the same testing. Frequently, a part of the course will be a nurse teaching and testing a group of doctors and nurses. A whole new esprit and teamwork exist in the ER. Now, seeking to put a needle into a difficult vein, a doctor may want to call on the skill of an ER or ICU nurse, or vice versa. Awareness that each nurse knows nearly as much about a lot of things as I do is both comforting and challenging, and brings forth the best skill and effort from all of us.

Fifty years ago women doctors were in the minority - 10 percent in my class - and male nurses were a rarity - none in my wife's class. In the last ER where I worked, at Mid-Columbia Medical Center (MCMC, or MC^2, as we liked to call it), we had three nurses named Bob, besides Dave and Kurt - men and women in almost equal numbers.

During the 1980s and 90s the range and availability of technology increased -- computer-assisted x-ray tomography (CAT scans), magnetic resonance imaging (MRI), ultrasound imaging of heart and blood flow; surgery with optic-fiber scopes through tiny incisions.

Wonders could be performed in diagnosis and treatment. And it became easy to subtly shift ones focus from the patient to the machines -- to watch the monitor on the wall instead of watching the patient's face and holding his hand as he approached death..

The ER hummed and bustled with clients until mid-morning. Finally there was a lull, and I had time to notice the arrangement of fresh flowers on the nurses' desk.

"Very pretty," I said to Joyce, the boss nurse. "Did somebody die, or get engaged?"

"No, this is National Nurses' Day. Dr. Chambers brought those in this morning."

And there, at the other end of the desk, was a tray of dried fruit with a card from Dr. Wilson. Curses! I had forgotten. And now it was too late. I wouldn't be free to go shopping until my shift ended at nine the next morning.

The matter simmered in my mind all day. This was the finest, most competent and congenial crew of nurses I had ever worked with. To be leader of such a team was a great pleasure, and this occasion couldn't be allowed to pass without proper acknowledgement.

195

During moments between patients, waiting for lab tests or x-rays, retreating into the doctors' windowless cave to gulp some supper and catch up on dictating records, snatching spare moments, I pieced together strings of ideas and words. After several naps and interruptions, by dawn I finally had it all penned out on a clean sheet of paper in time to present it before the shift change:

THE DAY OF THE NURSE
A Tribute

'Mid blood and broken bones and pain
Or airways clogged and battered brain,
When clerks pass out and surgeons curse,
Whom do we seek? Of course! A nurse.

She takes the pulse and wipes the blood,
Whips in a shot and mops up mud.
She hands us things with all four hands
And fulfills everyone's demands.

In triage skill she can't be beat;
She checks the patient, head to feet.
She notes each missing breath or part
And always writes it on the chart.

She's on the phone and on the run;
She never fails to get things done.
If some small wound I fail to see,
She's sure to point it out to me.

She turns the oxygen up high
And notes when PVCs go by.
When any patient feels afraid,
The nurse is there to offer aid.

She serves up coffee, Silvadene,
Some sterile gloves, or linen clean.
She always knows right where things are
And fetches them from near or far.

Sometimes the nurse I'm calling "she"
Turns out instead to be a "he."
But never fear; with life or limb
You still can trust a nurse that's "him."

In time of trouble, time of pain,
Time of sickness, fear, and strain -
When things have gone from bad to worse,
The cry on people's lips is, "Nurse!"

Safety

Blood is a cosmic fluid. It flows abundantly in the veins of mythology, through the pages of legend and religion. It stains the battlefields of history and carries the stuff of life to the cells of all creatures great and small.

In my third year of medical school I worked nights in the blood bank, crossmatching the blood for tomorrow's surgeries. We tested each unit of blood for syphilis - the only disease which, in that time in New York, offered any significant threat of being transmitted by a blood transfusion. The year was 1947.

Blood remained much the same, its place in society and politics and medicine changing little, for another four decades.

In the 1980s new mysterious hazards began appearing - Hepatitis B, then Human Immunodeficiency Virus (HIV); most often in gay men, then in intravenous drug users, then among recipients of blood transfusions, and on rare occasions in health workers after trivial needle or scalpel injuries. Eventually most victims of hemophilia also became victims of HIV infection because the clotting factor that they received intravenously came from plasma pooled from many donors.

All this cast a complex web of controversy over medical thought, practice, and politics. It pitted health departments against gay bath houses; gay communities against health departments; the Center for Disease Control against city officials; gays against pharmaceutical companies, and them against the FDA; gays against the president and congress. Moral issues. Privacy. Human rights. Individual rights. Denial. Political correctness. Social justice. Responsibility.

Larry Kramer, gay social activist, ranted and organized protests. Randy Schilts, gay newspaper man, studied and reported. Insurance companies worried and scurried. Medical groups studied, postured, agonized, learned and taught. Schilts wrote a book, a piercing documentary, "And the Band Played On."

The politics, economics, and practice of medicine profoundly changed, the new fears became institutionalized and commercialized (if only I'd owned stock in latex gloves!), and for the past 20 years I have had an ongoing argument with my colleagues and with myself. It goes something like this:

[Entering the hospital cafeteria, in line behind the internist]
"How's it going, Joe? Hmm, sausage and sauerkraut again today," I say, sniffing the steamy air.

"Hi, Ted. Had a pretty busy morning in the ICU. Have you watched that video on Universal Precautions yet?"

"No," I reply, "and I'm trying to avoid it as long as possible."

"But you can get an hour of CME credit for sleeping through a 28-minute training film," he says with mock seriousness.

"It's too high a price to pay, Joe. If the liability insurer didn't force it on us, I wouldn't watch it at all. I hate the whole idea of 'universal precautions.' It's ridiculous."

"Well, I hear that if the inspector comes around and finds you messing with blood without gloves on, even cleaning a scratch or putting on a Band Aid, you can get a $3,000 fine."

"Yeah. Isn't that just tyrannical? Like the Inquisition in the middle ages."

"But Ted, don't you think that in the Emergency Department, especially, it makes a lot of sense? Wearing gloves and goggles, or whatever, to protect yourself? I'll tell you, I don't want to be spattered with body fluids from any of my AIDS patients. And in the E.R. you never know who you'll be dealing with next. I'd think you'd find that kind of scary, some broken-up biker bleeding and puking and struggling and spitting blood all over while you're trying to establish an airway and put in IV lines."

[We sit down at a table in the corner.]
"Yeah, that's true, of course. But scariness needs to be selective. You hit the problem on the head. In the E.R. - or anywhere else, for that matter - we never know for sure who or what we're dealing with. Theoretically I'm also supposed to be

afraid of the terrified little kid who fell against the coffee table and got a half-inch nick in his scalp, and I'm supposed to put on gloves while I feel around through his clotted-up hair to find the cut. But I just refuse to be afraid of that. Being afraid of people's blood or spit or tears is totally foreign to me. Hell, I've been dipping into or getting spattered with people's blood for forty years and it's never done me any harm. When I was in general practice and doing C-sections, where you have a big gush of bloody fluid, the nurses used to joke about the surgeon trying to tilt the drapes so most of the blood would run down the front of his assistant. I kept a pair of old shoes in my locker for delivering babies; they were crusted with the spilled blood of hundreds of moaning and panting mothers. Christ, blood is sacred, it's a ritual substance that unites the souls of the surgeon and his patient --"

"Now, Ted, you're getting carried away."

"Yeah, maybe" I concede, stabbing another piece of sausage. "But I'm serious about this. This isn't the way to do medicine. This AIDS thing has us all screwed up. We aren't dealing with disease like we used to. Sure, I've always taken precautions. I wash my hands when they've been in blood or feces or other slimy stuff, or when I've been touching a sick patient - partly to protect myself and partly to protect the next person I'm going to touch. And of course I always wear gloves during surgery - to protect the patient from all the germs on my hands and floating around in the world, not to protect him from me or me from him. And we've always had isolation precautions when we thought it mattered, like masks on people with TB to protect those around them, or GI precautions for people with hepatitis or typhoid, and even quarantine in the past, to protect well people from sick people. And it makes sense to use masks and gowns and all that to protect someone with a compromised immune system, like somebody on chemotherapy or with AIDS, from the germs that we well people carry around. But now we're not allowed to know who to be afraid of, we can't test high-risk people and track down their contacts like we've always been <u>required </u>to do with syphilis and gonorrhea and tuberculosis, and we can't confine or

200

quarantine anybody with HIV infection like we used to do with scarlet fever and measles and - yeah, I know that was way back before your time. But now, because of our mandatory blindfold, we have to treat everybody off the street as a hazard to us. That's just nuts. Politically correct isn't necessarily medically correct."

"But you know as well as I do, Ted, that anybody off the street now <u>may be</u> a hazard to us. You can't tell any better than I can, from looking at somebody, whether he or she is HIV positive. You don't know his sexual practices, you may not even know whether he's been shooting up with a borrowed needle. So what are you gonn'a do, just float along and take your chances? Then maybe <u>you'll</u> become a hazard to the rest of us. And besides, if it's known that you don't use universal precautions, and if you ever, God forbid, get HIV, your insurance company will probably refuse to pay for it as worker's compensation, because you were asking for it."

"Oh, come on, Joe! That's just part of the hysteria and distortion we've gotten ourselves into, by treating the whole thing as politics and liability instead of medicine. I'll tell you what, if the AIDS epidemic had first shown up in some other demographic group, like nuns or professional athletes or kindergarten kids, instead of gay men, it would be a whole different ballgame. The morality question wouldn't have confused us, and we'd be treating it just like we have other infectious and even other sexually transmitted diseases in the past - mandatory testing, identifying and testing contacts - "

"Now wait a minute, Ted. Identifying and testing contacts? That may work for gonorrhea, where the incubation period is maybe three days and you can tell within a week whether the contact person has gotten the infection. And even then the contact may have spread it on to half a dozen more people before you catch up with him or her. So how about HIV with an incubation period of three months, or maybe a year, before it's detectable, and two or three or five years before any symptoms? And mandatory testing - whom are you going to test? To do what you want you'd have to test everybody in the world every three months, and even then a lot would fall through the cracks.

"And the other part of it is, what do you do when you identify the 'contact' and find that he's HIV positive? What do you do? How do you change anything? You can't cure it. If there was a good treatment for HIV folks who aren't sick yet, it might be different. But anybody in a high risk group now will still be in a high risk group after you've done your mandatory blood test and proven that he has HIV. Maybe knowing it will make him act more responsibly, but don't count on it. Or would you legislate abstinence, or legislate using condoms? Or maybe you could clamp an electronic device on the person's ankle that would shout out 'Beware, HIV!' every five minutes. Come on, Ted; universal precautions is the only way to go now."

"Yeah," I flare," what you really mean is universal denial and universal fear. We've got both of those, all right. In the past the only patients I've been afraid of were the ones who were crazy and violent. Now I'm supposed to be afraid of all of them. And what does that do for the doctor-patient relationship, the therapeutic interaction? You know, Joe, it may sound corny to you, but a big part of healing goes with touch, the 'laying on of hands.' I mean this. I had a patient just the other day complaining about another doctor she'd been to, and she felt he didn't care, he was cold and aloof. 'He just talked to me, and didn't even touch me,' she said. Said that had never happened to her with a doctor before. That's real, Joe. Something of value passes between people with that touch, something that really makes a difference to the experience, and I'd bet that in some subtle way it even makes a difference to the outcome."

[We eat in silence - briefly.]

"You know," I rave on, "one place I've always worn gloves is doing a pelvic exam. It just occurred to me, now there you don't need gloves to protect either party from becoming ill. You wear them - you're never told this, but you wear them specifically as a psychological barrier, a barrier against the intimacy of touch. Well, it'll have the same effect where you don't want that barrier. If you come to me for comforting and I put on gloves before patting your arm or feeling your pulse, will

202

this distort our psychic transaction? Of course it will! 'Universal precautions' means universal separation, an unspoken agreement that all humans must accept fear of each other as the norm, especially in a crisis, instead of facing and dealing with the crisis together."

"Now Ted, I think you're blowing this thing all out of proportion. The world has changed, and you've got to go along with it." I shake my head. Joe stuffs a bite of bread into his mouth.

"I once talked to an old guy," I say, "he'd been a missionary doctor in China. He could speak just a little of the language of the natives, not nearly as much as the other missionaries who'd been there a long time; yet he said he almost felt guilty because he could communicate more effectively with the Chinese than the others could. The reason? He had an excuse, a context for touching the people, and it was a two-way communication. He felt their pulse and their fever and the hardness in their belly, and they felt his care and his compassion and his brotherhood. I wonder how that would have worked if he'd pulled on a pair of gloves and a gown and goggles whenever a patient came into the room."

Joe looks at his watch. "Ted, you're a dreamer. You're a great guy, and you're still a helluva good doctor, but you're from another age. You'd better either retire or join the real world." He swallows the last of his coffee. "I've got to get on over to the office."

"Yeah. Thanks, Joe. See ya later." *[I stare unseeing at my half-eaten meal. At last I pick up my tray and follow Joe toward the door.]*

Around 1990 it became mandatory in our hospital for all health care workers to be vaccinated against Hepatitis B virus (HBV). Special classes were given on how to handle needles defensively and safely; and a standard protocol was established for managing cases of accidental needle sticks. I followed the rest of the flock and got the HBV vaccine. And I filled out the forms and ordered the testing whenever a nurse accidentally stuck herself drawing blood or giving a shot.

I have gone along with the tide, and I follow the rules, but I still hate Universal Precautions, the cowardly barrier between souls. Larry Kramer and Randy Schilts are dead now, but my only risk factor is being a health care worker.

In 1992 I underwent replacement of a crusted-up heart valve. Afterward I was told that I could no longer be a blood donor, because the routine blood tests showed that sometime in the past - presumably before my vaccination, presumably from some random and unsuspected patient contact and minor skin penetration - I had become infected with Hepatitis B. Some people die from Hepatitis B; I did not. I never had any symptoms, and probably never will.

Yes, the discovery that I was infected, I suppose, makes a mockery of my disdain for Universal Precautions. Just how safe can you be?

Chocolate Syrup

The emergency entry buzzer sounded and the door swung open. I could hear a child whimper, and then only the sound of hurrying feet. I stepped out from the Emergency Room into the hall as a mother approached the check-in counter. She carried a toddler in her right arm, and with her left hand steadied the object apparently attached to the child's right forefinger. The little blonde boy on her hip showed quiet consternation, waiting to learn what fate awaited him in this intimidating place. Meanwhile, he continued carefully to point into the depths of a Hershey's chocolate syrup can.

"I know this sounds foolish," said the mother in a tone of agitation and embarrassment, "but we can't get his finger out."

The can had been opened with the pointed kind of opener that curls a triangle of metal down inside the can. Finding the almost empty can, the boy had probed for a taste of the yummy stuff. His finger was seized by the sharp prong of metal, and efforts to pull the finger out caused the point to dig in more firmly.

We didn't bother with any paperwork. I gently persuaded the boy to set his can on the counter and, with soothing words of reassurance, slipped the blunt blade of my pocket knife alongside the finger. The blade easily enlarged the hole, then pressed the offending point of metal back and away from its victim. The boy withdrew the finger and gave a broad smile.

"Do you want the can?" I asked. "For a souvenir?"

"No, thanks!" said the lady hastily. "We're finished with it."

They gratefully departed, and I was forced to scrape out and consume what little chocolate syrup remained.

In Praise of Useless Action

In my childhood our school-teacher father had the summers free and we spent many of them camping and fishing on Idaho's upper Salmon River.

From time to time - perhaps in deference to our mother - instead of spending the morning fishing we would simply go for a drive, see some sights. Mom would fix a picnic lunch (and we might have some fishing gear along, just in case).

On one such a day in midsummer, the sky crystal clear and the air pleasantly warm and fragrant of pine and sage, we drove down river toward no hard destination. Four miles below Sunbeam we crossed the bridge at Robinson's Bar and continued on down the east side. At one place, from the road high above the river you could look down a stretch of canyon for what appeared to be many miles, with shadowed ravines and small valleys feeding their mysterious secrets into the main channel. Our parents were chatting about some bit of business or politics and my brother and I were taking turns holding a little home-made windmill out the window.

Suddenly Mom gave a gasping cry. I looked up in time to see her clutch at her neck or chest. She said, "I hurt!"

Dad stopped the car abruptly in the middle of the road (there was no other place to stop). All three of us leaned toward Mom, hovering, not knowing what was happening. She looked frightened, fists still clenched against her bosom. Dad reached and touched her shoulder, but nothing changed; she didn't speak.

"I'll get you some water!" Dad said. He fumbled in the picnic box, found a white enameled metal cup, looked at her once more, and plunged over the shoulder of the road toward the river. He leaped, strode, slid, and clattered down the steep shale slope, down a hundred feet or so to the bottom. He scooped up a cup of water and started back up toward the car. Scrambling and clawing, he climbed up and slid back, fell at least twice, all the while holding the cup, and made gradual headway. A couple of times I glanced at Mom; she seemed to be improving, so I worried more now about Dad. At last he reached the edge of the road, crawled on his knees to the car's running board, stretched his arm out to hand the cup (still, incredibly, half full of water) to Mom, then collapsed gasping against the wheel of the car.

Mom's sudden attack of pain had quit. In ten minutes Dad had recovered enough to drive on. We had a nice picnic lunch, and completed our excursion uneventfully. But a half-century later I can still feel deep inside of me a reprise of that scene: my father racing, at considerable peril to life and limb, to deliver to his wife a half cup of water *because something had to be done,* and *because he didn't know anything better to do.*

Examples occur all the time where futile actions, useless gestures are absolutely required: A mother picks up her dead child and holds him tightly against her. A man holding his neighbor's garden hose sprinkles the dying embers of the remains of his own house. A funeral, however you want to do it.

Years later, as Emergency Department physician, I was on duty when the patient being rushed in by ambulance was Marty, one of our own ER nurses, a close member of our professional family, shot in the chest by a drunken boyfriend.

We worked on her for an hour, four doctors and a lot of nurses and technicians - CPR, tracheal intubation, heart monitor, multiple IVs, blood transfusions, finally opening her chest and massaging her naked heart - even though we really knew after the first few minutes that she was dead beyond rescue. We all had to go through these motions before any of us was ready to say, "Stop."

At last we were able to lay down our tools, brush away tears, and concede defeat. Suddenly I thought of Dad, desperate on the crumbling hillside, holding out the cup.

Somewhat Informed Consent

In medical school I was taught that it sometimes is permissible to lie to a patient in order to spare him or her the trauma of an unfavorable diagnosis or prognosis, and that the doctor knows best what is good for the patient. This is no longer the prevailing view.

It is universal practice now to obtain from the patient a signed Informed Consent document before any invasive or potentially risky procedure, especially surgery. This custom has grown from the litigious nature of our present society, but also from the enlightened modern idea that a patient should have a major role in decisions about his health care.

The pre-op dictation by the surgeon now must state that "a PAR conference has been held with the patient" - Procedure being recommended; Alternatives to the proposed procedure (including doing nothing); and Results to be expected from each choice. But truly informed consent would go far beyond the usual streamlined discussion of procedures, alternatives, and expected results.

Some thirty years ago, when I signed the consent form and lay down for repair of my inguinal hernia, I had a large advantage over other patients. Though "informed" consent was much less clearly defined at that time, mine was indeed informed, for several reasons.

First, I understood well the anatomy of a hernia and what would be required to repair it.

Second, I had repaired many hernias myself, and knew the potential pitfalls and errors or accidents that might occur, from anesthetic to surgical to mechanical to pharmacologic, and had a sense of the odds on each.

Third, the surgeon was my partner, with whom I had worked for years. He and I had assisted each other on numerous hernia repairs, so I knew exactly how he would handle the tissues, how he would place that first stitch in Cooper's ligament, what was the chance that he might skewer my spermatic artery or tighten the external ring too snugly or leave a blood vessel leaking inside as he closed the wound. And I knew and trusted the anesthetist and her methods. All went well, as I had expected.

Many years later I signed a consent form again. This time, however, it was with much less assurance, for despite all my knowledge and the best intentions of the health care providers, my "informedness" was full of gaps, uncertainties, hesitant faith and hopeful assumptions. I had developed aortic stenosis, and was bargaining for a new heart valve.

I had once referred a patient to Albert Starr, a prominent cardiac surgeon and a pioneer in the field, and watched him install a Starr-Edwards valve. Since that time, the technology had advanced, mortality had decreased, and many accomplished heart surgeons were available. But most of what I knew about it was third-hand and sketchy. I knew that I had the choice between a mechanical valve and a pig valve; that the pig valve might fail before the rest of me did, since I was otherwise in good health despite being near seventy; that with the mechanical valve I would have to take coumadin the rest of my life to prevent blood clots from forming on the valve; and that I would have to choose a surgeon, sight-unseen.

I had never watched the placement of a pig valve nor a St. Jude mechanical valve. My knowledge of anesthetic techniques was obsolete. I had never operated a heart-lung machine, nor met the person who would keep me alive by running it while my heart was stopped and open. I had only the sketchiest knowledge of all the niceties of craftsmanship that were required, the complications that could occur, little glitches in technique, mechanical or electronic failures, problems with blood replacement, the details of stopping and restarting the heart, preventing clots or air emboli, and numerous other problems that wouldn't even occur to me.

When I first noticed an aortic systolic murmur I consulted an internist, Dr. Hodge. I went back for the report on the echocardiogram, and he said the stenosis was quite mild.

"Dr. Schutz, who read the test, is a superb echocardiographer," said Dr. Hodge. I had never met Dr.

Schutz, but from that moment he became the cardiologist who would follow my four-year progression from "mild stenosis" to "moderate" to "critical degree of obstruction," and who did the angiogram and ventriculography. I signed the "informed consent" for this procedure (snaking a thin tube up from my groin into my heart to inject dye and take x-rays), though I had never seen him do one, nor had I compared his mortality/morbidity track record with that of other cardiologists.

Dr. Schutz regularly worked with several surgeons, doing echocardiograms in the operating room to check the newly placed valves for leakage and pressure gradients. Since he had watched them work, he should be in a good position to give an opinion.

"If you were choosing a surgeon to give you a new valve," I said, "whom would you pick?"

"I know several that I'd be happy with," he replied.

"I've heard someone speak well of Albert Krause."

"Yes," he said, "Al would be a great choice. He works quickly, gets in and out with no wasted time, and he's an excellent craftsman."

Since I had not yet experienced any of the "big three" symptoms of aortic stenosis - dizziness, angina, or sudden death - there was no clear consensus as to when was the right time for my surgery. I decided to get a second opinion from another cardiologist whom I knew. Dr. Ames reviewed the history and the records, listened to my heart and lungs, then took from his shelf a brand new textbook on heart disease.

"The question is not yet fully resolved," the author wrote, "but at this time I do not favor aortic valve replacement in an asymptomatic patient merely on the basis of echocardiographic findings."

Dr. Ames agreed that my tests showed I would indeed need the surgery. "But I would say that you don't need to rush it; it doesn't have to be done before the holidays. I'd plan it for early next year."

I thanked him and we stepped out into the hall. Dr. Hattenhauer, another cardiologist, was just walking by. Dr.

Ames introduced us, and I briefly described my mission with Dr. Ames.

"Oh, yes," said Dr. Hattenhauer. "I'm familiar with that dilemma. When I was in my cardiology fellowship I had three patients worked up and scheduled for aortic valve replacement in one week. Two of them died before they got to the operating table."

I swallowed hard, then mentioned the choices of kinds of valves.

"Go for the St. Jude valve," said Dr. Hattenhauer. "It's been perfected and tested and will last a hundred years."

"Yes, "I said, "but the anticoagulant . . . ?"

"That's a minor problem," he said. "You wouldn't want to have to go through the surgery again because the pig valve didn't last."

This was the same advice I had had from two internists and another cardiologist. But I could not agree with their view that the lifelong nuisance and discipline required - frequent blood tests and daily anti-clot medicine, with risks of either bleeding or stroke - were trivial matters.

Fortunately, my appointment with the surgeon was that same afternoon. Thinking of Dr. Hattenhauer's three patients, I walked eagerly but gingerly down the block to Dr. Krause's office.

He was as brisk in his conversation as in his surgery, and as careful and thorough. On his desk were samples of different valves: a St. Jude valve with its fracture-proof, carbon-fiber, eccentrically-pivoted disc, serviceable life indefinite; a pig's aortic valve with a ring attached for sewing, estimated durability seven to ten years; a modified version of the pig valve with a metal stent added, which it was hoped would add a bit to its life expectancy; and a newer type of valve fabricated from calf's pericardium, durability maybe about comparable to the modified pig valve.

The choice was going to be even more complicated than I had thought. I sat silently looking over this array.

"Another possibility is a human allograft - a preserved valve from an organ donor," Dr. Krause said. "We haven't done

211

many of them in this country, but they've been used quite a lot in Australia."

I hadn't known this option existed. "And how long will that last?"

"It's not certain, but we think some may be good for up to twenty years."

"Would it require long-term anticoagulant?"

"No."

I looked from one of the specimens to another. There wasn't a human valve to look at.

"Before the surgery you'll have to make a first, second, third, and fourth choice," he said, "in case for some reason one or more turn out not to be technically feasible while we're in there." He seemed to be pressing me for a decision now. I thought some more.

"Suppose you were in need of a new valve. Which would you choose?" I asked.

He paused for a moment. "I'm fifty-two." Another pause. "I'd probably take the human allograft."

"That sounds good enough to me," I replied. "I'd like the allograft."

I requested the earliest available surgery date. He explained that the human valve procedure was still under an FDA-controlled research program, which would mean some additional tests beyond the usual; and that there was no guarantee that a donor valve in my size would be available. A date was set for ten days hence. I went off to make two blood donations during that time, so my own risk-free blood could be used if needed during the operation, and to get a precise measurement of my aortic annulus by an MRI so a computer search could be sent out to various tissue banks for an appropriate-sized valve.

My wife and I were shown two videos to orient us as to what to expect before and after the surgery - but they did not show any surgical details, nor did they show Dr. Krause at work.

I got my first choice of valves. I received - without being consulted - two units of bank blood in addition to the two that I had donated, which gave my wife and me some uneasiness for a few months until HIV tests continued to be negative. I had not been informed that two little barbed electrodes would be stuck into my heart muscle with wires connected to a pacemaker, just in case, nor that they were to be summarily jerked out by the intern on the day I went home. But this too went without a hitch.

Looking back now, with my new valve already 12 years old and functioning flawlessly, taking no medication and without any cardiovascular limitations on my activities, I feel only gratitude for the technology, the craftsmanship, the resources, and the unfortunate donor and his family who made this extension of my life possible. I know that as a physician talking to other physicians, I had the best information possible under the circumstances. But it wasn't the same as with the hernia repair. I realized that for most of our patients - even for a physician - "informed consent" as I once experienced it is not really possible.

Some years ago the Journal of the American Medical Association published a study of about 1000 taped interviews on routine visits between physicians - family doctors, internists, and surgeons - and their patients. The report concluded that in 9 out of 10 cases "the doctor did not discuss the issue enough to allow the patient to make an informed choice." The article went on, "The findings suggest that the ethical model of informed consent is not routinely applied in office practice."

What information does a patient need? What, indeed, are the implications of designating a person as a "patient"?

When one desires help with a health-related problem, the first move is to decide what health-care discipline makes sense. Counseling? Chiropractic? Homeopathy? Naturopathy? "Alternative" medicine? Surgery?

This decision requires some information, which the patient may or may not already possess to his satisfaction. And one can never say glibly that his choice is correct and therefore all the others are wrong.

213

What are the differences and the similarities between a patient and a doctor that make a useful encounter possible? Information, knowledge and skill are of course the primary differences, the resources the patient seeks.

He must then choose (or accept) a specific individual doctor, and by entering the encounter he is acknowledging - or at least hoping - that the doctor has skills and knowledge that he himself lacks.

He is now ready to seek more information about the nature of his problem. But the amount and kind of information he can accept is different for every patient. How is his command of the English language? How much does he understand about the body, about anatomy and physiology and pathology? How much does he <u>want</u> to know about dangers of his condition, side effects of treatment, the odds of complications, the real prognosis?

As a physician I must evaluate the patient with respect to all of these factors, and then try to convey as much information as he needs, in a form and language that he can understand. One patient says, "But why not . . . ? What if . . . ? How do you know . . . ?" Another says, "Never mind all that. Just give me the prescription. I'm in a hurry."

What the patient really needs is <u>advice</u>, and just enough information to *validate a decision about it to his satisfaction.* The true measure of the encounter is not so much the outcome, but the <u>satisfaction</u> that results on both sides.

Everyone's point of satisfaction with information lies at a different level, so no simple formula is possible. The evening before my heart surgery, Dr. Krause came into my room. Though my mind was awash with small technical details, questions that I knew could not be answered, I was as satisfied as would be possible.

My wife did not know the anatomy of the heart and aorta nor any of the technical trivia, so none of these questions occurred to her; her satisfaction point lay in a different place. The surgeon asked, "Mrs. Merrill, do you have any further questions about tomorrow morning?"

"No, thank you," she said. "Just get a good night's sleep."

Ambroise Paré

The town of Turin, in northwestern Italy, lies on the left bank of the Po River amid flat, fertile fields and farms, ringed farther out by gentle hills. It has had a troubled existence off and on since Hannibal destroyed most of it in the year 218. It has seen many onslaughts by dukes and kings and generals of various nationalities and political adventurisms.

When the French came over the hills from the west, yet again, and laid siege to Turin in 1536, one among them was a young man named Ambroise Paré. In his teens he had left his home town and gone to Paris to be apprenticed to a barber-surgeon. He received further training, such as it was, by physicians of the day, and became employed as surgeon in the Royal Army. At Turin, Paré was new on the job.

I was not present at the siege of Turin, nor was anyone who knew anyone who knew anyone now alive. But from scattered and flimsy records, from historical accounts, from movies, from talking with veterans of recent wars, and extrapolating massively from injuries I have seen in the hospital emergency room, I imagine the scene at Turin.

Hundreds of foot soldiers armed with pikes and lances, swords hanging at their waists, round a bend of the river. Mounted troops follow, banners flying. Lookouts sound the alarm. The home boys retire behind the moat and climb to their places on the wall; the archers man the narrow slots in the ramparts. Then cannons belch smoke, fire, shrapnel and noise. Small individual flashes and explosions announce the newly invented harquebuss, the first shoulder-fired weapon. On top of the fortress and on the fields below, cries of the wounded mingle with the heavier sounds. Bodies fall, blood pours onto the grass and soaks the soil. All is pandemonium, the inevitable chaos of war, of disordered plans and disordered ranks and disordered flesh, of dust and noise, of disembodied limbs, of men's life dreams switched off in a flash or trickling slowly

215

away. Lifeless bodies lying everywhere. Soldiers, pressed into the service of the Crown, doing their job.

And somewhere not far off is the surgeon. He is organizing litter-bearers, bringing up his cart of supplies, unbundling his tools and bandages.

It is the teaching of the day that gunpowder carries a poison which must be neutralized by pouring boiling oil into the wound. Somewhere a fire must be built to heat the oil, while the wounded - those considered salvageable - are being gathered up.

Paré became a well-known and popular surgeon, and over some 50 years he served four kings of France. On one busy day early in his career he encountered so many battlefield casualties that he ran out of boiling oil. He did the best he could, devising a salve for the wounds using egg yolk, oil of roses, and turpentine. He finally went to bed, exhausted, grieving and guilt-ridden.

Next morning, checking on his patients and changing dressings, he was astonished to find that the pain and fever were much less in those who had been deprived of the sizzling oil.

Paré took this observation to heart, and discontinued the use of the oil. He developed a method of controlling bleeding vessels by ligature instead of by cautery; and twelve years after his debut at Turin, he wrote a book on "The Method of Treating Wounds From the Harquebuss and Other Guns."

Ambroise Paré is perhaps most famous for bringing an end to the boiling oil as a surgical aid, but what I remember him for is a brief comment he made. When praised for his surgical skill on the battlefield, he replied, "I only dress the wounds. God heals them."

I couldn't have said it better myself. Nothing a doctor does can "heal" a wound or "cure" an illness. It is all very well, as a jest or as a shortcut of thought, to call myself "a healer." But my prescription for penicillin doesn't <u>cure</u> the streptococcal infection in the throat; it merely impairs the growth of the streptococci, thus giving the body's immune system improved odds of overcoming the infection. Appendicitis is often fatal if untreated; but when I remove an appendix, I leave traumatic wreckage behind: cut skin, severed muscles, inflamed peritoneum, blood in the tissues, angry nerve fibers - which the body must clear away and put back together. That part of it, the actual healing, is way beyond my power. To hold onto the understanding of this, the humility of it, I just remind myself of Ambroise Paré.

Two Images

My first look through a microscope introduced me to another world, an imaginary, fantasy world. Seventy years later I still live in that world and see almost everything in terms of that world. Everything has its basic dimension in the microscopic realm of molecules, cells, fibers, crystals. Even vast outer space is best characterized by the absence - almost, but not quite - of molecules, atoms, micromatter.

My medical education, all sixty years of it, has been replete with mental pictures that remain, explicitly or subconsciously, in my mind; but there are two images, both of them in the form of microscope slides, that remain crystal clear, hovering behind everyday decisions and actions and beliefs.

CREATION: THE FIVE-MILLIMETER PIG.

Yes, an ordinary pig, at one point in its life, is 5 mm. long, just under a quarter of an inch, about the length of a small ant.

Picture such a pig, removed from its mother's interior, pickled in formalin solution, and then, in a series of meticulous steps, embedded in paraffin and shaved into 300 cross-sectional slices, which are laid out sequentially and cemented in place on a series of glass slides and stained to bring out cellular detail. At this stage the pig is a near-perfect model of the developing human.

I came upon this box of slides in an elective embryology class, but I wistfully imagine a view of this pig as being required of every human who would wish to be literate.

By looking at the sections one after another, one could mentally reassemble the tiny creature, caught in the very act of being created: the partially formed brain with prominent eyes; the spinal cord, with primordial nerve cells reaching outward toward the future muscle cells in the beginnings of limbs; the heart, already with its four chambers nearly formed; the digestive tract beginning its rotation by which it is able to change from a nearly straight tube into its eventual tortuous form some 4 to 5 times the length of the entire animal. This and much more, contained in 300 consecutive pictures. Here, I was stunned to realize, was an almost perfect effigy of my very self and my mysterious entry into sentient and functional humanness.

As I viewed this scene, the most pressing question was: How do those cells organize themselves? How do the future nerve cells "know" to grow outward toward cells which have yet to differentiate themselves into either muscle or bone? How do the cells of the heart figure out how to form into the elaborate four-chambered structure, and connect in tubular form with all the other tubular forms? How can this happen?

That it happens doesn't prove that it's magic, but only that I and other, smarter people don't understand how. But it happens, and because of it, here I am.

RE-CREATION: INFLAMMATION

It wasn't my dog's fault that she bit my hand. She reached for the smaller dog at the same time that I did. Nevertheless, I had a one-inch gash on my palm, gaping open about a quarter of an inch. Because of the high risk of infection, one doesn't suture a dog bite. I washed it under the tap and trimmed off a protruding tag of fat, and my wife bandaged me up. I got a booster shot against tetanus, took antibiotics for a couple of days, and for the next week constantly changed dressings and explained the bandage to each patient.

Now, seventeen days later, the wound has magically healed and I can hardly stop inspecting and admiring it.

Fifty years ago last month I walked into that second-year pathology class in medical school and sat down at the microscope. Time and events are compressed and distorted in my mind by the passing decades, but that microscope slide shines there in my inner vision as if it were yesterday. "Inflammation: Healing Laceration," the label said.

We had already spent a year learning gross anatomy and the microscopic structure of normal tissues, along with

219

physiology. On the hair-thin and stained tissue slides in histology class I could recognize muscle cells, collagen fibers, epithelium and glands of various kinds, the specific layers in the walls of blood vessels, the capillaries and the various kinds of blood cells they contained. These were all static images, the fascinating steady-state nature of the tissues of which I am made. Each new discovery was a pleasure, adding to the repertoire of concepts that are the infrastructure of all medical practice.

But now we had moved to the next step, pathology, and this picture of inflammation opened a whole new dimension. Though it too was a static picture, it depicted a frozen moment in a dynamic process playing out before my eyes. The traumatic cleft in the skin was visible at one edge of the slide, the margins raised by all that lay below. Deeper in the tissues was a jumble of new capillaries - many more than in the tissues a half-centimeter to either side. The fibroblasts, usually showing only their thin, shriveled, hibernating nuclei against the collagen strands, now were plump and eager and full of cytoplasm, manufacturing collagen threads that would knit the severed tissues back together. Troops of granulocytes swarmed through the area, consuming the invading bacteria and bits of dead tissue. The normal organized structure was blurred and distorted by the numerous cells, like a crowded marketplace where the brisk commerce going on is hard to make sense of when seen from a block away.

From this slide one could understand the Latin description, by ancient physicians, of the four basic signs of inflammation: "rubor" or redness (the color of blood in all those dilated new capillaries); "calor" or warmth (the heat of that copious blood); "tumor" or swelling (the increased mass of cells and leaked-out fluid in the tissues); and "dolor" or pain (the mechanical and chemical stimuli tweaking nerve fibers in the area).

All those different cells - how do they "know" what to do, to work together in such apparent teamwork to kill bacteria, build new vessels, haul away debris, weave in new collagen and even bone if needed, pull the surviving parts together, adjust the structure to the tensions and mechanical demands of this particular location in the body, clean up the area, refinish the surface, remodel the scar, then go back into their normal quiescence?

In the 5 mm. pig we saw creation; here we see re-creation, restoration - a remarkably parallel and similarly mysterious kind of cellular choreography. Again, how does it happen?

The simplest answer would be the oldest one: Divine intervention and direction, the Creator creating, by means that seem more and more complicated as our observational methods become more advanced. Now, a half-century after my Pig and Inflammation encounters, scientists are developing even more penetrating methods, trying to explain the "intelligence" of the developing cells in mechanical and chemical terms. But in the meantime, I just find intense pleasure in being mystified.

I have a big advantage over Ambroise Paré. He figured out that after he finished dressing a wound, he could only stand back and wait for God to heal it. And now I have had a peek at how God does it! He just calls out the troops: the hordes of leukocytes - martyrs all, for after they have cleaned away the garbage they themselves become garbage; the eager cells of the capillaries cranking out many times their original numbers; the exuberant fibroblasts, emerging from sleep to braid the tissues back together; and the epithelial cells of the skin, healing, healing, always laying down their tiles of healing even if the area to be healed is too big for them ever to cover it over.

The picture of that microscope slide of inflammation still flashes into my mind whenever I'm confronted by an abscess, an injury, an infection, a laceration to be sutured. I can hardly wait to dress another wound! And when involved in the processes of pregnancy and delivering a baby, I always flash back to that other enchanting picture, the itsy bitsy pig.

Teleology and God

The question on the Comparative Anatomy quiz was, "Compare the esophagus of a dog with that of a human, and explain the differences."

My answer was, "The dog's esophagus contains more muscle, and the tougher epidermal lining extends the full length of the esophagus in a dog. From a teleological point of view, this is to allow the dog to swallow rough objects such as pieces of bone that might injure a human."

Dr. Stough's remark on the test paper: "I didn't know you knew the word 'teleological.'"

Oh, yes, I know it. I can't recall when I learned the word, but I have grappled with its meaning, with the question, for as long as I can remember: Do things happen because they're *designed and planned* to happen that way, or because that's *just the way things work out*?

I've been almost obsessed with those words: God, and teleology.

The question "Why?" usually implies teleologic assumptions: "Toward what end?" or "For what purpose?" or "According to what design?" But to me, "Why?" means "From what cause?" This may seem like a trivial distinction, but not so! One's whole world view hinges on this apparently subtle difference.

Pierre Teilhard de Chardin, a scientist-philosopher turned Catholic priest, was a prince of teleology, arguing that man is a creature risen from lower stages and is evolving mentally and socially toward a final spiritual god-like unity: the Omega Point.

Even most evolutionists - sometimes without realizing it - swallow the idea of some future goal or purpose. The terms "ecological niche," and the "selection pressure" of natural selection toward an apparently useful trait are subtle examples of this.

In his book, *The Emergence of Everything*, Harold Morowitz states nicely the opposite view: that from the Big

Bang to the formation of stars and solar systems to the origins of life and on to the human mind - in 28 somewhat arbitrary steps - each change in the universe arises naturally from the properties of the previous stage. We are the product of a continually self-creating world, not just random rolls of the dice.

The late great Stephen Jay Gould, a modern paleontologist and thinker, teacher and student of evolution, tried hard to counter the teleologic view of the world. In Gould's view things happen because other things have happened because other things have happened, not because it was all planned out in advance. He points out that if one could rewind the entire tape of evolution to the Eocene era and then play it again, it wouldn't come out the same and the chance that we would be in it is very small. The System has created itself by its own stern internal rules, patterns and structures of interacting particles, and the rules allow for infinite variation but permit no cheating. It all works without any intervention. Man is the only glorious and terrible exception, the animal who knows how to think and to worry, to have intentions, to make designs. Hence man easily concludes that everything happens according to a predetermined plan or purpose, and tries to explain who designed it, and - most dangerous of all - tries always to improve upon it.

If you accept - if you are stuck with - the teleological view of the world, then you need God with a capital "G" to account for all the mystery of the world, some sort of plan or intent that the human brain can never entirely encompass.

The easy, the conventional ways to understand God and all the happenings or conditions that are attributed to Him involve some sort of magic, something beyond "natural" laws and events: that is, a God that cheats, having his whimsical way with nature.

I once read a book called *Your God Is Too Small.* The writer observed that some people see God as a Supreme Santa Claus who provides us with incredible gifts. Some see him as an Angry Tyrant threatening us with whips and fire. Others see him as a Grand Choreographer or Puppeteer, in charge of all that happens; and some as a Compassionate Caregiver concerned with the fate of every sparrow, even me.

After the author had explained how each of these views is inadequate, I came away convinced that even he didn't get it, that his grandly Composite or Superlative God was still too small.

I have a problem with all of the formal religions. A formal religion indeed provides a context for a dogma that can be widely shared, and to share a set of specified beliefs or ideas is a comforting means for mutual reinforcement and validation among believers, whatever their beliefs, and provides a common context for approaching their god, whether in supplication or gratitude or fear. (It's a powerful feeling to be in the presence of a bunch of serious Catholics as they worship.) But language itself is a problem; it not only can provide a common statement of what God is and what he does, but in doing so it also limits the ways of understanding. Thus a formal religion in a sense trivializes God. Even giving him, or it, a name is limiting. In ancient Hebrew times, Jaweh was considered so sacred and awesome that ordinary people were forbidden to speak his name.

I'm uncomfortable even with the <u>word</u> God - with the smallness of it; with what it means to capitalize it, as I would Jones or Seattle; and especially with the implications of putting a pronoun with the word: he/she/it.

A good Catholic friend of mine (my wife) complains that I worship the creation instead of the Creator. *Nolo contendere* - I do not deny this charge. After all, the creation is what I can see and feel, is what I am made of, is all that I can love and fear. The creation deserves my worship and adoration because it is all I can conceive of, and much more.

Aldo Leopold, noted naturalist, said something like, "The ecosystem is more complex than we think. In fact, it's more complex than we <u>can</u> think."

Some say that belief in God, a religious belief, is the necessary and only basis for morality. Maybe for some this is true; I can only speak for myself. But morality based on fear - fear of getting caught, or fear of Hell and Final Judgment -

seems to me a poor excuse for morality, and an unnecessary stretch when a perfectly good pragmatic basis for morality is right there before my eyes: the "Golden Rule." I might sometimes want to ask myself, "What would Jesus do?" or "What would my Dad do?" or "What would my respected peers do?" But mostly I need only ask, "How would I want it done to me?" If you are willing to go outside of yourself, to see yourself as others see you, to try to understand the point of view of another person and to treat him as you would want to be treated, this is as close as you can get to a "god-induced" morality. It doesn't always work perfectly, but in the long run it's the best road map I can find.

Some say belief in a "divine" deity is what gives purpose to life; otherwise it would all be pointless, life would be meaningless without that. I suppose this means that what gives life value is the attempt to earn an eternal life after this one. (Questions about an afterlife are meat for a whole other discussion.) But I can't relate, viscerally, to the meaning of "divine"; it just won't fit into the way I see things.

I reject the word and the very idea of "supernatural." If something happens, it has to be "natural." If it seems unnatural, or supernatural, it's only because there's something about it that I don't understand.

Existentialists think along this line. There are two kinds of existentialists: the sad-faced, tragic kind (like Jean-Paul Sartre) and the non-tragic, happy kind (like me). The first kind say that yes, life would be meaningless without God; and since God is an illusion created by us in our own image, life indeed has no meaning and the whole thing is a pointless and hideous sham.

We others somehow find life, the adventure and the challenge, full of meaning in and of itself - a meaning which, of course, we create from our past and assign to it ourselves. The tragic ones, speaking of life, say, "Oh, woe!" We others, speaking of life, say "Oh, wow!" Or as astronaut Alan Shepard exclaimed on climbing out of the space capsule after the first manned space shot, "Man, what a ride!"

I couldn't do this medical job without some concept of God - of what happens, that is, after I dress the wound - because

I wouldn't know where to stop. I might make a fool of myself, like those who create "healing salves," trying to <u>force</u> a miraculous healing instead of just helping clear the path and then stepping back and letting the healing happen. When my sister-in-law was dying of a recurrent pneumonia, her doctor said, "We can only slow the bugs down some with our medicines. She has to do the rest."

To deny the traditional caricatures of "God" is certainly not to deny that there is something bigger and more than me. It is merely to deny that I have the possibility of access, control or knowledge of whatever the Great Is is.

They say that a young man thinks of sex every 90 seconds, and that in later life this is stretched to a minute and a half. Probably so; and for me, thoughts of god are at least as frequent. I find god under the microscope, in the laboratory, in the field and stream and sky, on my plate, and in my own pulse and bellyache. What else is there but godness everywhere?

And so the word God, or some evasive equivalent of it, is a necessary shorthand - may I say nickname? - for the mysteries of the Infinite Complexity, for those things that are beyond my conceptual reach and that will always run on tantalizingly just beyond the edge of our latest insights. I recently heard an elderly philosopher (who happened to be a priest) extolling ". . . this day fresh-minted from the hand of God, a day which has never been before and will never be again." How nicely said!

Four and a half centuries have given time for a lot of discoveries and a lot of inventions, developments that would overwhelm Ambroise Paré's understanding were he to return today. Few of these new things or new ideas pertain directly to God; yet in combination they have given me an extensive matrix for believing and understanding what Paré was talking about when he said, "I only dress the wounds."

I offer up - to the Great Whatever - a prayer of thanks for life, thanks for this ride, like rafting down an unknown river, some white water behind and pretty calm right here, with the breeze in the pines covering up the distant roar of the falls that I know lie somewhere ahead.

That which is, is as god as it gets. Thanks again for all of it.

Amen.

The Pulse

It is said that a skillful Chinese physician can make many diagnoses exclusively by feeling the pulse. I do not know how far this can be carried, and even to judge the truth of this claim would bring two different ways of thinking, of believing and of knowing, into collision. There are in fact several conditions that I, too, can diagnose or suspect by feeling the pulse, sometimes by comparing the pulse in different locations. But there is more to it than this.

Thousands of times throughout my life I have placed my fingers at the wrist or at the groin or at the throat or beneath the breast or on the foot to examine the pulse. When I am first talking to a patient my greeting, like offering part of myself, is to lay my hand on his wrist and feel the radial pulse. It enables me to look deeper inside, a transparent window to the action inside the flesh. At the same time, touching gently at the wrist is an invitation to speak, to share the truth with me.

The electronic monitor, the oscilloscope on the wall can tell me some things I need to know. But touching the pulse tells me different things, plugs my spirit into the other in a way that no machines or electrodes or devices can match.

The rhythm, the musical cadence of the heartbeat is a thing miraculous and always fresh, always vital. It sings the melody of life itself, and one inwardly trembles lest it fall silent. The cellular elixirs and gears, the electron-shifts of ions flowing through membranes, the graceful oar-strokes of the heart muscle rowing endlessly in place, the smoothly rising and falling pressures and movement of fluid moderated by friction and viscosity translate in my fingertips to a sense of life-energy, an automatic gauge of health and vitality, and a communion achievable no other way.

Sexuality and Doctoring

Am I a sexual being? You bet. My penis with its accessories has been with me all my life, in my mind and heart and body.

Through the middle years of life - from roughly, say, 13 to 73 - sexual awareness and sensations and physiologic functions are never far below the surface of one's outward life. Through those years the genitals play a strong though mostly covert role in social interactions, identity-building, power trips, pride, and maintenance of fundamental self-image.

Now, in life's twilight, the thing hunkers down there like an old work shirt hung behind the door. It lives, with the rest of me, in memory and fantasy and in any minor achievements of which I am still capable.

On arriving at medical school, I was still a virgin - certainly not from lack of interest, but rather from a blend of naivete, timidity, and scruples. I wondered how dealing in a clinical setting with other people's genitalia would feel - for both parties - and how a doctor separates himself from the emotional complications of that.

I don't recall a single word of instruction or advice or guidance on the subject in medical school. It was done, I saw in retrospect, entirely by role models, by seeing how other people acted.

On our first day in the anatomy lab, after the breath-taking chore of whisking away the stiff malodorous brown canvas to expose our first "patient," we all stood around as if dismounting from a spinning rope swing, waiting for the vertigo to pass. The second thing that I noticed, after the dark, depleted, obviously dead appearance, was that it was a "she."

We were told to study the exterior of our cadaver. A couple of the fellows in my foursome (they happened all to be men) raised the question: when and how do we approach the various body orifices? (There are several, you know.)

"Well, I guess we'll have to do this sooner or later," said one, and gingerly inserted a finger into the mouth, then the vagina, then the rectum. Like a leather pouch. We all (because someone, at the moment, was taking the lead) checked it out to make sure it was OK.

Gynecology Clinic, two years later, was the first place where I actually put my fingers into a live vagina. The young woman was "up in stirrups" and fully covered with a sheet from the chin down past the knees, with only the vaguely familiar external anatomy exposed. The gynecology resident stood just behind me, describing a lemon-sized lump that I was supposed to be able to feel in the vicinity of the right ovary, while a nurse stood at the patient's head and offered comfort and reassurance (to the patient, not to me).

When the examination was finished, I casually realized, with relief and a bit of surprise, that I hadn't been sexually aroused by this experience. The purpose and context of the encounter was definitely not sexual. The rubber gloves, the large expanse of white sheet, the avoidance of eye contact, the presence of other people, and trying to find that lump all helped to establish the context and the atmosphere of the event. From there on, it was never a problem.

The answer was clear and simple: <u>context</u> <u>is</u> <u>everything</u>. And the context is always under complete control of the doctor.

It is widely agreed that any sexual interaction or relationship between a doctor and patient is inappropriate, unprofessional, and a cause for disciplinary action. It is an abuse of the psychological power of the physician over his patient -- a highly asymmetrical relationship -- and causes a serious distortion of the clinical process with potentially grave consequences.

The Oregon Board of Medical Examiners reports several cases each year in which it has received complaints against a doctor, has investigated, and has rendered judgment on sexual transgression. The gravity with which it is treated shows the sanctity of the doctor-patient relationship in the eyes of these keepers of the rules of conduct.

230

After living in the town of John Day for several years, I received a call one evening from one of my patients, in her forties, who had a pain in the lower abdomen. She was troubled more by worry than by pain. I told her - as was my custom with most evening calls - to meet me at my office in 20 minutes.

She lay on the examining table and I spread a sheet over her from the waist down. We pulled clothing upward and downward so I could examine her abdomen. It didn't seem like appendicitis, probably something with the ovary, but I explained to her that we needed to be sure.

"For safety's sake," I said, "I really need to do a pelvic exam."

"Well," she said, "whatever's necessary."

I stepped out of the room for a couple of minutes while she removed her underpants and climbed back onto the table with the sheet over her. I adjusted the stirrups, asked her to scoot down on the table a bit, and moved the end section of the table out of the way. I put on the latex gloves and, lifting the sheet barely enough to locate my target, I proceeded with a vaginal exam, at the same time probing her abdomen with my left hand through the sheet to try to bring the ovary within reach.

Suddenly she said, "You must really trust me."

I generally don't make eye contact during a pelvic examination except when I'm speaking to the patient. I swung my gaze to meet hers and said, "And you must really trust me." Thus ended that discussion, and I finished the exam.

I concluded that she had probably a bit of bleeding from the ovary resulting from ovulation, and told her that if it got worse, or was not better in two days, she should call me.

In today's medical climate I would not recommend this kind of unaccompanied doctor-patient interaction. But an established doctor-patient relationship based on mutual trust, respect, and openness is still a priceless asset for both doctor and patient.

Just keep a firm grip on the context, and you'll be fine.

Risk Management

Ben Dodds dozed off coming down Long Creek Mountain. His pickup bounced through a ditch and stopped in some brush. The constable from Long Creek came by a half hour later.

When they arrived in the hospital parking lot I found Ben curled on his side on the back seat of the station wagon, holding his head tightly with one hand over each ear.

"He's been doing that ever since I found him," said the constable.

"My neck hurts," said Ben.

We moved him very carefully onto a stretcher. He had normal sensation and movement in arms and legs, but the x-rays showed his 6th cervical vertebra broken and slid forward nearly a fourth of its width. Another quarter of an inch and he would have been paralyzed for life.

I phoned a neurosurgeon for detailed instructions, and had my first experience at applying Crutchfield tongs. This device - like old-fashioned ice tongs, two sharp points that grip the skull just above the ears - along with cord, pulley, and a few pounds of weight helps to keep the neck bones in alignment while the fracture heals. From another hospital we borrowed a Stryker frame. A sort of sandwich stretcher with pivots at the ends, it permits turning the patient like a chicken on a spit, removing the top piece for bathing, toileting, and moving arms and legs with the neck traction always precisely in place.

After just over three weeks in this contraption Ben was ready for a cast - an upper body jacket that extended up under his chin and the back of his head. It took him about two days to get used to being vertical without nearly fainting, and in another couple of days he left the hospital.

The second day after he went home was opening day of deer season. Almost everybody in Grant County observes opening day, and Ben was a dedicated hunter. The plaster cast around his shoulders wouldn't let him hold the gun in a normal way; but at daylight he was out there creeping through the woods with his rifle in his right hand and a forked stick in his left. He spotted a three-point buck, stood the stick up in the path, laid the gun in the crotch, turned enough to bring his eye around in line with the sights - and shot the deer. I heard the story two days later when he came in for a followup visit.

In Vermont, coming down from Maple Hill and heading for home at dusk, I was admiring the silhouette of an old farmhouse on a knoll against a deeply violet sky, and almost missed seeing a car on its side in some weeds near the road. It hadn't been there a couple of hours before.

Walking down to investigate, I heard a faint voice. In the swampy grass a few yards from the upset car lay a body, partly on its side and belly-down. I squatted down and asked, "Are you all right?"

The body didn't move but the voice said, "Is that you, Ted?"

"Jeff!" I said, leaning down to see his face, which rested in shallow mud. "What happened?" He was one of my students at the college.

"I can't feel my hands or feet."

"All right," I said, "whatever you do, don't try to move your head." I gently felt his scalp, and tried sketchily to survey the rest of him but found no sign of other injuries. He couldn't feel me touch him anywhere below his shoulders.

About then a heavyset boy walked up to the edge of the road above us. "I thought I heard something down here," he said.

"Yeah, there's a man hurt here. You live up there in that house? Will you go and call Central Vermont Hospital and ask them to send an ambulance out here as fast as possible? You can explain to them exactly where it is." He took off in a waddling trot.

While we waited I cradled Jeff's head between my hands, with a bit of traction in line with his spine, mainly to remind him not to try to move. When the ambulance finally arrived we very carefully "log-rolled" him onto the stretcher while I held his head. Once we had securely strapped him in place and stabilized his head with sandbags and adhesive tape, we headed for the hospital.

A few minutes later Jeff said, "I think I can feel my fingers a little bit." Sure enough, the fingers of his left hand moved slightly. During the rest of the forty-minute ride he had gradual increase in movement and sensation, and when we arrived at the hospital he could move and feel all four extremities. I had never seen such miraculous improvement after a spine injury. We sent him off to University of Vermont Hospital, and he eventually made a full recovery.

A lady from Dufur lived only two miles from her workplace. One morning, in a hurry, she didn't bother to fasten her seat belt. On a curve the car struck a patch of ice and failed to turn when the road did. It did not tip over, but struck a large rock, bounced into the air, and came to rest on the rock. When the ambulance arrived a short time later she was conscious, sitting in the driver's seat but unable to move or feel her arms or feet. The fracture was below the third vertebra where the nerve to the diaphragm emerges, so she hadn't died immediately from suffocation. But she was a permanent quadriplegic.

These three cases are excellent arguments for the use of seat belts. They also emphasize the frailty and vulnerability of the vertebrae in the neck. In the lower spine the five lumbar vertebrae are solid, hefty blocks of bone surrounded by the big muscles of back and belly. The twelve thoracic vertebrae are largely splinted by both muscles and ribs. But the seven cervical vertebrae are small and delicate within a skimpy bundle of muscles, holding up the head like a heavy blossom on a slender stem. Even just being tossed up against the top of your car can crunch these little bones. And the scary part is that the bony arches on the backs of the vertebrae bravely enclose the spinal cord, a structure about the diameter of my finger with a consistency somewhere between a stalk of celery and cooked spaghetti, which extends down from the brain and holds in its microscopic neural tracery your entire future.

234

I left general practice in 1986 to work in the Emergency Department at Mid-Columbia Medical Center in The Dalles, Oregon. The hospital had hired a management company to supervise and maintain "quality control" in the Department. The company sent someone around every month or so to review our charts and to give us pep talks and lectures on "risk management."

When I first heard that term I thought it referred to some kind of risk to patients. In a twisted way it did, but what they were really addressing was risk to the hospital: the risk of lawsuit over malpractice. "Risk management" was a mantra thrown about so relentlessly that it began to feel almost like a personal insult.

The theme, of course, was reasonable enough: constant care and vigilance against any mistakes, but especially care not to overlook some potentially disastrous condition. The "big three" risk cases- the problems that experience had shown were the most treacherous even for skilled and well-meaning doctors - were: 1) meningitis in a baby, which could go from apparently mild flu-like symptoms to fatal outcome in a matter of hours; 2) ruptured ectopic pregnancy - "If a woman bleeds to death internally while she sits out there in the waiting room, remember you're the one in charge here!" we were told; and 3) fracture of a cervical vertebra, which, if not detected and protected, can shift and destroy the spinal cord when you try to rise to a sitting position or bend to pull up your pants.

They tried to scare us, and it worked. (I fondly glimpsed a shimmering vision of Robert Rife in the distance.) The hospital even sent me with one of our ER nurses, all expenses paid, to Orlando, Florida to a two-day conference on risk management. We had heard it all before, but at least we got a half day in Disney World before our return flight.

Having been in private general practice in a small town, I was accustomed to reading all the x-rays that I ordered, and in the Emergency Department this didn't change, even though the hospital staff had three good radiologists. Two of them welcomed me in the x-ray department and shared pearls and tidbits of knowledge. Dr. Three, however, seemed a bit annoyed at my desire to see the films myself rather than just accept his report. Amid the flurry of action in the ER, I would order an x-ray of a wrist. Dr. Three would read it and send back a written note: "left wrist negative." Then between maneuvers I would trot back to the x-ray department to look at the pictures, and he would subtly act offended.

One evening the EMTs brought a patient from a motor vehicle accident, properly secured on a back board with head stabilized and cervical collar in place as was, by then, standard procedure. She complained of neck pain, and after finishing the rest of the examination I ordered neck x-rays. A note soon came back: "C-spine negative."

When I went in to view the films the radiologist said, "I just sent out the report; they're OK."

"Yes, thanks, I saw your note; but I always feel better when I look at them too."

"There's nothing to see; but whatever you want." He motioned to the technician to get out the films that had already been filed away.

I looked at them for quite a while before I said anything.

"The transverse processes of C-1 - they don't sit quite symmetrically on C-2."

Dr. Three hesitated, then got up from his desk and came over to the view box. After a moment of looking he said, "It's just positional. There's no fracture." He went back to his seat. I tried to convince myself that he was right.

"I'd feel better if we had a CT scan, just to make sure."

"It isn't necessary," he said.

I looked at each millimeter of the lateral view, looking for some clue, some reassurance.

"You're probably entirely right," I said, "but I just can't quite get comfortable with that view of C-1. If there was a fracture there that we're missing, it'd be my neck in the noose. I'd like to get a CT."

He shook his head and didn't look at me, but said, "Send her back over."

A half hour later, looking at the CT films, the radiologist and I shared a moment of silent astonishment. Not only did the ring of C-1 indeed have a fracture through it, but C-2 also had a vertical fracture completely through its body.

This would give the risk management guys nightmares for sure. We both studied the original films yet again, but could see no clues that we hadn't already seen.

I referred the lady to an orthopedist. I never mentioned the episode to anyone; but from then on Dr. Three was friendly as one could wish, and we got along fine.

When I entered practice in California in 1950, the premium for malpractice insurance was $150 per year. It gradually rose, and eight years later it was $275. I moved that year, and found the premium in Oregon was $150. Eleven years later, in 1969, it had risen to $350. I moved to Vermont and the premium was only $125, and rose a little bit during six years.

In 1975 I returned to Oregon and to a shocking $3,000 annual premium. Luckily Good Samaritan Hospital in Corvallis, in whose ER I was working, paid our malpractice premiums.

Three years later I returned to private general practice in John Day, my old stomping ground. I was trying to limit my hours of work per week. This reduced my income, but didn't reduce the insurance cost. I decided - from a combination, I suppose, of stinginess, resentment, and reckless confidence - to go without malpractice insurance. I was somewhat comforted in this by the fact that Dr. Clair Spalding, the surgeon in town, also was working without insurance.

This continued for eight years, when Blue Mountain Hospital's board of directors voted - under pressure from the hospital's insurance carrier - to require all members of the medical staff to carry individual malpractice insurance. At this point (I had considered moving anyway) Clair Spalding bought insurance, and I resigned from the staff. The next month I started in the ER in The Dalles, where again the hospital paid the cost of insurance - upward of $4,000.

What has changed? Do doctors know less? Are they more careless and prone to stupid mistakes than they used to be? Or is the rising level of insurance premiums just "normal" inflation, the same trend that has multiplied ten-fold the price of a loaf of bread or a gallon of gasoline?

You could propose many explanations:

Doctors have brought it on themselves. With their fancy technology and headlines of "breakthrough" discoveries they seem to be promising perfection, a cure for every problem. And they have tried to turn everybody into a patient by urging people who feel well to get checkups for this and that (diabetes, high blood pressure, cancer, high cholesterol) and by ever more confusing statistics - a glass of wine is good for your heart, but two glasses may kill liver and brain cells; hormone replacement therapy will prevent hot flashes and osteoporosis but may give you cancer, and we were wrong about its preventing heart attacks; there's good cholesterol and bad cholesterol and you need constant monitoring to know where you stand, and eating fish may help your cholesterol level but mercury in the fish may cause brain damage to your unborn baby. And now you can buy a genome analysis and find out your odds for the future, like buying a lottery ticket. We pay for all of this; a lottery ticket is a bargain by comparison.

Or maybe it's the fault of the insurance industry, which has thrust itself between the doctor and the patient and plays games with the money from both of them and gets rich, while forcing the doctor to feel defensive and to order expensive and needless tests to protect himself.

Or perhaps it's the pharmaceutical industry, urging you on TV to "Ask your doctor if a free trial of Immortalis is right for you!" (You can be sure that any prescription medicine advertised on TV will cost you a few dollars per pill.)

No, it must be the lawyers who caused it, with their "contingent" fee so that the higher the malpractice award, the more money they make. Again the TV commercial: "If you or a loved one has been diagnosed with Condition X, call the law offices of your friendly Attorney Y. We may be able to help you collect a bundle from somebody."

I fear, dear reader, that as a society we have all done it to ourselves. It's inflation, all right - inflation of expectations.

There's a built-in conflict of interest just in being alive. There are two of me: me as <u>myself</u>, and me as <u>one of us</u>. In today's world, "myself" has gained dominance over "us." The risk we need to manage now is the risk to our entire system, to the way people relate to each other individually and politically and economically.

It seems obvious that mutual trust and respect are the strongest safeguards against malpractice suits. If the doctor takes the time to listen to the patient, to try to understand his concerns, and to explain things in terms that the patient can understand, and if he shows proper diligence and attention in his management of the problem, and if the patient recognizes the doctor's good intentions and the inevitable bounds of his capabilities, the patient should have little motivation to attack the doctor in court.

Now prenatal care and delivery have joined the "big three" triggers of malpractice suits. If your child turns up with a learning disability or a behavior disorder, you may be able to blame it on the doctor who delivered him. Today the malpractice premium, for general practice including obstetrics, costs from $30,000 to $60,000 a year and rising. The doctors in Grant County say they can no longer afford the premiums, so this year they discussed maybe having to quit delivering babies.

We've come a long way!

The Mind

My favorite organ - the one I would choose over all others to keep functionally intact - is my brain. I consider the mind to be a function of the brain, a product of the actions or conditions of the billions of neurons, each one a tiny chemical generator of an electrical charge.

Yet I am furtively ambivalent about thinking of my mind as merely a quart of chemicals reflecting upon themselves, just a set of sequential and shifting molecular interactions. I try to demystify the principles of the body, all the life processes; but with the mind I can't quite make it work. Is there something more to it than simple chemistry?

The late, great, but under-appreciated Thomas Szasz, professor of psychiatry at the State University of New York (who called himself "a psychiatrist of sorts") argued fervently - as did the bold social critic Ivan Illich - that psychiatry is not a true medical discipline based on science, not equivalent to anatomy or physiology or pharmacology (despite the practice of applying chemicals to the brain). It is, instead, a cultural and political system of values and beliefs. They argue especially that involuntary psychiatric intervention - whether by incarceration or by surgical assault on the brain, by electric shock therapy or by drugs - is a state-supported form of tyranny analogous to the church/state tyranny common in the Middle Ages.

Looking back now at ancient yellowing transcripts, I am surprised to see that I had psychiatry classes scattered through three separate years of medical school, yet I have only one sharp and vivid memory from the course. The professor stands at the lectern, his dark glued-down hair half concealing his scalp. A squarish chin is rigid below thin tight lips. He adjusts his glasses, his eyes averted from ours to his page of notes.

"Cunnilingus," he intones with obvious discomfort, "is invariably a request for fellatio."

240

This isolated pearl, the one clear residue from that course, was a piece of information that I never found strikingly useful in my professional life.

Why do I remember so little of it? It's because the pieces of the puzzle didn't ever click into place in my mental model of the world, didn't fit comfortably with the other parts of medicine that I was learning. The behaviors of mental illness never seemed connected as clearly to the structure of the brain, for example, as did diabetes to the function of the pancreas and the chemistry of the blood.

Psychiatry, like surgery, is a discipline that doesn't lend itself well to learning just from books; it has to be experienced, to be put into practice, in order to be understood. That was a time when Sigmund Freud's authority was slipping only a little, before he had been placed in a jar on the museum shelf of academe. People then who had any doubts about Freud's beliefs or techniques tried to cast their dissent in Freudian terms, to propose amendments rather than repeal of the psychoanalyst's couch as the essential tool for "mental healing." Carl Jung, Freud's associate, had partially broken step with his mentor and was developing ideas about the role of symbol and myth in the human mind.

What I gradually learned of psychiatry came much later, from such sources as Carl Rogers, a clinical psychologist who promoted "client-centered" therapy; Abraham Maslow, another clinical psychologist, who tried to understand psychological disorders by studying "normal people" and "self-actualized" people; a Quaker psychiatrist who, in a little essay that I came across, gave me permission to open myself, to let my own sense and feelings enter into the dialogue with troubled patients; and from my bride, who worked at the New York State Psychiatric Institute and was assigned to a ward full of folks who had been subjected to surgical slicing of the frontal lobes of their minds - excuse me, their brains.

The lesson in psychology which I recall most clearly from medical school did not occur in Psychiatry Class, but rather in General Clinic. In our third year we were brought for the first time into contact with actual patients. General Clinic was a public facility for the use of patients from the neighborhood around Presbyterian Hospital and the school, and we were sent down to see patients there.

On my first day I was assigned to do a history and physical exam on a 32-year-old woman and then present my findings and my diagnosis to one of the teachers.

The patient's complaints were nervousness, fatigue, slight shakiness, sometimes a feeling that her heart was beating fast. The symptoms had increased over the past few months, and she said she had lost about five pounds.

The physical exam showed indeed a mildly rapid pulse, slight tremor of her outstretched hands, and I was pretty sure I could feel a little enlargement of her thyroid gland. The rest of the very detailed exam was normal.

Not a very difficult diagnosis, I thought, though the findings were rather subtle. I had almost finished my write-up when the attending physician arrived, and I confidently presented my conclusion: overactivity of the thyroid gland - hyperthyroidism in an early stage.

The mentor listened carefully, and glanced over my written notes. He had the patient hold out her hands for a moment, checked her pulse, looked at her tongue, and briefly but carefully felt her neck.

He then sat down and faced her, looked her in the eye. "Are you happy?" he asked.

She burst into tears, sobbing and covering her face with her hands.

So much for the "subtly overactive thyroid." This doctor had had clinically close encounters with more unhappy people than I had, and knew that every illness, disorder, or complaint has an emotional and a mental aspect to it. Often, as in this case, the mental and emotional side is the disorder. Her life pattern itself, not the thyroid gland, was the culprit.

My efforts at psychotherapy through my years of practice were simple, limited, intuitive, and probably sometimes mildly useful. I developed some standard spiels for common situations:

"The term 'psychosomatic' doesn't mean you're imagining it," I would say. "It means body and mind are one, and

242

constantly affect each other. Your high blood pressure, upset stomach, insomnia, [fill in the blank] is caused by anxiety and stress.

"Suppose someone steps out of dark shadows, puts a gun to your ribs and says, 'Give me your money!'

"In your mind you will be afraid, and your body automatically reacts to the fear. Your heart speeds up, blood pressure rises, muscles tighten, stomach contracts and produces more acid; you perspire and may even wet yourself.

"These are normal fear reactions; you'd be abnormal if you didn't do these things. After the gun is gone and the episode is past, your body functions return to normal.

"But if, instead of a gun, the threat is from your overdue rent, or fear of being fired, or wondering whether your marriage is crumbling, or questioning whether you're a good enough person, the phantom gun never goes away. The threat persists and so do your body's responses, which eventually causes harm."

Occasionally I certified a psychotic and disturbed person as both "mentally ill and a danger to self or others," and arranged for the sheriff to transport him to the State Psychiatric Hospital for evaluation and treatment.

A few years ago I worked for another doctor, seeing his patients in his office on his day off each week. He was a master of "psychopharmacy." He attended numerous medical conferences (usually dinner meetings sponsored by the company whose drug was to be discussed) and knew in fine detail the therapeutic profile of each mind-adjusting medicine, its recognized side effects and the subtle ways in which one drug might differ slightly from another as to effects on sleep, blood pressure, appetite, sex, anxiety, and so on. He had many patients taking so-called "psychotropic" drugs - antidepressants, anti-anxiety medicines, insomnia drugs, appetite suppressants, and especially children taking Ritalin, or even this plus another "upper," for a presumed diagnosis of Attention Deficit Hyperactivity Disorder.

Already something of a skeptic, during this time I became further disillusioned with the over-generous use of such drugs. Little was known of long-term effects; and in at least two ADHD families I was sure that the child was pretty much OK and the mother was furtively taking his medicine.

An impressive thing about the mind is its capacity to confuse itself, to selectively conceal important things from itself, to build a convincing case for whatever its host has decided to do.

My wife Betsy and I had gone twice, during our time together, to personal or marriage counselors (they were not psychiatrists), and it helped us to see what we were doing to each other. But only once did I ever have occasion personally to visit a psychiatrist, and it seemed important to me to choose the right one.

I had watched Dr. George Saszlow, professor of psychiatry at Oregon Health Sciences University, in action at a medical conference titled "Death, Dying, and Doctoring." He interviewed a couple, onstage, before a large audience of doctors.

The patient had pancreatic cancer and only a few more months to live. He and his wife discussed how the pair were facing and coping with the impending death and its attendant fears and pain. I was impressed at Dr. Saszlow's conduct of the interview - such kindness, such sensitivity and class, even a bit of humor, so that the couple felt comforted and empowered.

Unknown to my wife, I had been having a brief affair outside of our marriage, and was increasingly agonizing over a tangle of conflicting feelings - guilt, self-justifications, anxieties, trying to balance things out and continue to function. Dr. Saszlow seemed like a professional who could get to the depths of my pain, to help me unravel these tangled threads of emotion, to find perhaps some hidden problem deep within my past and to show me a way to proceed.

I called and made an appointment and drove the 250 miles, my foot heavy on the throttle and my spirit hopefully optimistic.

Somehow his schedule had been altered. As I arrived at the appointed time Dr. Saszlow was just leaving to catch a plane. I argued and pleaded with his receptionist, and finally she retrieved him from the back door.

We sat down. I briefly explained my situation, and he understood.

"So," he said, "you've come here for me to tell you that what you've been doing is all right?"

With one swift, clean stroke he had cut to the heart of the matter.

He still had time to catch his plane, and I drove the five hours home, not exactly with peace of mind but with a clearer view, a firm foundation on which to start rebuilding.

Now there's a psychiatrist for you!

Bus Stop

The Greyhound station in Seattle is long and narrow, with restrooms at one end and Burger King at the other. At one side, electronic grunts and groans issue from a small video game arcade.

A brief gust of luggage-laden passengers has blown in through the wide-open doors, bringing with them a bracing whiff of Puget Sound; they have trickled on through, evaporating individually or fusing with significant others and vanishing into waiting vehicles. A blue-uniformed clerk with an Afro drifts about languidly behind the counter, her mission now in suspension until the next bus approaches. The place is placid again, and the scent of French fries and stale coffee drifts back in like returning tide.

Sculptured wire benches lined back-to-back down the center of the room are tolerably comfortable if you sit carefully and firmly against the backrest. I am reading a story about a war in Spain.

Lowering my book for a moment to shift weight and relieve pressure points, I am aware of snippets of talk behind me.

" Virginia . . . back and forth across the country a couple of times."

". . . retired?"

"No . . . sabbatical."

"Oh? You're a teacher?"

"I'm a psychiatrist. I've done some teaching, but not lately . . . ."

"Well, I've got a degree in clinical psychology that I've never used . . . ."

(The book lies dead in my lap.)

". . . looking for work?"

"Not exactly, just looking around. I was thinking of stopping in Port Angeles . . . ."

246

I'm twisted around in my seat, and can just glimpse the un-psychologist's face from behind. I make eye contact with the psychiatrist; he acknowledges me with a fleeting smile and turns back to his discussion.

"I wonder what it's like there, whether a psychiatrist could make a living." They fall silent for a moment.

Over the bench backs between us I lunge into the pause, become the hypotenuse of the conversation. "The economics of medicine has changed so much, it's harder to make a living anywhere these days."

Psychiatrist: *[Thirty-degree body shift, re-orienting to the sudden invasion.]* "You can, but it's so controlled, you have to comply, have to jump through the hoops of the insurance companies. There's no independence, no freedom <u>to treat all people equally</u>. You can't do that; it would be an attack on their corporate principles."

His triangular face reminds me of a dog I once knew (a German shepherd - very intense dog, and totally faithful). Cleanshaven, skin barely hinting at a few wrinkles about dark blue eyes. Jaws angular. Soft felt hat squarely set over a residue of light brown hair. Probably yesterday's shirt, with plain brown tie and fitted rain jacket. Yes, you might pick him out as a professor.

He relaxes from combative to wistful, sighs, leans back a little and adds, "When the people in charge of your care are eager for you to die, you've got a bad situation."

Un-Psychologist: *[Turns a verbal page.]* "What do you think of these new psychotropic drugs?"

[Pause.] "Like what?"

"Well . . . like Trilafon."

"That's not new, that's an old one."

"Really?"

"We sometimes used Triavil - that's Trilafon and Elavil combined; we never used Trilafon much by itself."

"I thought they were making some breakthroughs in that area."

"They have. Some of the medicines are quite useful."

247

"From what I've seen, there are places where they just warehouse the mentally ill people, load 'em up on Thorazine or Haldol and just warehouse 'em."

He still hasn't turned around. I can just see the edge of his face past his ear: rounded, meaty, with large incurving moustache of dark salt-and-pepper gray like the hair showing beneath his sagging cap. Like a walrus without the tusks. His blue denim shirt looks new. He could use a haircut. I think an unjustified thought: Is he perhaps taking Trilafon?

I: "They used Thorazine and Haldol and Mellaril to empty out the mental hospitals, so now the warehouses are on the streets."

P: *[Quietly; a hint of raised eyebrow; maybe I was getting carried away a bit.]* "Yes there's quite a lot of mental illness among the homeless."

[U-P leaves to go to restroom or counter or somewhere.]

I: *[By way of non-contrite apology]* I'm a GP, or have been most of my life."

P: "Where?"

I: "A small town in eastern Oregon - surgery, delivering babies, house calls. Then I phased down to emergency rooms for a few years, and now I've phased down again to a doc-in-a-box walk-in clinic in Portland - owned by a hospital, of course. Did you say you're from Virginia?"

P: "Yes, northern Virginia."

I: "Yeah, the insurance industry sure has a tight control on medicine now."

P: *[Shifts into heavier gear again.]* "You no longer have the freedom to treat everybody the same. *[We're both now twisted around at forty-five degrees, leaning over the backs of the seats to face each other.]* "It's not fashionable or permitted any more to practice your profession just for the passionate love of people, of human beings." *[Gesticulating now with both hands, clutching a basketball-sized chunk of air in front of him.]*

[U-P returns and sits down.]

P: *[Turns to him.]* "He's a doctor too." *[Brief acknowledgements all around. The verbal ground tilts a bit.]*

"When two out of three people in the bus station are doctors, there must be something going on."

I: "I've just been up here visiting my daughter." *[To U-P]* "And what do you do?"

U-P: *[Turns head slightly.]* "I have a degree in clinical psychology, but I've never used it."

I: "What kind of work do you do?"

U-P: "I'm retired." *[I am silenced. Actively silenced.]*

P: "Yeah, I don't think it's likely to get better until we can get out of the corporate noose."

U-P: "You mean socialized medicine?"

P: "No, I don't believe this country has the strength of love for humanity, of caring for each other, to go against the corporate power that controls it now. I don't see the will in Congress now, or any power that can overthrow the present system. I see it as Hillary's Revenge: 'If you don't like it the other way, we'll see that you get a full dose of it this way.'"

I: "You know, there is a grassroots movement for a single-payor system, to get it out of the corporate jaws of the insurance system; but it would take a lot bigger revolt than I can see coming - yet, anyway."

U-P: *[Gets up, picks up a bag, turns to P.]* "Well, good luck." *[Exits. I still have never seen his eyes.]*

I: "One evening a man came into our clinic because his doctor wasn't around. While I was writing a prescription for his strep throat I asked what kind of work he does. He said, 'I'm CEO of an HMO.'

"Wow! I couldn't resist. I said, 'Things have sure changed since I started in medicine. I used to be just a doctor caring for my patients the best I could. But now I'm a "provider" and the patient is a "consumer of health care," and we're both parts of the "health care industry." What used to be a service and transaction between two people has now become a market commodity. And now doctors and patients are bought and sold in the marketplace like herds of cattle.' He said, 'Oh, it's not quite like that.' I said, 'Well, it feels like that.' And he said, 'Well, I guess it is like that.'"

P: *[Nods.]* "We used to <u>care</u> for people. Now the emphasis is all on curing. There's no money in caring; it's all in curing.

I: "Yeah, but it's nice to have some of each. I was talking recently with an eighty-five-year-old general practitioner. He was six years ahead of me in graduating, and retired fifteen years ago. We were reminiscing, comparing our first experiences with penicillin, when it was first discovered, and there was no such thing as CPR or heart surgery or organ transplants. And he said, 'You know, we had the best years to be in medicine. The generation before us could only do diagnosis and prognosis, and some caring. In our time we were able to <u>do</u> something of therapeutic value for people; and we could do it in the way we thought best for the patient, follow our own lead. But now they've taken that away from us - first the specialists, and all the fancy technology, and now the insurance companies. I'm glad I got out when I did.'"

P: "I've been traveling around. I'm trying to learn about New Age medicine, but I don't quite get it yet."

I: "New Age - is that what you could call alternative medicine? As opposed to the medicine that you and I were taught?"

P: "Yes. All the people I know and respect - people that are enlightened - they're crazy about it, devoted to it. And I know they must be right; I <u>intuitively</u> know they're right. I just am searching for the answers, to see where the truth lies."

I: "I agree. I think there's a lot of good to be found in those ideas. For a small instance, I'm taking saw palmetto myself."

P: "That's for . . . for . . . inflammation?"

I: "It's for the prostate, for prostate enlargement."

P: "And take St. John's wort. That works well. In Europe, for treating depression, they use that first."

[The wires of the bench are biting mercilessly into my rear.]

I: "I know a lot of people who believe in the alternative kind of medicine; but I'm not sure I'd call them 'enlightened'. I don't consider myself enlightened. I don't think any of us are really enlightened. It used to be that an educated man, a philosopher, knew it all - medicine, astrology, mathematics, physics - all the central content of human knowledge. But now there's too much knowledge, so everybody knows a tiny piece of it and feels smug and satisfied. But I don't think anybody really has the Truth. How can you be enlightened now?"

P: "I was in Iran - the eastern part, near Afghanistan - and I tried to find out why the people are so devoted to the old ways - why they don't want to change. They plow their fields with oxen, like they've done for 1,000 years. And you can just see the love, the religious passion, the love of God in the way they do things." *[He is massaging the air again, now hugging a full armload of it, with fists clenched.]*

I: "It seems like for a lot of those ancient peoples, indigenous peoples, God and work and the activities of life and things around them were all one, not separate compartments."

P: *[Nods.]* "I think Islam's a fresher, a more recent religion - only 600 years old or so -"

I: "You mean in comparison with - ?"

P: "Christianity."

I: "Maybe. But there's both love and cruelty in all religions - or rather in people under the banner of all religions. Like the Crusades and the Spanish inquisition, for Christianity; and the bombings in Nairobi and Dar es Salaam and the Jerusalem markets, for Islam. And I've seen the passionate love of both people and God among some Christians - some Catholic nuns and priests, for instance. But I guess most of the ones I've known seem to operate more from respect, reverence, or fear than from pure love of God or of people. And the Jewish people too, especially the Jewish people, their respect for God and the Jewish history as the ground of being. But I regret that I don't know any Muslims."

P: "I'd never been to a Jewish service, and there was this girl who didn't have a ride to the synagogue, so I said OK, I'd give her a ride, and I went with her. And there was love, certainly, expressed in their service, just as in a Catholic mass."

I: "I'm not really a Christian. My wife is a devout Catholic. But I take Jesus as an excellent role model, not as a personal savior; and I don't know - not viscerally, or existentially - the

251

meaning of the word 'divine'. So I'm disqualified as a Christian."

P: "Maybe you could make it as a Muslim. They say 'hey, Jesus was a man!'"

I: "No, I think I'll just take my chances on making it as 'Other'. I'm optimistic about that; I'm comfortable just struggling along as I am, trying to do right as I can find it."

[Squirming, shifting, feeling the vicious gnawing of the wires; but I like the geometry, the spacing and diagonal symmetry of our conversation, and don't want to violate it by changing my stance.]

"Where are you going from here?"

P: *[Hesitates; glances around the room.]* "Vancouver, British Columbia." *[Frowns slightly.]* "I have some family here in Seattle, I could . . . . Yeah, Vancouver."

I: "My brother lives in British Columbia."

[Abruptly more animated, his eyes shining, he leans forward.] "What does he tell you? Do they treat all people equally there?"

I: *[Hesitant. Wanting to be truthful, choosing my words carefully.]* "I'm not quite sure, actually, but I think so, pretty much. Except maybe the indigenous people, the Indians; I don't know about them."

P: *[Quickly]* "Aren't they under the government system?"

I: "I don't know." *[Stand up, cautiously flex my limbs, let the inner juices adjust themselves.]*

"My bus is about to leave." *[Pick up bags, walk around the bench to face him.]* "Are you on a mission? Not a jihad?"

P: *[Pause.]* "No, a sabbatical from a jihad, a jihad of twenty years back home, to get the doctors to insist on their independence, freedom to do their own credentialing, as a group. We've been pretty much successful so far, at least in the hospital bylaws. It's gotten eroded some, but it could be worse. The struggle goes on."

I: "Well, good luck on your pilgrimage to find Truth." *[Shake hands.]*

P: "Thank you. I've enjoyed the discussion."

252

I: "And I." *[Pick up bags and exit into the stained but refreshingly chilly air of Gate 5.]*

Whatever Works

> I said to my friend Dr. Bill Stahl,
> "Each person lives in his own individual
> and unique world, created from all of his
> past experiences and observations and
> integrations."
>
> "Yeah," he said, "that's the nice thing
> about reality: you can make it up as you
> go along."

The articles and lectures on acupuncture that I have encountered usually started with the almost dismissive warning: "You can't understand acupuncture until you understand Eastern thought and philosophy." I believe this is true: the mystical, subjective, non-quantitative, soft ways of seeing the workings of the world.

And I am tempted to reply: "You can't understand Western medicine until you understand the objective, reductionist, linear, mechanistic, hard view of the world that underlies Western science and technology of medicine."

We enter a room where straight wooden chairs flank a long narrow table. Graceful cups with delicate lids and no handles line either side of the table. The tea in them is hot.

Our host gestures for us to be seated along one side of the table, then takes the chair at the end. A dozen white-coated men occupy the other side, smiling and faintly nodding whenever we make eye contact. Everyone appears cordial and friendly, but movements and body language seem unsure, tentative. I am reminded of two strange dogs, their tails wagging as they circle and sniff each other's backsides to make their evaluations.

This is the conference room in the China Medical College in Taichung, on the west coast of Taiwan. Twenty-two family practice doctors from the U.S. are on a three-week tour of

China, Taiwan, Hong Kong, and South Korea in a Science and Technology Exchange Program.

Here sit two groups of official "healers" facing each other, joined in common intention and profession, yet still separated in 1984 by millennia of language, philosophy, experience, knowledge and belief accumulated and passed on from one person and one generation to the next.

On one side of the table sits the ancient philosophy of Yin and Yang, the cosmic principles that must be in harmony and balance in the body and spirit in order to maintain health; the *Nei Ching*, classic treatise of medical lore, written perhaps by the Yellow Emperor some 5,000 years ago, or maybe by others 2,300 years ago; the *Pen-ts'ao Kang-mu*, The Great Pharmacopoeia, about 450 years old, in 52 volumes and containing over 1,000 herbs; a concept of anatomy built almost entirely on speculation, since religious rules of the past have forbidden cutting into corpses. This hypothetical anatomy produced charts of acupuncture points and the connecting meridians - straight dotted lines on the charts. The life force "chi" flows along these channels, and obstructions or imbalance of the flow leads to disease. I note that the points and meridians do not correspond to actual nerves, blood vessels, or specific body structures.

And facing the other line of tea cups sits Aesclepius, ancient God of Medicine; Hippocrates, Greek "father of medicine" in the 4th century BC; Galen, who circumvented the prohibitions on corpse dissection by studying pigs and apes; William Harvey, discovering less than 400 years ago that blood circulates from and returns to the heart; Anton Leeuwenhoek and his microscopes; Louis Pasteur and the birth of bacteriology; the Curie family and Wilhelm Roentgen finding radioactivity and x-rays; Sir Alexander Fleming noticing, in my own century, the first actual antibiotic; and a bursting escalation of knowledge and change since then.

Each line feels secure in its own knowing, its own roots, its history, each individual ascending the prescribed ladder of knowledge and custom and belief and practice, each generation testing itself against those who have gone before, rejecting and replacing some elements, confirming and building on others. And now at last each side reaches across the divide, across the seas, across the table, testing the waters on the other side and trying to make some sense of what they find. And each remains dedicated to applying time-tested knowledge and methods toward helping ailing fellow humans.

The president of the college, at the head of the table, gives a short welcoming speech. Then he and Dr. John Gayman, professor from the University of Washington, exchange statements of appreciation for the opportunity to meet with colleagues and to share and exchange medical and scientific knowledge.

The China Medical College was established in 1958. It has three goals, its president tells us: first, to advance Chinese traditional medicine; second, to absorb knowledge of Western medicine; and third, to integrate the two. Actually it is two colleges closely connected, a "College of Traditional Chinese Medicine" and a "College of Western Medicine." The main traditional courses of study are herbal medicine and acupuncture.

We tour the herbal gardens, a demonstration plot of perhaps a half-acre.

We stop and look in briefly on a classroom; the majority of the students are women.

Dr. Chen, from the College of Western Medicine, then gives a slide presentation of a Western-style "controlled" treatment study. A series of patients with essential hypertension (high blood pressure of unknown cause) are being treated with *san-huang-hseih-hsin-tang,* an ancient formula containing three herbs, prescribed for people with "epigastric fullness, flushing up, restlessness, constipation, and a hard pulse." (A "hard pulse" indeed often signifies high blood pressure.) Patients are given a placebo for one week, then the medicine - 500 mg. three times a day - for two weeks, then no medication for one week. Their blood pressure is monitored, along with heart rate, liver and kidney function, electrolytes, serum cholesterol, and any observed side effects.

The herbs in the ancient recipe are not tested separately, only in combination. The patients' records do appear to show mild reduction in blood pressure, but which part or parts of the mixture may have produced the change is not addressed. The one-month trial is too short to draw convincing conclusions.

Our procession moves next to the Department of Acupuncture Research. The sign above this door at the end of a short hall is painted on a wooden board, in English. (We never felt sure, on this entire trip, just what we were seeing, how authentic were the demonstrations, how much things were dressed up or changed or swept out of sight for our visit.)

This area seems more like a museum than a research laboratory. There are display cases of assorted needles; old-looking books with diagrams of acupuncture points and meridians and drawings of hands inserting needles. At one side stands a hollow copper manikin, full life size, with a light inside and numerous perforations representing the precise numbered points worked out by masters in ancient times.

In the Fu Xing District Hospital in Beijing the previous week, after a demonstration of acupuncture, I asked Dr. Xu Zu Mo, professor of internal medicine, "How does it work?"

He hesitated briefly (perhaps, I thought, because of the language gap; perhaps searching for an answer he believed would satisfy me). Then, "It stimulates the nerves," he said, "and increases the circulation."

Here in Taiwan, after a brief description of acupuncture by the chief research doctor, I ask him, "How does this relate to anatomy and physiology as we Westerners know it?"

His answer is prompt and emphatic. "There is no relation," he says. "It's an entirely different thing."

One of our group, Dr. Cleve Enriques from Pasco, Washington, sometimes uses acupuncture in his practice - mainly to help patients stop smoking - and "it quite often works." We had discussed this among ourselves.

"It's all in the power of suggestion," said Dr. Ron Horn, from Seattle.

"So what?" said Cleve. "As long as it works, who cares?"

257

Back again in Beijing, I bought a set of acupuncture charts and needles. Cleve was pleased to see my purchase. "Are you going to start using acupuncture?" he asked.

"No," I said, "These are just a souvenir. I don't plan to use them. You know it works for you, so that's fine. But it will only work if both the patient and the doctor believe it. And since I don't believe it would work, I wouldn't be able to convince the patient that it would work. This kit will stay on my curio shelf, along with my sample capsule of *san-huang-hseih-hsin-tang*."

Since the dawn of history the healing professions have been successful and highly esteemed. This is true whether their methods were songs and incantations, powdered deer horn, herbal teas, acupuncture, penicillin, sharpened knives, homeopathy, or drugs aimed at the mind. All of these treatment methods have been found, by observation and popular acclaim, to work.

How is this possible? Could it all be a scam?

Medicine is not an exact science. Life is much more complex than we like to think. In fact, to paraphrase again the late naturalist Aldo Leopold, life and the workings of the world are more complex than we can think.

So we are forced to face the question: How do we decide whether a medicine or treatment "works"? What does "it works" mean? How can we know whether a drug or a procedure actually causes the result we hope or believe it will cause?

That should be easy. Common sense says just try it out. You invent a new medicine - say an antidepressant - and give it to 100 depressed people. Six weeks later 40 of them feel better. *Voila!* It works!

But just to be sure, you compare it with something else; you give sugar pills to another 100 depressed folks.

Oops! Thirty of them feel better too, almost as many as with your drug. Now what?

Well, you conclude, at least your Heavenweed is better than the placebo, by 10 per cent. It works - but only in 1 out of 10 people?

With some arm twisting you can get the records of 47 clinical trials done on the six antidepressants most commonly prescribed in the U.S. in 2003 - trials done by the drug manufacturing companies themselves. About half show <u>no difference</u> between the drug and placebo; but the drug makers didn't show those trials to the Food and Drug Administration. The trials that they did submit indicate a few percent of difference - enough to persuade the FDA to approve the drug and allow it to be patented and marketed.

What is generally ignored is the 25% to 40% of folks who feel better after taking a placebo. <u>Why</u> do they feel better?

Every ailment or injury - from a broken nail to a near-fatal crash, from a common cold to Ebola fever - has both a physical and an emotional component. It's convenient to think of them separately, but they are not really separable. One's <u>experience</u> and <u>interpretation</u> of a sensation become part of the sensation.

If I touch the bottom of my foot, or my genitals, it's just a sensation of touching. But if someone else touches the same spots in exactly the same way, the feeling is entirely different because my interpretation of it is different.

If we call the feelings of childbirth "labor pains" it implies one thing; if instead we call them "muscle contractions" the implication is very different and the experience of them often changes dramatically. This type of conceptual difference is the central basis for "natural childbirth."

Despite many ingenious attempts, no one has been able to devise an objective method or instrument to take an actual measurement of pain. When I get a headache or a pain in my chest, do I feel bad, or just different? How bad? What does it mean? What does it portend? Brain tumor or hangover? Indigestion or heart attack? Am I supposed to fear this feeling, or to ignore it? How do I know the difference? When is denial the preferred and practical response, and when might denial prove fatal?

The causes of the placebo effect may be roughly summarized as *hope, expectation, and faith.* If you *hope* to be relieved of your discomfort, and *expect* that calling on your doctor may achieve this, and have *faith* that his skill and his intentions are directed toward making you better, you will interpret your subsequent sensations in the context of this faith and will likely feel better.

My brother's wife had symptoms from an early age that were eventually diagnosed as lupus. He pointed out that "a medical problem is easier to deal with if you have a name for it." Naming it makes it easier for you to focus your hope, expectations, and faith; and naming it makes it easier for the doctor because he can tell you what he is intending to treat. The name provides the music for the dance.

The acupuncturist with his needles can't set a broken leg, correct an inflamed appendix, or stop a significant hemorrhage. He alone cannot not heal meningitis, pneumonia, or a collapsed lung. What he will treat is arthritis, or eczema, or paralysis after a stroke, or other chronic, persistent and painful conditions, subjective symptoms whose natural course has ups and downs.

The more skilled the acupuncturist, we are told, the fewer needles he will use and the farther he will place them from the area being treated. Meaning, I presume, that the more charismatic and convincing the acupuncturist, the more powerful will be the placebo effect as he locates the points and inserts his threads of steel. Yes, I confess, I can't avoid the belief that the effectiveness of acupuncture is a prime example of the placebo effect.

What is the "art" of medicine? I believe this is mainly the validation of the patient's faith. By eye contact, demeanor, body language, attentiveness, respect, and experience of past meetings the doctor enhances the placebo effect of the encounter. Abruptness, condescension, accusation, preoccupation or annoyance, being in a hurry, or apparent lack of respect for the patient or his beliefs will diminish the available placebo effect.

If I am sick, the healing begins when I make the appointment or walk in the Emergency Room door.

I know what I believe and believe what I know, and can only practice what I see as true. I know how I would wish to be treated. But this does not mean that all else is false. The real measure of a medical transaction is not just the outcome, but rather the resulting degree of satisfaction for both parties. A mutual, shared experience of hope, expectation, and faith between healer and seeker, like a magnetic field of force, draws the two together in a process from which they both emerge satisfied and feeling better. When the patient and the "health care provider" - doctor, nurse, herbalist, counselor, shaman - fully share the hopes, expectations, and faith in the process, this force field becomes the Grand Placebo. All the rest is mere technical details.

House Calls

My mother never spoke to me about it in advance. I don't know how she knew, whom she may have consulted, or where in San Francisco she bought it, but she made the perfect choice.

Her gift to me on my graduation from medical school was a black bag, a doctor's bag, which still, 55 years later, says in tastefully small, plain gold letters embossed on one side between the leather tabs that anchor the handles: M. T. MERRILL, M.D. Thus - as if it were not already so - she assured herself a permanent place in my life.

I have no way of knowing, or even making a credible estimate; but counting the years, and the days, and the memories, I have to guess the bag's visits in the tens of thousands. It went with me every day to the office for restocking and for retrieval of my notes and records of house calls; and home with me every evening to be ready for whatever might come. The bag's handles are wrapped, where the leather seams started to separate, with black electrician's tape, and the edges of the flaps that close the compartments inside the lid are a bit scuffed; otherwise the bag has changed hardly at all through its lifetime.

That bag, I am sure, has been a powerful catalyst to my effectiveness as a "healer." It has a strong symbolic significance both to me and to my patients. Subliminally, subconsciously when I pick up that bag it is Dr. Parkinson's bag, the old tattered brown leather one with the past-maroon cloth lining and the latched drawer in the bottom. My bag has only traces of a scent of medicine; but without meaning to be trite or maudlin, I have carried the ghosts of Aesclepius and Hippocrates and Paré, and Semmelweis of Hungary - and Dana Atchley and Robert Loeb of P&S and Robert Rife of SCCH - on all of the times that bag has gone with me to home and highway, forest and field, on emergencies or mere concerns - baby with fever or cough; mother hemorrhaging; rancher with chest pain; logger on whom a tree has fallen; rider with whom a horse has fallen;

grandmother fallen on the floor or found cold and pulseless in bed at dawn. To see a serious man come through the door carrying that bag lays a firm foundation for whatever is to follow.

Under the auspices of the black bag, I have collected, in living rooms ("Would you mind turning off the TV?") or kitchens or bedrooms or bathrooms or roadsides, blood samples or urine samples or stool samples; felt bellies and arms and ribs and backs; listened to hearts and lungs; checked pulses and blood pressures and measured temperatures via various orifices; inspected gunshot wounds; delivered bad news and good news and babies; dispensed samples of pills and sympathy and advice; written prescriptions and time-off-work excuses; given instructions on how to use the vaporizer, the enema bag, the hot pack or the ice.

One day toward the end of medical school a visiting doctor came - a "real" doctor, a practitioner, they said - to tell us about being a doctor outside the hallowed halls of P&S, to give us homely hands-on advice on house calls and on what to carry in the doctor bag.

The man turned out to be a New York City surgeon - all they could find for the job, perhaps. He said that he often rode the subway from hospital to hospital, and that his bag contained a ham sandwich and a copy of the New York Times. The other thing he told us was that if you are in a situation where you have to do a rectal examination but don't have a rubber glove with you, be sure to put soap under your finger nail.

His talk was merely a letdown for me at the time, but in retrospect it seemed like a parody of actual doctoring, reflecting the disdain at P&S for the very concept of "general practice." In recording medical histories, we were taught the term "LMD" - local medical doctor - which carried a suggestion of someone of lesser skill or knowledge who had probably missed the true diagnosis or botched the treatment.

The bag, reposing now under the desk where I can touch it with my foot as I write, contains the crystallized remains, the hardened residue of a life's calling.

Down the Other Side

We strolled along by the water of Puget Sound, my son and daughter and their spouses. The ladies were up ahead, chatting, their skirts fluttering in the saline breeze like a pair of butterflies. We three men casually brought up the rear, speaking of jobs and houses and cars and my son-in-law's fishing boat.

Then I saw and felt it. The fellows were moving just a bit slowly, imperceptibly adjusting their gait to mine. And the conversation, the subjects - theirs had been vigorous, forward, into the future; mine were retrospective, skimpy and nostalgic. The lads were kind, loving, and respectful, all right; it wasn't anything they did or failed to do. But it suddenly hit me: I don't feel like the alpha male in this group any more!

How do you know when it's time to be left behind on an ice floe?

After eight years in the emergency department at Mid-Columbia Medical Center, I had finally tired of the 75-mile commute from Portland to The Dalles; the 24-hour shifts, leaping into full alert between naps in the middle of the night; recuperating in a motel room and then doing another 24 hours on duty before dragging back down the Columbia Gorge to home for the rest of the week.

I found a job in an "Urgent Care" clinic close to home, a doc-in-a-box place where we didn't do 9-1-1 problems, just small cuts and bladder infections and babies with earaches and people with ingenious excuses for needing pain pills, and maybe an occasional broken wrist. Then I moved even farther out, down to the other end of the hall in the Occupational Medicine unit, doing physical exams on bus and truck drivers and follow-up on workmen's compensation cases and going to industrial sites to do lung-function tests on workers who labored in clouds of silica dust.

Retiring is a slow, gradual thing. It comes on you furtively season by season, one spring and autumn at a time, one snow after another. Your perspective subtly changes - and then it hits you all at once.

I had just come back inside for the second lecture of the afternoon, second day of a three-day Scientific Session of the Oregon Academy of Family Physicians. The air outside was pleasantly cool, the sunshine gentle on the bit of grass by the entry below the off-white of the faux-marble building, and I hesitated before reentering the cavern and taking my seat.

The topic - against the background of the new controversial law allowing physician-assisted suicide - was "Appropriate Prescribing for Pain in Terminal Illness." Did the doctor-assisted suicide movement reflect failure of doctors to give adequate comfort measures in end-of-life care? Clearly it did. But as the speaker got under way, I suddenly didn't want to hear it. I couldn't bring myself to concentrate on the talk, or on the topic. I quietly picked up my syllabus and bag of notes and papers, walked out, and drove home.

The next morning I forced myself into the car and across the city to the conference center. This time I didn't last until noon.

Doctoring, I told myself, has been gutted, the juice squeezed out of it leaving just a desiccated rind of words and priorities: peer review organization, recredentialing, utilization review committee, chart reviews, cost containment, approved procedures, double-blind studies, co-payments, panels of approved providers, evidence-based medicine, outcomes survey, standard of care, risk management, research and development - always confrontational or competitive or defensive or money-centered, and so little about the one-on-one interaction between a doctor and his patient.

I think of old Wayne Grodrian, 15 years retired. "Before the 1930s," he said, "a patient barely had a fifty-fifty chance of benefiting from a visit to a doctor. About the time we arrived antibiotics were making a big difference in infectious diseases. Anesthesia and surgical techniques were improving. General practice was about to enter a new level of competency and respect and recognition. And then the whole new field of cardiology - monitors and CPR and defibrillation and cardiac surgery, and on and on. And now it's all ruined, taken over by the insurance industry and the pharmaceutical industry and the huge for-profit hospital corporations and the relentless rush to make yesterday's technology obsolete."

Sure, and maybe I'd like to be again on my mother's lap, feeling her arms around me and sucking at her breast. This sentimental, whining, mawkish talk I suppose is just part of the old-man syndrome, like limping, clutching at hand rails, cupping the hand at the ear and lingering at the urinal.

Yes, there still is some fun in practicing medicine, even if you have to poke around to find it like picking about for the raisins in a bowl of oatmeal. I see third-year students sent out from Oregon's medical school to spend a few weeks working with practitioners in rural settings. They seem innocent and bright and happy and are soaking up new experiences like eager sponges - just where I was a lifetime ago. To them the world is fresh and clean and the way it's meant to be. I've had my day, and now they'll have theirs. God love and help them!

But time is a one-way street, and here I am now. I know that if I can't motivate myself to stay on top of all the new information, to be the best I can, and don't have the gumption to meet each new situation head-on, the odds are against me - and against my patients.

I read somewhere that, on average, a doctor gets sued (not necessarily convicted) for malpractice about every 10 years. I certainly have made my share of mistakes, but in 50 years of practice I have never been sued. It occurred to me one day what a pity it would be to spoil that record, and what a handy excuse for retiring. I must jump off the merry-go-round before some disastrous error or oversight brings me down. So at last, in my 76th year, I quit while I was ahead.

Getting It Right

Yesterday a loud bang, a concussion near my head stopped me in my tracks, and I saw a bird drop to the floor of the patio just outside the window.

A kingfisher sprawled limply on the cold stone. Its left wing was hidden under the body. The other, angled off to the right, very slowly relaxed and folded itself in against the breast. The head, with the powerful spear-like beak and familiar bushy crest, was twisted backward, and the eyelids slowly closed as I watched.

I picked the bird up; it lay completely flaccid and motionless in my hand. When I grasped the tip of a blue-grey feather and drew the wing out as if asking it to fly, bright white bars blinked into view. Below the wings, soft, rosy-brown feathers framed the white of breast and belly.

One tiny bit of white down clung to the glass beside my shoulder.

Along the small creek in our back yard, air and water and ground are inhabited or visited by a wide variety of creatures - deer, mink, ducks, quail, finches, hummingbirds and many other kinds of birds. Of all of these, the kingfisher strikes within me the strongest emotional chord. Its harsh, grating cry draws my attention barely in time to see one, or rarely two together, flash down the creek, over or perhaps under the little bridge, clearly on some terribly urgent mission. Sometimes one perches briefly on the bridge rail to look and dive for a crayfish. Their presence is a periodic reassurance that the larger system of life is functioning well enough for now.

The kingfisher seems so clearly focused, so utterly competent, far above making stupid mistakes. That of all possible birds it was a kingfisher that self-destructed against my window seemed baffling; there must be some hidden message here to which I was blind. I could only suppose that somehow the early sun on the glass cast a reflection of stream or trees that appeared to the hunter like a new inviting vista.

Feeling vaguely intrusive and embarrassed, I spread the bird out on the picnic table and took a photograph - just to document the event, I told myself - and I placed a half-dozen feathers in an envelope labeled "Feathers from Left Wing of Kingfisher." After admiring and stroking the lifeless form once more, I tossed it in the garbage barrel and went back to my chores around the house.

Last night, lying in bed, I awakened from a half-dream with the kingfisher heavy on my mind. Suddenly I was in a different time, memory vivid over thirty passing years. The telephone was ringing late at night, the woman two and a half months along, her first pregnancy after three years of trying.

I started bleeding this afternoon, she said. *Now it's worse and I'm having cramps and I've soaked three towels.*

"I'll meet you at the hospital right away, I said."

No, my husband's away and I have no transportation.

"Just lie down and wait," I said. "I'll be there in twenty minutes."

By the time I arrived, the miscarriage had nearly completed itself. In the bed, along with some large blood clots, was the glob of placental tissue. Inside its small fluid-filled cavity floated a pale remnant, big as a medium-sized grasshopper, suspended by a wispy thread. The bleeding had all but stopped.

"Do you want to see it?" I asked.

Brief hesitation.

No.

"I'm sorry," I said. "I know how important it was to you. About one pregnancy in four ends this way." She dabbed the tears.

Yes, I know.

I carried away the towels, ran some water, cleaned up my instruments and put them in my bag. It had been a long day.

She raised her head abruptly from the pillow, voice suddenly intense.

Did you flush it down the toilet?

I stared at her, speechless. Three seconds crept by. Why had I not waited until I got back to the clinic? How could I. . . .

268

"Yes," I said. "It was just dead tissue, like the blood clots."

Her face was rigid, a mask. She nodded stiffly, then turned on her side, facing the wall. I finished packing my things.

"Call me tomorrow to let me know how you're doing," I said. "At the clinic they'll know where I am any time. Everything should be all right now."

Still facing away, she was silent. I closed the door behind me.

This morning after daylight I carried a shovel and heavy crowbar down to the creek. The air was motionless, but against that silence that dawn brings with it, the gentle sounds of the moving water were sharp and brittle as glass. I scraped out a shallow hole among the rocks on the bank, down to where the soil was dark and wet.

I returned to the house, moved bags of garbage in the barrel and found the bird, stiff now, cold but still mutely elegant. I carried it down the bank and laid it in the hole, feathers smoothed, wings carefully folded, beak pointing upstream. I covered the bird gently with dirt and stones, smoothed the surface over, then stood looking, listening to the water.

End Game

With a single phone call to me at the nurses' desk in the hospital, from his second wife in their motel room, after a morning of golf, lounging on the bed and going over some of his papers, without warning, my father was dead. Cardiac arrest.

I arrived the next morning in the village in Idaho where he had lived. Strolling at dawn through the streets so familiar from my childhood, I met my brother Bill - who had also driven 300 miles - strolling from the other end of town.

Bill and I picked a late-summer bouquet from roadsides and vacant lots and fencerows: cattails, dry full-headed wild grasses, teasel, some small shrub with colorful crisp leaves. We stuck these into a coffee can full of sand, wrapped the can in tasteful brown paper, and brought this offering, this symbol of our deepest love and respect for our father, to the simple funeral and placed it among the conventional lilies and roses. He was 60 years old.

I have never been to his grave.

I was not yet forty when I last talked with Dad. How sweet it would be to visit with him now! Not as son to father, but man to man. We never really got around to that.

Albert and Mary Good were my wife's parents, a retired missionary couple, fastidious in word and thought and deed. In later life she suffered from spastic colitis. The couple moved from a retirement center into our home in Vermont.

There was plenty of room, and they looked after each other in a way, sitting together on the couch, holding hands, dozing. But her bowel function - her apparent need to be helped to the bathroom repeatedly in the night - so exhausted Grandpa Good (who suspected that her demands were partly a struggle for control, hence was less sympathetic as time passed) that at last we all agreed that she should be in a nursing home. Some member of the family visited her three times a week. She had no appetite, complained incessantly, lost weight, became ever more forgetful and weak and frail.

When she was brought home for Thanksgiving dinner she smiled and ate heartily, even ravenously, for the first time in months. The reality was inescapable: her major clinical problem was simply the corrosive effect of being discarded.

In mid-winter I went to visit. She was gaunt, shrunken, like the stick figures in news clips from Bangladesh. She lay motionless, her gaze fixed on the ceiling.

"Mother?" I said. Her head and eyes turned slowly toward me and her parched, parted lips, sticking to her teeth in the center, twitched upward perceptibly at the corners.

I held her hand, bathed her forehead, smoothed her wispy white hair, persuaded her to take a few small sips of water. She responded feebly, every movement delayed like a mechanical toy with failing batteries.

She couldn't have weighed more than seventy pounds. Suddenly I felt an urge to pick her up from the bed and hold her on my lap.

I started to lean over the bed - then something stopped me. I don't know what it was. Fear that the aide would enter the room? That she might soil my lap? That I would be awkward in handling her, or hurt her? Instead I squeezed her hand, kissed her cheek, and walked away.

After two more weeks she died. Thirty years later I am still plagued with guilt and shame that I didn't take Mother Good onto my lap and hold her in my arms.

Albert had known that her end was near. They had been married for more than sixty years.

A month after her passing he said to me, "Ted, I wish I could go back to Africa one more time. I believe that in three months I could bring 200 souls to Christ." He cautiously inquired whether it might be possible for me to go with him.

No. But I lit 90 candles on his birthday cake. (Don't try it. In that miniature firestorm the candles collapsed into the icing in seconds.)

That summer Dad Good and I had some nice times together, and some separately. He loved to fish, but his macular degeneration made his eyesight marginal. When I set him adrift in North Montpelier Pond in the aluminum rowboat for a few hours, with his lunch and a supply of worms, a bucket for the fish and a coffee can to pee in, he took two fishing outfits because if one got tangled he couldn't see to unsnarl it.

A few months later, crunching through the snow on Creamery Street on a sub-zero evening, he had his first episode of chest pain. Then it happened a couple of times just lying in bed.

At 5:30 one morning he rang his bell; the pain was more severe, and different. I gave him a shot of Demerol from my bag, and called the ambulance over his protest.

"They can give you some oxygen. That will help," I said.

A smile, a strange glow of resignation and finality, flitted like a moth's wing across his face. "It doesn't matter," he said softly.

In the ICU Dr. Bill Allard examined him. An ECG showed, as expected, a myocardial infarction - a section of muscle dead from blockage of a coronary artery. They put an oxygen cannula in his nose, connected him to the heart monitor, and started an IV. In that time and place there was nothing more to do. His pulse was regular, the pain was nearly gone, but his blood pressure had dropped to 80 and the skin of his brow and neck was cool and moist.

I thought of asking if he would like me to pray with him, but the question died on my lips. Perhaps I feared exposing his uncertainty - or mine - as to what comes after this. It was 7:15 am.

This was the day of the monthly Medical Staff meeting. For two weeks I had been preparing, editing, and rewriting a paper I wanted to present to the community's doctors and the hospital's board of directors. They were about to embark on a building program that I considered unnecessary, excessive, and misdirected; this would be my last chance to register a futile but passionate objection.

272

I had been sitting and fidgeting. I took his hand. "Dad," I said, "I have to go downstairs for about fifteen or twenty minutes and then I'll be right back."

His eyes met mine. "Can't you stay with me?" he asked, not quite pleading.

My gut tightened. I hesitated. Then I said, "I really need to go down, just for a few minutes." His hand lay limply in mine. He looked away.

I had been sitting in the conference room for maybe ten minutes, awaiting my turn, when the intercom announced, "Code Blue, ICU. Code Blue, ICU." Dr. Allard and I jumped from our seats and rushed upstairs.

He was still alive, breathing, blood pressure down to 40, rhythm regular on the screen but no detectable pulse. He was unresponsive. Unconscious? Who can say? That's always a mystery.

"Dad, I'm here," I said. In moments his blood pressure was gone. I stood and watched as Dr. Allard and the nurses did the CPR and resuscitation drill according to standard American Heart Association protocols, an obviously useless formality. After a decent period, with a glance between us we agreed and he gave the signal to stop.

Priorities are everything: I didn't really get to say goodbye.

My mother called from San Francisco to tell me that her leg had been inflamed just above the ankle for a couple of days. I advised her to see her doctor right away to make sure it wasn't anything serious. The next day Duncan Johnston, my stepfather, called to say that Mom was in the hospital with cellulitis in her leg. It didn't sound too bad, but it was puzzling because no cause had been put to it.

Later, on the way to the airport, I pieced together the bits of information:

The day after she was admitted to the hospital someone noticed that she appeared jaundiced. Blood tests confirmed that she had some kind of liver disorder, and she was scheduled for an ultrasound of her gall bladder and bile ducts the following morning.

"Why couldn't Ted be here when I need him?" she had asked. But she never got the ultrasound test done because in the hall on the way to the imaging department she suddenly started vomiting up large amounts of blood. They did what they could to stop the bleeding, from veins in her esophagus, but from there it was all downhill.

When I arrived I found Duncan and Bill already in her hospital room. She was receiving blood transfusions; had a tube through her nose holding an inflated balloon in her esophagus to try to compress the veins; and had been unresponsive for three or four hours, Duncan said. I got to speak briefly to the doctor, but at her age of 90 it was obviously a hopeless situation and I had nothing to say to him but "Thanks."

There was a Chinese woman who most of her life had called our mother "Mom," a sort of honorary sister to Bill and me. I went to try to call her. It took me a few minutes to find a phone, and she didn't answer.

When I returned to the room, Mom was no longer breathing. And I hadn't been there when she quit.

Duncan lived at home for a few weeks, then moved into a retirement center, and finally to a nursing home. I called him occasionally. A couple of months or more had elapsed, and I decided to talk to him. The nurse who answered said, "Yes, I just saw him down the hall in his wheel chair. I'll bring him to the phone." I waited. I waited. Several minutes passed.

At last she returned to the phone. "Mr. Johnston isn't doing real well just now; could you call back in an hour or so?"

"I'm a physician," I said, "and I'm his son. I'd like to know just what's happening."

"Well," she said, "when I got down there he was slumped over in his chair. We got him in bed and they're doing CPR on him now."

It was futile, of course.

Betsy began to get short of breath walking up to where I was digging post holes. A doctor's visit led to referral to a cardiologist in the city. The ECG was normal, and he

274

recommended a coronary angiogram. This involves local anesthetic in the groin, a long plastic catheter inserted all the way up and into the top of the heart, then maneuvered by means of its specially curved tip into the right coronary artery - a vessel the size of a wooden match - and then into the left coronary artery. At each point a machine injects a gush of dye and takes a rapid series of x-ray pictures as the dye spreads through the arteries.

The angiogram requires, externally, only one tiny nick in the groin; but on the inside, what goes on is invasive indeed and not without hazard. Equipment and skills are always at the ready to deal with cardiac arrest or other life-threatening things that can happen.

I said to Dr Ames, "I'd like to be present when you do the catheterization. She'll want me to be there."

"No," he said, "I don't think that would be advisable. We never have the family members present for this procedure."

"But I've always been there when she has had major things done before - scrubbed in on the breast surgery, and on the hysterectomy, been at the birthings when I could, and delivered one of our sons. I've always been there. You can ask her what she would want."

"I still don't think so. It's against our policy, and I wouldn't be comfortable with that. It's not a harmless procedure, you know. She might die."

"I know. That's exactly why I need to be there - especially if she should die. This is no way a question of trust or implied criticism, and I don't want to make you uncomfortable. I know that you know your business very well, and whatever happens I will stay completely out of your way. If she dies, I know that you will have done everything possible to handle the problems. But this is her life on the line, and she is my wife, and we just need for her to know that I'm there, for better or for worse."

For a few moments he studied his hands in silence, then looked at me. "I'll have to think about it. I may discuss it with my partner."

"Thank you," I said. "We'll check into the hospital in the morning before seven."

275

The entire procedure went smoothly. As instructed, she held perfectly still, and looked up at me with a wan smile.

I thanked Dr. Ames for letting me stand in. He smiled thinly, looked at the monitor once more, and hurried away.

That afternoon he came to her room to check the sandbag and pressure dressing on her groin, and to tell us what the pictures had shown.

"Your coronary arteries are all beautifully clear," he said. "The entire heart muscle is just weak, not doing its job as it should. Cardiomyopathy is the name for it - sick heart muscle. None of your other tests explain it, and you don't have the known risk factors for it, like alcoholism or diabetes. So it's what we call idiopathic cardiomyopathy. Meaning 'it causes itself.' Meaning we just don't know the cause. We know some things to do to help with the symptoms, but not to make it well."

Betsy and I didn't look at each other, but I laid my hand on hers. "Then talk to me about the future," she said. "What happens now?"

Dr. Ames, standing by her bed, turned slightly to face both of us, and shifted into a formal posture. His voice was gentle, sad, and firm. "The average survival time after this condition is diagnosed," he said, "is two years." He paused. "I'll be in touch with your local doctor about our findings and our recommendations."

The shortness of breath slowly increased. The predicted two years stretched toward three. She had two bouts of erratic rhythm, and finally only high doses of prednisone would prevent her going back into atrial fibrillation. After a time prednisone causes fluid retention in the tissues, a puffy "moon face" appearance, and increasing muscle loss and weakness.

The slow downhill slide continued. A "monkey bar" trapeze in the living room helped her to get up from the couch, and raising the toilet seat a couple of inches on blocks made it easier to dismount. She had to pass a full length mirror by the door as she left or entered the bedroom, and she made me take it down because she hated bitterly the sight of her swollen, disfigured face, the eyes like mere slits in a pumpkin, as she made her way to the bathroom. Even this small exertion made her gasp for breath. Finally she couldn't leave the bed.

On July 29 she looked and talked the same as the day before, but I couldn't feel a pulse or hear a heartbeat. She and I discussed it, and I called Dr. Stahl, our family doctor.

"It's not that I expect you to do anything the cardiologists haven't been able to do," I said. "But I'm trying here to manage something I've never faced before, and I want to come out of it feeling that we've done it all as right as possible."

He came out, twenty miles from town, a little hesitantly - not, I realized, because he was already over-scheduled at the office, but because the slow death of a colleague's wife was a new experience for him as well, and the visit could only make him feel more helpless.

Though she was speaking to him quite lucidly, he confirmed that she had no detectable pulse or blood pressure.

"In different circumstances," he said, "I might want to send a blood specimen to check the potassium level. But here it wouldn't make any difference."

Betsy and I both thanked him. She drank a little fruit juice. A few hours went by, and nothing changed.

We had our routine. At 10 pm I set out the little cup with the pills: prednisone, digoxin, diuretic, cardiac after-load reducer. As I raised her head for a sip of water to wet her mouth she looked at me and said, "Let's stop pouring meds for now, OK?"

It wasn't easy to answer, to know what to say.

After what felt like a long pause: "OK." I thought that movement of her swollen lips was meant to be a smile.

She took the water. I crawled into bed beside her, stroked her cheek and her arm. She didn't move, didn't speak, but her breathing was still steady.

About midnight she stirred a little, and asked to be turned on her side. When this was done, and a pillow propped at her back, she nodded but didn't want to talk. I propped myself on the other pillow. I thought forward, to what to do after; thought backward, to some of the good times, to that last anniversary six weeks before when all the kids came to the hospital and we had

277

a wonderful party in the yard, sipping a taste of champagne while the children sang the song to Mom and Dad that they had composed the night before. The picture we took of Betsy, in the wheelchair on the grass, in her hospital gown, with the IV bottle hanging above, was one of the best pictures she had ever had.

When I awoke with a start it was just getting light. I quickly looked over at her. Her position hadn't changed. Her skin was a bluish hue, her puffy eyelids closed. A wisp of froth on her swollen lips moved faintly in and out, in and out, a jerky but regular movement, slowing as I watched. The pauses became gradually longer. At last the tiny bubbles lay still at the corner of her mouth.

We had had three years in which to grieve, to mourn together, and I had recently spoken to her of my gratitude for this. Her words still ring in my ears: "Yes, that's all very well. But when you die, you die alone."

I am haunted by having fallen asleep, by failing to keep the final watch.

There's always been something wrong, something missing, something left out. I seem destined always, with someone I care for, to feel inadequate in the end. Is it possible ever to find that moment, that perfect, final moment to be fully present, to close the magic circle?

The Chemistry of a Little Dog

It was my good fortune to have a father who was a high school teacher. He taught chemistry, physics, algebra, English literature, grammar, and football. He was a Jack of all trades and master, perhaps, of none - except teaching, and providing a living example of doing what he believed was the right thing, unswayed by the opinions of others. A significant part of what I know and believe was transferred almost directly, though gently and bit by bit, from his brain to mine. As our family rode in the car on camping or fishing trips he would patiently and eagerly explain to my brother and me the nature of an atom, or how water evaporates, or why ice floats in water.

I shudder to think of living without the picture I have in my mind of the physical world, of how it all works - without the vision of the heat transfers and molecular dance as water evaporates from my face and steams up my glasses, or of how gravity and the pressure, temperature, volume and density of gases make the autumn breeze swoop in and tousel my hair. How could I know the true position of the fish that I see lurking there in the deep pool if I were unaware of how light is refracted in passing from air into water and back? Perhaps I might, with blind luck, learn to catch a fly ball or occasionally to knock a pool ball into the pocket; but to fail to understand the parabola, the acceleration of the ball from its initial course by the force of gravity, or the quantitative transfer of energy from the cue ball to the other, would be a pitiable disability.

Dad was not a biologist. That part I learned from other sources - from a nearby pond, and a microscope which my parents gave me for a birthday; from books that explained the carbon cycle, how the oxygen that animals need to breathe is discarded in the form of carbon dioxide that plants need to breathe so that the whole system supports itself.

I once saw a large wall chart, published by the American Chemical Society, showing - in small print - most of the chemical reactions and energy paths known in human metabolism, with little arrows to show the sequences and connections among all of the substances and their interactions. It was an astounding - though of course very limited - view of what goes on inside me, unbidden, unseen, unnoticed.

On a recent sunny morning in late fall I sat on the steps outside my study. Canyon Creek runs through the back yard, gushing and dancing over the rocks in spring but now low, slow, and barely murmuring. Leaves of the elderberry tree across the water were turning yellow below the brilliant red of the sumac on the hillside beyond. The iris blooms were gone, as were most of the daisies. Apples on two of the trees were nearly ripe. The big willow tree had already been dropping leaves for a while.

As I sat idly surveying the scene, Roger, my little black and white terrier, trotted over and stood on the step between my knees, looking up at me. We stared into each other's eyes while I stroked his ears.

Suddenly the scene began to change, to expand, the details becoming at once hopelessly entangled and blindingly clear. I could see that Roger and I are identical, in our DNA and our chemical dynamics, except for a few minor details. I could see the air, perhaps the cleanest air in the world, coming over 3,000 miles of living ocean and 400 miles of field and forest (and only a few thousand internal combustion engines), visible in the riffling of the willow leaves, air moving because the sun's energy changes the temperature and thus the density of the air so it always runs away from itself.

I could see the water flowing over stones and green slime, moving, like the air, under the force of gravity, moving leisurely toward the river, joining other rivers, toward the ocean, and then returning, endlessly flowing down and returning, in clouds now trivial and fleecy but sometimes heavy and dark, drifting on the moving air. Upstream the drops were seeping through the soil and replenishing the stream. And the water seeped through the ground beneath us, and into the roots of the trees, and up to their tops, and through their leaves back into the air. And I looked again into Roger's black and white face, his soft brown bulging eyes as he stood and stared and wondered what happens next.

We hung there in space, motionless. I could see the water and the air moving in his body and in mine, carrying with them the other elements constantly circling and shifting in and out of our cells, the molecular gears of our chemical factories grinding and silently clanking, his blood and breath inseparable from mine and both of us joined and continuous with the creek and the willow tree and the hanging apples and the ants and the finches and the green scum at the edge of the stream, all being pushed gently along by our sole source of energy shining down now so modestly from over my left shoulder, as Roger and the willow tree and I rode the grand carousel through that segment of space overseen by the star Polaris.

Time was frozen. I was stunned at the sight, at the vast and seamless beauty of the world. Roger licked my face as I sobbed with gratitude and reverence and awe.

Epilogue

I dread the word "dread," the ominous, mind-choking heaviness of it like stacked stones and earth coming down.

I dread it because in these later times it's so personal. High places. Slippery ground. Bones of porcelain and egg shell. Snow, the bite of winter and a dwindling firewood pile. The possibility of running out of money, of falling. Dread lurks always behind the real-time picture of this present moment.

I have walked the tops of forty-foot walls under construction, clambered happily through branches of big trees, worked on roofs and scaffolds, and leaped from rock to slippery rock in a river. But in my eighth decade the boundaries of life are shrunken. I have drawn into the crusted shell of age like a barnacle startled in its feeding. Flesh once solid, robust, passionate is now stringy, cautious, and wistful. My mind is faint and fearful; in thought and word and in the actions of daily life I am constrained by rote, ritual, and routine. The flavor of derring-do is all in memory, all in the nostalgic view of what was once so rich in possibility and promise.

Most of all I dread the meaning of forgetting a name or a word that I know well, of reaching into a drawer and coming out with the wrong utensil, of having to say to myself, "Now what was I coming to the basement for?" What are the bounds of normal forgetfulness, and where does it cross over into something more sinister, the beginning of the loss of self itself?

One recent night my wife was away and I was in the house alone with our small dog. The thermostat for the upstairs was set at its usual 72 degrees. I had carelessly let the wood fire downstairs almost go out, so that I had to add kindling and blow on the embers to bring the stove back to life. Outside the temperature was just below freezing and the prediction was for "low 20s" when I went to throw out feed for the wild things.

I was only out a few minutes, in a warm jacket. Darkness came quickly. The burbling of the creek, usually a cheery and uplifting music, suddenly sounded cold, crackling, threatening.

282

Standing on the sloping bank on the far side to toss grains of corn at the edge of the black, shimmering water, I felt waves of near-vertigo, of tipping downhill, balance precarious on the uneven stones. Though the stream is only ankle deep I pictured falling into freezing water, deep water, flailing helpless under ice.

I scrambled back across the little bridge above the dark and cheerless stream - which now reminded me of a moat - and hurried with the last of the chores, then scuttled inside, put more wood on the fire, and closed the drapes. Upstairs the readings were normal but I couldn't feel the warmth. The thermometer outside now stood at 27°. The dark and the chill were closing in, surrounding and pressing on the house.

I turned on the brightest lights in the kitchen; this only intensified the pervading sense of cold. I tried a thick wool sweater, but it felt dank and clammy to the touch.

Huddling near the wood stove was scant solace. I remembered a story in which a fugitive treks through Siberia alone, on foot, in the dead of winter, making a fire from nothing in a cave at 40 degrees below zero. The frozen fist of this vision plunged into the very core of me and I closed my eyes, curled up and hugged myself.

At last I resorted to a hot shower, but in disrobing I was more vividly aware of the coldness around and through me. The hot water felt good, but by the time I had dried off the effect was gone.

Strangely, I was not shivering. Might I have some febrile illness as justification for what I felt? Some reassuring sore throat or congested nose? A survey of myself showed no such consoling explanation. Maybe this was hypothermia of the soul.

I finally put on a heavy cotton sweat suit and crawled into bed, and after a long time the bed covers absorbed enough warmth from me to become tolerably comforting. My limbs, though tense, were still but my spirit cringed and quivered. With the little dog clutched against my chest, at last I slept.

When I awoke and dressed the air was crisp and clear. The sun shone brightly on the trees, like tinsel on their bare and bony fingers. The mercury had dropped to 22° but the inner chill had drained away. Though my hands were cold to my cheek I felt warm inside, the fire crackled and danced merrily, the birds broke the night's fast on what the deer had left behind. The earth leaned and sidled toward the sun, and life again like a gleaming cord stretched on ahead and out of sight - for now.